THE FIRST SCHOOL HOUSE IN SAN FRANCISCO.
Erected on the Plaza in 1847.

HISTORY

OF THE

PUBLIC SCHOOL SYSTEM

OF

CALIFORNIA.

BY

JOHN SWETT.

SAN FRANCISCO:
A. L. BANCROFT AND COMPANY.
1876.

A. L. BANCROFT & CO.,
PRINTERS.

PREFACE.

This history contains an outline of school legislation, school reports, and educational conventions, from 1850 to 1876, and a statement of the leading facts connected with the organization of the school system of California.

This Centennial year seems a fitting time to gather up the scattered and fragmentary records of the beginnings of our schools, and to trace the development of our system of public instruction during the first quarter of a century of our history as a State.

I have undertaken the work, because I felt that it ought to be done, and no one else seemed ready to do it. I have endeavored to make it accurate and impartial. It is published on my own responsibility solely, and at my own expense.

Only a limited number of copies has been printed; it is not stereotyped, and the type is distributed. It is submitted to the pioneer teachers and school officers of California, with the hope that this record of the history they helped *to make* may not be wholly devoid of interest.

J. S.

San Francisco,
August, 1876.

TABLE OF CONTENTS.

PART I.

SPECIAL HISTORY OF SAN FRANCISCO.

PART II.

I. CONVENTIONS AND INSTITUTES.

II. INSTITUTE ADDRESSES.

III. STATE UNIVERSITY.

IV. STATE NORMAL SCHOOL.

V. STATE BOARDS OF EDUCATION.

VI. TEACHERS' CERTIFICATES AND BOARDS OF EXAMINATION.

PART III.

PRESENT CONDITION OF THE SCHOOL SYSTEM.

THE

PUBLIC SCHOOL SYSTEM OF CALIFORNIA.

PART I.

I. FOUNDATION.

THE foundation of the public school system of California was laid in the Constitutional Convention held in Monterey, September, 1849.

The Select Committee on the State Constitution reported, in Committee of the Whole, in favor of appropriating the five hundred thousand acres of land granted by Congress to new States for the purpose of internal improvements, to constitute a perpetual School Fund, with a *proviso*, however, that the Legislature might appropriate the revenue so derived to other purposes if the exigencies of the State required it. An animated debate occurred on this *proviso*, in which Mr. Sherwood of Sacramento, and Mr. Jones of San Joaquin, were the principal speakers in favor of it; and Mr. Semple of Sonoma, and Mr. McCarver, opposed to it. The *proviso* was stricken out by the close vote of eighteen ayes to seventeen noes, thus securing an inviolable fund for school purposes. In the progress of the debate Mr. Semple spoke as follows:

"This is a subject upon which I have thought probably more than upon any other subject that has ever engrossed my attention. I regard it as a subject of peculiar importance here in California, from our location and the circumstances under which we are placed, the immense value of our lands, and the extent and wealth of the country. I think that here, above all places in the Union, we should have, and we possess the resources to have, a well-regulated system of education.

"It is the duty of members of this House to unite together and secure that reputation, character and ability in our public teachers which can only be obtained by a liberal and permanent fund. It is the basis of a well-regulated school system that it shall be uniform throughout the State; that any surplus funds collected in one district shall not be appropriated in that district, but that the aggregate fund from all the districts shall be appropriated strictly to school purposes, and distributed equally throughout the State.

* * * * * * * *

"We should therefore carefully provide that this fund shall be used for no other purpose."

A section providing that a school should be kept in each district at least three months in each year, in order to secure any share of the State Fund, was adopted; an amendment by Mr. Hastings, to insert "six" months instead of "three," having been rejected.

SIXTEENTH AND THIRTY-SIXTH SECTIONS.

Mr. Semple, of Sonoma, whose opinions on school matters seem to have been remarkably clear and correct, moved, as a substitute for a rejected section relating to collecting and disbursing the proceeds of fines for breach of penal laws, that all funds collected from any source, including, of course, the proceeds from the sales of the sixteenth and thirty-sixth sections of township school lands, *be paid into a common fund, to be apportioned according to the number of children.*

William M. Gwin and Henry W. Halleck, both of San Francisco, spoke against the measure; and Mr. Semple defended it in an able speech. It was rejected, however, and the way was left open for a great deal of cumbersome legislation in vain attempts to form township school funds. Finally, after fifty thousand acres had been sold by various townships, the proceeds of which have never been heard of since, in 1861 a law was passed consolidating the proceeds into one common State School Fund, as proposed by Mr. Semple in 1849.

THE TEST VOTE.

When Article IX, on education, came up for final adoption in the Convention, there was a lengthy debate on the policy of concurring with the action in Committee of the Whole in striking out the *proviso* in section second before mentioned. The opinion prevailed in the Convention that this grant would be of immense value; that the lands would be located in mineral regions, and sold for fabulous sums; that the fund derived would be the most munificent in the world; and the argument was used in favor of the *proviso*, that the fund would be more than sufficient to educate the children, and would prove a source of corruption and speculation. Hence the question was made an important one, which brought out the full strength of the friends of free schools.

W. M. Stewart and Messrs. Sherwood and Vermeule, spoke in favor of retaining the *proviso*, and Messrs. Gwin, Halleck, Botts, Hoppe, Semple, and McDougal, in favor of striking it out.

After various amendments offered and rejected, the *proviso* was stricken out by the following vote:

AYES.—Messrs. Aram, Botts, Brown, Covarrubias, Gwin, Hanks, Hill, Hoppe, Halleck, Hastings, Hollingsworth, Larkin, Lippitt, Lippincott, McCarver, McDougal, Ord, Price, Reid, Sutter, Stearns, Sansevaine, Tefft, Vermeule, Walker, and President Semple—26.

NOES.—Messrs. Dimmick, Dominguez, Foster, Gilbert, Hobson, Norton, Pico, Sherwood and Wozencraft—10.

And so was laid the foundation of our School Fund and School System.

CONSTITUTIONAL PROVISIONS.

Article IX of the Constitution, as adopted, was as follows:

"ARTICLE IX.—*Education.*

"SECTION 1. The Legislature shall provide for the election by the people of a Superintendent of Public Instruction, who shall hold his office for three years, and whose duties shall be prescribed by law, and who shall receive such compensation as the Legislature may direct.*

"SEC. 2. The Legislature shall encourage by all suitable means the promotion of intellectual, scientific, moral and agricultural improvement. The proceeds of all land that may be granted by the United States to this State for the support of schools which may be sold or disposed of, and the five hundred thousand acres of land granted to the new States, under an act of Congress distributing the proceeds of the public lands among the several States of the Union, approved A. D. 1841, such per cent. as may be granted by Congress on the sale of lands in this State shall be and remain a

* Amended in 1862 so as to provide for the election of State Superintendent at the Special Judicial Election, for a term of four years.

perpetual fund, the interest of which, together with all the rents of the unsold lands, and such other means as the Legislature may provide, shall be inviolably appropriated to the support of common schools throughout the State.

"SEC. 3. The Legislature shall provide for a system of common schools, by which a school shall be kept up and supported in each district at least three months in every year; and any district neglecting to keep and support such a school, may be deprived of its proportion of the interest of the public fund during such neglect.

"SEC. 4. The Legislature shall take measures for the protection, improvement, or other disposition of such lands as have been or may hereafter be reserved or granted by the United States, or any person or persons, to the State, for the use of a university; and the funds accruing from the rents or sale of such lands, or from any other source, for the purpose aforesaid, shall be and remain a permanent fund, the interest of which shall be applied to the support of said university, with such branches as the public convenience may demand, for the promotion of literature, the arts and sciences, as may be authorized by the terms of such grant. And it shall be the duty of the Legislature, as soon as may be, to provide effectual means for the improvement and permanent security of the funds of said university."

2. SCHOOL LEGISLATION, 1849-50.

Near the close of the first session of the Legislature, 1849–50, held in the city of San Jose, Mr. Corey, from the Committee on Education, reported that the taxes laid on the people for State, county, and municipal purposes, were so heavy the committee did not consider it advisable to report a bill to tax the people still further for the support of public schools, and, accordingly, the school bill, of which no record remains, was indefinitely postponed. But while the school bill, thus defeated, has been forgotten, the reason advanced by Mr. Corey has been the standing argument urged against every school bill which has contained any provision for maintaining by taxation a system of public schools.

3. THE FIRST FREE PUBLIC SCHOOL.

A solid foundation for a school system was laid by the framers of the State Constitution, but San Francisco was the first place in the State to organize, independent of State law, by her Common Council, a *free public school.*

The Ayuntamiento, or City Council, adopted, April 8, 1850, the following ordinance, drawn by H. C. Murray, which was the *first public school ordinance of any kind passed in California,* and consequently made the school taught by Mr. Pelton the first free public school in the State. The ordinance was crude, it is true, but it was the germ of all succeeding city ordinances.

The following is a copy of the ordinance:

"1st. *Be it ordained by the Common Council of San Francisco*, That from and after the passage of this act, it shall be the duty of J. C. Pelton, who has been employed by the Council as a public teacher, to open a school in the Baptist Chapel.

"2d. Said school shall be opened from half-past eight o'clock A. M. to twelve o'clock M., and from two o'clock P. M. until five o'clock P. M., and shall continue open from Monday until Friday at five o'clock P. M.

"3d. The number of scholars shall not exceed the number of one hundred; and no scholar shall be admitted under the age of four or over the age of sixteen.

"4th. All persons desirous of having their children instructed in said school shall first obtain an order from the Chairman of the Committee on Education, and all children obtaining said order shall be instructed in said school free of charge.

"5th. It shall be the duty of said Pelton to report to the Council on the first of each and every month the number of scholars and the progress of said school.

"H. C. MURRAY.
"F. TILFORD."

4. THE PIONEER SCHOOLS.

On October 11, 1847, a committee of the Town Council contracted for the erection of a small schoolhouse of one room, on the southwest corner of the Plaza, at the corner of Clay Street and Brenham Place.

On February 23, 1848, a small number of voters assembled and elected a Board of School Trustees, consisting of Dr. Townsend, Dr. Fourgeaud, C. L. Ross, Wm. H. Davis and J. Serine. This board elected Thomas Douglass as teacher, at a salary of one thousand dollars a year, and the school opened on the 3d of April, 1848, with 6 pupils. This was in fact a *tuition* school under public auspices, it being free only to *indigent* pupils. The Town Council agreed to make up any deficiency in the salary of the teacher, to the extent of four hundred dollars. The estimated population of the town, April 1, 1848, was one thousand, with 60 children of school age. In May the school numbered 37 pupils.

On May 13, 1848, a new election of Trustees was ordered, and after a spirited contest the old board was re-elected. Soon after gold was discovered, the school dwindled to 8 pupils, and Schoolmaster Douglass closed his doors and started for the mines.

Prior to the opening of this *quasi* public school, Mr. Marston, a Mormon, opened a private school, April, 1847, and soon had 20 pupils in attendance. Schoolmaster Marston also became a miner when the stampede for the "diggings" took place.

In April, 1849, Rev. Albert Williams opened a private school of about 25 pupils, and continued it until the September following.

On the 11th of October, 1849, John C. Pelton and wife arrived from Boston, with school furniture, books, etc., for the purpose of establishing a school on the New England plan. He opened school December, 1849, with *three* pupils. This school was to be supported by voluntary contributions, but was free to indigent children. This school was made a *free public school* soon after.

The school so established soon numbered 150 pupils, and in addition to Mr. Pelton and his wife, two assistants had to be employed. At one time the school numbered 300 pupils. The salary of Mr. and Mrs. Pelton was $500 a month.

This school was continued until September 25, 1851, when it was suspended by the adoption of a new school ordinance, under which T. J. Nevins became Superintendent, new teachers were elected, and Mr. Pelton temporarily retired from school.

5. SCHOOL LEGISLATION, 1850–1851.

The Chairman of the Senate Committee on Education, Mr Heydenfelt, early in the second session of the Legislature, at San Jose, 1850–51, reported a bill "Concerning common schools," which dragged slowly along, was indefinitely postponed in the Assembly, submitted to a Committee of Conference, and finally passed on the very last day of the session, May 1, 1851.

The original bill was mainly drawn by Hon. George B. Tingley, a member of the Legislature. John G. Marvin, Superintendent of Public Instruction, and John C. Pelton, teacher of the public school in San Francisco, under a local school ordinance, assisted in preparing and perfecting the bill, and in securing its passage. David C. Broderick, then a member of the Legislature, was an active supporter of the bill.

THE FIRST SCHOOL LAW.

The school law of 1851 was cumbersome and imperfect in many of its provisions. It provided for the survey and sale of school lands in so impracticable a manner that no lands were ever sold under its operation. The Governor was to order a survey; the surveyor was to lay off the land in lots not exceeding eighty acres, nor less than forty, and to furnish the State Superintendent with a schedule of the same; the lands were to be sold at auction, on an order from the Court of Sessions—the purchaser to pay one third down, and ten per cent. per annum interest on the remainder; the County Treasurer to give a certificate of payment, and report to the State Superintendent; the State Superintendent to direct the District Attorney to make out a deed; the County Recorder to report annually to the State Superintendent.

It provided for the apportionment of the interest of the State School Fund to the counties, on the basis of the number of children between seven and eighteen years of age; but the County Treasurers were to apportion to districts according to the number actually attending school; no district was to receive its share of State money unless school was maintained three months, and unless it raised a sum equal to at least one half its share of the State Fund. It defined the duties of the Superintendent of Public Instruction; provided for a "Superintending School Committee" of three, elected annually, with power to examine and appoint teachers, disburse the School Fund, build schoolhouses, and report annually to the State Superintendent. It divided schools into primary, intermediate and grammar, specifying the studies in each, and provided for the establishment of high schools.

DIVISION OF THE SCHOOL MONEYS.

It also provided for the distribution of the School Fund among religious and sectarian schools, in the following sections:

"SEC. 10. If a school be formed by the enterprise of a religious society, in which all the educational branches of the district schools shall be taught, and which, from its private and public examination, the committee will it to be well conducted, such school shall be allowed a compensation from the Public School Fund in proportion to the number of its pupils, in the same manner as provided for district schools by this act.

"SEC. 11. Schools established under charitable auspices, orphan asylums, schools for blind, almshouse schools, etc., such as shall be subject to the general supervision of laws on education, but under the immediate management of their respective trustees, managers, or directors; and said schools shall participate in the apportionment of the school moneys in the same manner as other common schools."

6. SCHOOLS IN SAN FRANCISCO, 1851-52.

The first school ordinance passed under the State school law of 1851 was that of San Francisco, adopted in September, 1851, which made provision for a City Board of Education, composed of seven members, and for a City Superintendent, and appropriated $35,000 for the support of schools. Thomas J. Nevins, who mainly prepared the ordinance, was elected Superintendent of Schools, and proceeded to organize the department. The first schools organized under this ordinance were the Happy Valley School, of which Mr. James Denman was elected the first teacher, and the Powell Street School, of which Mr. Joel Tracy was appointed teacher.

Both schools opened on the 17th of December, 1851.

The *Washington* Grammar School opened December 22, Mr. F. E. Jones, Principal.

During 1852 the following new schools were organized: Rincon School, January 28, Silas Weston, Principal; Spring Valley Grammar, February 9, Asa W. Cole, Principal; Union Grammar, June, Ahira Holmes, Principal; Mission Grammar, May, Alfred Rix, Principal.

The average daily attendance in all the schools for 1852 was 445; in 1853, 703 pupils.

Among the teachers elected in 1853 were Ellis H. Holmes, Principal of the Washington School, March 1; John Swett, Principal Rincon School, December 4; Joseph C. Morrill, Principal Spring Valley School, October 1.

The salary of Principals of Grammar Schools in 1853 was $1500 a year.

7. FIRST STATE SCHOOL REPORT, 1851.

John G. Marvin, the first Superintendent of Public Instruction, made his first annual report to the third Legislature on the 5th of January, 1852. He recommended that a carefully prepared school law should be passed, as that of the previous year was meagre in its provisions; that an appropriation of $50,000 should be immediately made, and that next year a State school tax of five cents on a hundred dollars should be levied until some revenue could be derived from the State School Fund; that the office of County Superintendent be created; that provision be made for school libraries; and that the proceeds of the sales of tule lands be applied to the School Fund. He estimated the total amount of State school land, including the 16th and 36th sections, and the 500,000 acre grant, to be 6,380,320 acres, which would yield a prospective School Fund of $7,975,400, and says of this estimate: "This would be truly a magnificent bequest, and one worthy of the El Dorado State."

In an appendix to his report, Mr. Marvin gave extracts from letters of inquiry addressed by him to various county officers and to postmasters. A few extracts from these will show the educational condition of the State at that time: Butte County had 50 children, but no school; Calaveras County, 100 children, and no school; Colusa, 75 children, with some prospect of a school next year; El Dorado County, 100 children, but no school; Contra Costa County had some 400 children. Postmaster Coffin, of Martinez, wrote: "There are nearly 150 here. There is but just the breath of life existing in the apology for a school in the town. I presume it will be defunct ere one month passes away." Marin County had 60 children, and a mission school at San Rafael; Mariposa County, 100 children, "no school organized;" Mendocino County, 70 children, and a school of 20 pupils on Russian River; Monterey County, 500 children —two schools of 40 pupils each in the city—179 at San Juan, and no school; "morality and society in a desperate condition;" Napa County had 100 children, and three schools in the county, one of which was at Napa City, and numbered 25 scholars; Nevada County had 250, and four schools, two of which were at Nevada City, one at Grass Valley, and one at Rough and Ready; Placer County had 100 children, and one small school at Auburn; San Joaquin County had 250 children, and two schools, both at Stockton. Mr. Rogers, the teacher of a private school at Sacramento, reported that there were 400 children in that county, and no schools except two primary and one academy, a high school in the city of Sacramento, all private. He says: "This city has never spent a cent for elementary instruction. My sympathies are with the public free schools, but in their absence, I started a private school."

Santa Cruz County had 200 children, and two schools, both in the town, numbering 65 scholars.

Santa Clara County had 300 children. The Young Ladies' Seminary, at San Jose, in charge of the Sisters of Charity, had

90 pupils; and the San Jose Academy, Reverend E. Bannister, Principal, had 60 pupils. Through the exertions of Hon. George B. Tingley, a subscription of $5000 was raised for the benefit of this academy. There were two primary schools at Santa Clara, with 64 scholars, and two other schools in the township, numbering 35 scholars.

Santa Barbara County had 400 children, and one public school in the town, under supervision of the Common Council, who paid the two teachers together seventy dollars per month. There was also a small school at Santa Inez.

SAN FRANCISCO SCHOOLS.

Concerning San Francisco, it is reported: "In May last, the Common Council, under authority of the charter, authorized the raising of $35,000 as a School Fund for the present year. In September, 1851, the same body passed the present excellent school ordinance, and appointed Aldermen Ross, Atwell, John Wilson and Henry E. Lincoln, to form the Board of Education. These gentlemen chose T. J. Nevins Superintendent."

Three public schools were organized at that time—Happy Valley School, No. 1, 163 scholars, James Denman, Principal; District No. 2, Dupont Street School, 150 pupils, Mr. Jones, Principal; Powell Street School, No. 3, 60 pupils, Joel Tracy, Principal.

Among the private schools, the principal were as follows: San Francisco Academy, Rev. F. E. Prevaux, 31 pupils; Episcopal Parish School of Grace Church, 40 scholars, Dr. Ver Mehr; Wesleyan Chapel Select School, 33 scholars, Mr. Osborne, Instructor; St. Patrick's School, 150 children, Father McGinnis, Principal; Church of St. Francis School, 150 pupils, Father Langlois, Principal.

Sonoma County had 5 small schools, and 250 children; Solano County 200 children and one school, at Benicia, half public and half private; Trinity County 125 children, and one school of 50 pupils, at Uniontown; Tuolumne County 150 children, and no school; Yolo County 75 children, and no school; Yuba County had 150 children, and one school in Marysville, of 30 scholars, taught by Tyler Thatcher and his wife.

From these rough materials Mr. Marvin estimated the number of children in the State between 4 and 18 years of age to be about 6000. There was then no organized State school system, and most of the schools mentioned in the preceding items were private schools supported by tuition.

8. SCHOOL LEGISLATION, 1852.

At the third session of the Legislature, held in Vallejo and Sacramento, 1852, Hon. Frank Soulé, Chairman of the Senate Committee on Education, made an able report in favor of common schools, and introduced a revised school law much more complete than the law of 1851.

Hon. Paul K. Hubbs, of the Senate, afterwards Superintendent of Public Instruction, State Superintendent Marvin and Mr. Pelton, assisted Mr. Soulé in framing the bill.

A select committee of the Assembly on the Senate bill (Mr. Boggs, Chairman) reported strongly against many features of the bill; thought that parents could take care of their own children; that the State and the counties were in debt; that taxation ought not to be increased—the standing argument of Mr. Corey—and therefore recommended that the bill be postponed one year, and yet had the unblushing impudence to wind up their report by "declaring themselves faithful friends of common schools and loyal lovers of children!" Finally a committee of conference was appointed, on which appear the names of J. M. Estell, Henry A. Crabb and A. C. Peachy, who reported in favor of the bill with the sections relating to the sale of school lands stricken out, to be amended and passed as a separate bill. It was proposed by Mr. Soulé and others who assisted in framing the bill, that the 500,000 acres of school lands should be located by the State Board of Education, and held until the land should sell for a reasonable price.

But there was a big land speculation in the eyes of some members of the Legislature; and so the policy prevailed of disposing of these lands at $2.25 per acre, payable in depreciated State script. The total amount finally realized from this magnificent land grant was only about $600,000. It might have been made two or three millions.

FIRST STATE SCHOOL TAX.

The bill was passed, and a provision was inserted in the revenue law levying a *State school tax of five cents on each one hundred dollars of the taxable property of the State.* This school law made provision for a State Board of Education, consisting of the Governor, Surveyor-General and Superintendent of Public Instruction; made County Assessors *ex-officio* County Superintendents; three School Commissioners in each district, elected for one year; constables to be School Census Marshals; the school year to end October 31; State School Fund to be apportioned to districts according to the number of census children between five and eighteen years of age; State School Fund to be used exclusively for teachers' salaries, and fifty per cent. of County Fund for the same purpose; that no books of a denominational or sectarian character should be used in any common schools; defined the duties of County Superintendents, and of the State Superintendent and School Commissioners; authorized the Common Council in incorporated towns to raise a school tax not to exceed *three cents on a hundred dollars;* to provide for examination of teachers; to make rules and regulations for government of schools; authorized counties to levy a school tax not exceeding *three cents on a hundred dollars; provided that no school should receive any apportionment of public money, unless free from all denominational and sectarian bias, control or influence whatever;* and closed by giving permission to teachers to assemble at Sacramento, once a year, on the call of the Superintendent of Public Instruction, to discuss and recommend improvements in teaching. Approved May 3, 1862.

9. SECOND STATE SCHOOL REPORT, 1852.

In his second annual report, Mr. Marvin stated that the number of children between four and eighteen years of age was 17,821; that by a blunder of the Enrolling Clerk, the section creating the office of County Superintendent was omitted, and the duties were specified without creating the office, and in consequence thereof the State Board of Education had not been able to apportion the State Fund, which at that time amounted to $18,289, of which $14,874 was received from the five cent revenue tax; that the sales of school lands had amounted to 150,000 acres, yielding $300,000, on interest at the rate of seven per cent. per annum. He recommended that the County Assessors be made *ex-officio* County Superintendents; that Trustees be required to report to the State Superintendent as well as to County Superintendents; *that the Catholic schools be allowed their pro rata of the public fund;* that no necessity existed for a normal school, as the supply of teachers was greater than the demand; that the number of organized public schools was 20, the number of children attending public school 3314, and the total expenditure as reported, $28,000.

The report embraced twelve mission and church schools in various parts of the State, including 579 children in attendance.

10. SCHOOL LEGISLATION, 1853.

SALE OF SCHOOL LANDS.

The law regulating the sale of 500,000 acres of school lands, passed May 3, 1852, authorized the Governor to issue land warrants of not less than 160 acres, nor more than 320 acres; the State Treasurer was authorized to sell said lands at two dollars per acre, and to receive in payment Controller's warrants drawn upon the General Fund, or the bonds of the civil debt of the State; and to convert all moneys and all State three per cent. bonds or Controller's warrants so received by him into bonds of the civil funded debt of the State, bearing interest at seven per cent. per annum, and to keep such bonds as a special deposit, marked "School Fund," to the credit of said School Fund.

Under this provision the sales of land in 1852 amounted to 150,000 acres, yielding $300,000.

AMENDMENTS.

At the fourth session of the Legislature, 1853, the school law was amended by the following provisions: That Controller's warrants, received for school lands, should draw interest at seven per cent., the same rate as civil bonds; that the State Treasurer should keep a separate and distinct account of the Common School Fund, and of the interest and income thereof, and that no portion should be devoted to any other purpose; that County Assessors should be made *ex-officio* County Superintendents; that all county school officers should be paid such compensation as allowed by County Supervisors; that cities should have power to raise by tax whatever amount of money was necessary for school purposes; that counties should have power to levy a school tax not exceeding five cents on a hundred dollars; that religious and sectarian schools should receive a *pro rata* share of the School Fund.

The provision allowing the Catholic schools a share of the School Fund was as follows:

"SEC. 7. Article *five* of said act (1852) is hereby amended by adding after section *two* the following additional sections:

"'*Section Three.* The County Superintendent may and is hereby empowered, in incorporated cities, to appoint three School Commissioners for any common school or district, upon petition of the inhabitants thereof requesting the same.

"'*Section Four.* Such schools shall be and are hereby entitled to all the rights and privileges of any other city or common school, in the *pro rata* division of school money raised by taxation, and shall receive its proportion of money from the State School Fund in the annual distribution; *provided*, they are conducted in accordance with the requirements of this act.'"

This provision gave rise to the formation of the so-called "ward schools" of San Francisco.

11. THIRD ANNUAL SCHOOL REPORT, 1853.

Paul K. Hubbs, who had been a member of the last previous Legislature, was elected as successor to John G. Marvin, and took office on the first of January, 1854. In his very brief annual report, January 24, 1854, he stated that the School Fund, from the sale of school lands, amounted to $463,000, on which the annual interest was $32,000; that the sale of school lands had entirely ceased, and that there remained unsold 268,000 acres of the 500,000 acre grant. He dwelt on the necessity of reserving all sales of the sixteenth and thirty-sixth sections for township funds exclusively. Mr. Hubbs further recommended that the School Fund be apportioned according to the average attendance on school, instead of the number of census children, and urged the establishment of a State university.

No tabular statistics whatever were published with this report.

12. SCHOOL LEGISLATION, 1854.

In the fifth session of the Legislature, 1854, it was provided in the Revenue Act that fifteen per cent. of the State poll taxes should be paid into the School Fund. A well-prepared school law was introduced by Hon. D. R. Ashley, which, among other things, *repealed the sections allowing sectarian schools a pro rata share of the School Fund.* It met with strong opposition, finally passed to engrossment, but was buried in the rubbish of unfinished business at the end of the session.

13. FOURTH ANNUAL SCHOOL REPORT, 1854.

Superintendent Hubbs opened his second report with the statement, "that, though the average attendance on school had increased from 2000 in 1853 to 5751 in 1854, the report nevertheless exhibited the lamentable fact that the children of our State are growing up devoid of learning to read and write." He recommended the establishment of a State Industrial School; that School Commissioners be elected for three years, one annually; that the office of County Superintendent be abolished, as tending to unnecessary expense; that Township Treasurers be elected, to report to the State Superintendent; argued in favor of Township School Funds; stated that no income had ever been derived from "escheated estates," though it had been estimated that *millions* belonged of right to that fund; and urged a State university. A crude and confused tabular statement was attached to this report.

14. SCHOOL LEGISLATION, 1855.

During the sixth session of the Legislature, 1855, Hon. D. R. Ashley introduced a school bill which was in substance the same as that defeated at the last previous session. After some opposition, with a few amendments it became a law, approved May 3, 1855.

This revised law enlarged the powers of School Trustees; provided for the election of County Superintendents, and defined their duties; and empowered the Common Councils of incorporated cities to raise a school tax not exceeding twenty-five cents on a hundred dollars; to collect and disburse school moneys; to establish school districts; to provide by election or by appointment for City Boards of Education, and City Superintendents; to establish schools on petition of fifty heads of families, provided that no sectarian doctrines should be taught therein, and that such schools be under the same supervision as other schools.

SECULAR SCHOOLS.

It provided that no school should be entitled to any share of the public fund that had not been taught by teachers duly examined and approved by legal authority, and that no sectarian books should be used, and no sectarian doctrines should be taught in any public school under penalty of forfeiting the public funds. The stringent provision settled then, and probably forever, the question of an American system of public schools in this State, free from the bitterness of sectarian strife and the intolerance of religious bigotry. The public schools are free to the children of the people, and free from the influence of church or sect.

This law of 1855 also provided that Controller's warrants paid into the Treasury for school lands should draw the same rate of interest as civil bonds, and that the State Treasurer should indorse on such warrants, "Common School Fund," and that no portion of such securities should be sold or exchanged, except by special act of the Legislature; it authorized counties to raise a school tax not exceeding ten cents on a hundred dollars, to apportion the same on the same basis as the State Fund, and to appropriate the moneys so derived for building houses, purchasing libraries, or for salaries. This law contained many excellent provisions, and was a very great advance on all previous school bills. Its main features are retained in the school law of the present day.

15. FIFTH ANNUAL SCHOOL REPORT, 1856.

Superintendent Hubbs renewed his recommendations for the sale of school lands, and put in a special plea for Township Funds; recommended that all school lands and School Funds be placed under the control of the State Board of Education; asked a direct appropriation of $100,000; *considered the new school law behind the age;* recommended that the office of County Superintendent be abolished, and that the district township system be adopted; that the School Fund be apportioned according to the average daily attendance.

This report was accompanied by inaccurate statistical tables.

16. SIXTH ANNUAL SCHOOL REPORT, 1856.

The last report of Superintendent Hubbs was a brief one, without any statistical table whatever—not even the number of census children in the State.

He urged all his previous recommendations concerning school lands, and township lands in particular, the establishment of a grand university, with an agricultural department, and a military school; a legislative requirement that *a uniform series of elementary books be used in all the public schools;* entered his protest against certain "partisan and sectional" text-books sent him from the East; and closed by a eulogy on the English language and the Anglo-Saxon race.

17. SEVENTEENTH ANNUAL SCHOOL REPORT, 1857.

Paul K. Hubbs was succeeded in office, in 1857, by Andrew J. Moulder.

Mr. Moulder's first report opened as follows:

The number of schools has increased, in four years, from 53 to 367—nearly sevenfold; the number of teachers, from 50 to 486—nearly ninefold; the number of children reported by census, from 11,242 to 35,722—more than threefold; whilst the semi-annual contribution by the State has dwindled from $53,511.11 to $28,342.16, or nearly one half; and the average paid each teacher, from $955 to $58.32—that is to say, to less than one sixteenth of the average under the first apportionment.

I will not waste words on such an exhibit. If it be not convincing that the support derived from the State is altogether insufficient, and ought to be augmented, no appeal of mine could enforce it.

But this I may be permitted to say, that we have no such thing as public schools, in the full acceptation of the term—that is to say, schools at which all the children of the State may be educated, *free of expense.* That $9.72 per month, to each teacher, contributed by the State, never can maintain a public school; that the contributions by parents and guardians to keep up the schools are onerous, oftentimes unequal, and must, in time, damp their ardor in the cause of education; that our 367 schools are comparatively in their infancy, and now, above all other times, should be cherished and encouraged by the State. Lacking such fostering care and encouragement, it is to be feared they will languish, and gradually lose their hold upon the popular favor. Is it not worth more than an ordinary effort to avert such a calamity?

He recommended that the maximum rate of county school tax be increased from ten cents to twenty cents on a hundred dollars; that no warrants should be issued by Trustees on the District Funds, unless there was cash in the Treasury to pay them; and that all funds coming into the Treasury during one school year should be used exclusively for the payment of expenses of that year; asked an appropriation of $3000 for Teachers' Institutes; favored the establishment of a State Industrial School; recommended that all school lands be placed under the immediate charge of the State Board of Education, with power to locate and sell at one dollar and twenty-five cents per acre; that the proceeds of the sales of the 16th and 36th sections of township lands be consolidated into one general school fund, and that a State Military Institute be established.

The following extract will illustrate his views on a State University:

Ours is eminently a practical age. We want no pale and sickly scholars, profound in their knowledge of the dead or other languages and customs. We need energetic citizens, skilled in the arts of the living, and capable of instructing their less favored fellows in the pursuits that contribute to the material prosperity of our State. For what useful occupation are the graduates of most of our old colleges fit? and not of ours alone, but of the time-honored universities of England. Many of them are bright scholars, ornaments to their *alma mater*—they are perhaps all that the system under which they have been instructed could make them; they are learned in the antiquities of nations long since gone; they are eloquent in Latin; they may write a dissertation on the Greek particle; be masters of the rules of logic and the dogmas of ethics —all valuable acquirements, it is true; but when, after years of toil, they have received their diploma, their education for practical life has just commenced. They have still to study for a profession —are still dependent upon their parents.

This may do for old settled communities, but it will never answer for California. A young man at seventeen, eighteen, or twenty years of age, in this State, must expect to start in life for himself. He must have some occupation that will maintain him. Longer dependence is not to be tolerated or expected.

To fit our youth for such occupations, to end this dependence, must be the object of our university.

I would, therefore, urge that such professorships only shall be established at first as will turn out practical and scientific civil engineers; mining engineers; surveyors; metallurgists; smelters; assayers; geologists, or scientific prospectors; chemists, both manufacturing and agricultural; architects; builders; and last, but not least, school teachers.

Let me call your attention, however, to the necessity of educating a class of our young men in mining engineering.

The character of mining has undergone great changes since eighteen hundred and forty-nine and eighteen hundred and fifty. Enterprises are now conducted on an extensive scale. Tunnels of great magnitude, with labyrinthine galleries, are run into the mountains; deep shafts, with far-stretching drifts, are sunk; quartz works and mills are multiplying. In all these enterprises a skillful engineer would be a valuable acquisition; and, as they progress in magnitude, his services would become indispensable. It is from the want of such directing intelligence that we so often hear of accidents in the mines. Our State has scarcely started in the work of internal improvements. None offers more inducements—in none will more be needed. For these we shall require civil engineers and surveyors, and all such will, in a few years, find employment.

The statistical tables accompanying the report were very brief, embracing only the number of census children and the average daily attendance.

18. SCHOOL LEGISLATION, 1858.

The Legislatures of 1856 and 1857 did not trouble themselves about the school law, and no amendments worth mentioning were made.

The Legislature of 1858 made an advance in school legislation by providing that school districts, by a vote of the people, could levy a district tax for the support of schools or for building schoolhouses, under the restrictions that the district must have maintained a school four months; that the public money must be insufficient to defray one half the expense of another term; that a tax for supporting a school and for building a schoolhouse could not both be levied the same year, and that the trustees considered the tax advisable. This law was not well drawn, and great difficulty was experienced in collecting the taxes voted under it, the heavy taxpayers who chose to resist it generally escaping without payment. As a necessary result, comparatively few taxes were voted under it, and not till 1863 was a liberal and effective law passed whose provisions were as binding as those regulating the collection of State or county taxes.

The Legislature of 1856 passed a concurrent resolution instructing their representatives in Congress to use their influence to secure the surveys of the 16th and 36th sections of township school lands, and also to secure a law authorizing townships in the mineral districts to locate two sections in lieu thereof on the agricultural lands of the State.

The Legislature of 1858 passed a similar concurrent resolution.

A law was passed providing for the sale of the remainder of the 500,000 acre grant, and the 72 sections for a State university, which provided that the Governor should appoint a land locating agent in each land district of the State, who should locate in tracts not exceeding 320 acres; that purchasers should pay $1.25 per acre, or, if they preferred, twenty per cent. down, and interest on the remainder at ten per cent. per annum, in advance; that said agents should also locate lands in lieu of occupied 16th and 36th sections, at the request of the County Supervisors; that the State Board of Examiners, whenever it should appear that more than $10,000 had been received by the State Treasurer as purchase-money for such lands, should purchase bonds of the civil funded debt of the State, after advertising, at their lowest values; that such bonds should be marked "School Fund," and held in custody of the State Treasurer; that at the expiration of one year the State Board of Examiners should take and use $57,600 of any money belonging to the School Fund and purchase bonds, which should be marked "Seminary Fund," and that all interest on said fund should also be invested in bonds.

An act was also passed repealing that of 1855, and providing for the sale of the 16th and 36th sections of township lands by the Boards of Supervisors.

19. EIGHTH ANNUAL SCHOOL REPORT, 1858.

This was one of the longest and ablest of Mr. Moulder's reports. He opened with the statement that the schools of California were not creditable to the State, and showed the necessity of an immediate appropriation by the State of $100,000. Concerning this, he goes on to say:

A classification and analysis of the reports of full 2000 school officers to this department show that there are 40,530 children in the State between 4 and 18 years of age; that the whole number attending school during the year 1858 was 19,822, and that the daily average attendance was but 11,183. It follows that 20,708 children have not been inside of a public schoolhouse, and that 29,347 have, in effect, received no instruction during the year.

If this state of things is "very good for California," and we do not take instant and effective means to remedy it, these 29,347 neglected children will grow up into 29,347 benighted men and women; a number nearly sufficient, at ordinary times, to control the vote of the State, and, in consequence, to shape its legislation and its destiny!

Damning as the record is, it is yet lamentably true, that during the last five years the State of California has paid $754,193.80 for the support of criminals, and but $284,183.69 for the education of the young!

In other words, she has paid nearly three times as much for the support of an average of four hundred criminals as for the training and culture of thirty thousand children.

To make the point more forcible, the figures show that she has expended $1,885 on every criminal, and $9 on every child!

He recommended that districts should be required to maintain a school six months, instead of three, to entitle them to apportionment; that the authority of examining teachers should be transferred from Trustees to a County Board; that the maximum county tax should be raised to twenty cents on a hundred dollars; that County Treasurers should not be allowed a percentage for disbursing State school moneys; that County Superintendents, Marshals, and Trustees, should be paid out of the County General Fund; and that Negroes, Mongolians, and Indians, should not be allowed to attend the schools for white children, under penalty of the forfeiture of the public school money by districts admitting such children into school.

He reported that he had prepared a volume of "Commentaries on the School Law," containing suggestions on school architecture and extracts from the best authors on education. He argued at length the policy of consolidating the proceeds of the sales of the 16th and 36th sections into a State Fund.

This report closed by urging a Military Institute, and attached to the tabular statements, which were better arranged than those of any preceding report, were the reports of County Superintendents.

20. NINTH ANNUAL SCHOOL REPORT, 1859.

In this report Mr. Moulder renewed several of the recommendations of his previous report; recommended the establishment of a State Normal School; the organization of State and County Boards for examining teachers; the increase of the maximum county school tax to twenty-five cents on a hundred dollars; an appropriation for paying the expenses of State Institutes; an appropriation for traveling expenses to enable the State Superintendent to deliver lectures and visit schools throughout the State; that the Township School Funds should be consolidated into one common fund, which question he argued conclusively, supporting his position by letters from Land Commissioners at Washington, and from various State Superintendents, and concluded by an elaborate argument in favor of a Military Institute to be established at Monterey.

21. SCHOOL LEGISLATION, 1860.

Several important amendments were made to the school law by the Legislature of 1860. The maximum rate of county school tax was raised from ten cents to twenty-five cents on a hundred dollars; the State Superintendent was authorized to hold a State Teachers' Institute annually, and an appropriation of $3000 was made for payment of expenses; the State Superintendent was authorized to appoint a State Board of Examination, with power to grant State teachers' certificates, valid for two years, and the School Funds of any one year were required to be used exclusively for that year; County Superintendents were authorized to appoint County Boards of Examination, consisting exclusively of teachers, with power to grant teachers' certificates, valid for one year; the State Board of Education was authorized to adopt a State series of text-books, and to compel their adoption, under penalty of forfeiting the public school moneys, to go into effect in November, 1861; and an appropriation of $30,000 made for building a State Reform School at Marysville.

22. TENTH ANNUAL SCHOOL REPORT, 1860.

This report opened as follows:

> It is apparent, from an inspection of these statistics, that the amount contributed by the State to the cause of education is wretchedly insufficient. It is a pittance almost beneath contempt. It amounts to about one dollar and forty cents per annum for the education of each schoolable child in the State.
>
> With all the aid derived from local taxes, rate bills, and private subscription, it pays only an average of sixty-six dollars and seventy-two cents per month to each teacher in the State.
>
> A first-class bootblack obtains almost as much.
>
> I am almost disposed to believe that no teacher at all is better than an ignorant or unlettered one; but how can we expect to secure the services of highly educated and accomplished teachers for the pittance of sixty-six dollars and seventy-two cents per month?

He further urged a State Normal School, and a direct State appropriation for common schools; again argued in favor of consolidating Township Funds, and closed by stating that he had already exhausted argument in favor of a Military Institute.

23. SCHOOL LEGISLATION, 1861.

Early in the session of 1861, Hon. John Conness introduced a bill in the House, which was passed, providing for the sale of the sixteenth and thirty-sixth sections of school lands, and that the proceeds should be paid into the State School Fund. Thus, after many years of impracticable legislation, in which each successive Legislature tinkered on a township land bill, a plain and practicable law was passed, under the provisions of which, in less than a year, nearly 200,000 acres were sold, and the proceeds applied to the State School Fund.

DIVISION OF THE SCHOOL MONEYS.

During this session Mr. Montgomery introduced a bill providing—

That every school numbering thirty pupils, established by the parents or guardians of such pupils, should have the right on application to be enrolled as a public school; that the common school branches should be taught five hours a day, with religious instructions and catechism as an extra, at the will of the parents; that the parents or guardians should elect the trustees of such school, with full powers to control; and that the State Fund should be apportioned according to the number of children attending school.

This bill was accompanied by a petition extensively signed; and, at one time, there was some danger of its passage. Hon. John Conness defended secular public schools, and the following extracts from his speech are worthy of a place in school history:

A quarter of a century ago I landed from the deck of an emigrant ship, upon the shores of America. I was deposited there as a single grain of sand upon the sea shore by a wave of the ocean. Soon after my arrival I found my way to a free school, where I soon learned that my anticipations and fears were not realized. I found there, in lieu of intercourse with strangers, the greatest friendship that I have ever yet experienced at the hands of mankind. I was received into an institution established by the intelligence, the wisdom, the patriotism, and at the expense of a great and free people. I soon learned to appreciate the advantages that were placed before me. During the short period of seven months, being the interim between my arrival and my being placed, from the necessities that surrounded me, as an apprentice to a mechanic's trade, I enjoyed the opportunities for the acquirement of information and knowledge that was furnished by that common free school. Day by day, for I never missed a single day, nor fractional part of a day in my attendance, I experienced at the hands of the teachers appointed over me by the people, the most marked consideration and kindness. The very fact that I was a stranger seemed but to invite the attention and even the caresses of the noble man who stood at the head of that school. More than once—and I shall remember it to the last hour of my existence—I was desired to remain after the other children were dismissed from the school, to be spoken to, to be encouraged, to be led onward in the paths of education by my teacher. More than once he has placed his hand kindly upon my head, and familiarly, because not in the presence of other children, addressed me, saying, 'John, you must make effort in this and in that particular direction—you are wanting in these particular parts—if you will only bring yourself up in these, you will occupy a foremost position in this school.' He marked my attempts at progress, and to me as well as to others he always reached out the encouraging hand of kindness, and spoke the word that led to emulation and ambition in the acquirement of knowledge. For me to have found an institution like that was a great acquisition and a great wonder. I could scarcely understand it then, although I believe I fully appreciated it, as I do to-day. Up to the period of my advent into that school I had not been favored with great or any considerable advantages in the way of education. I had never attended other than the village schoolhouse, where the commonest branches of education were taught, perhaps in the commonest way; and for the two years preceding my arrival I had been deprived of even these poor advantages by circumstances that I will not undertake to detail here. And to have found not only the means so abundant placed before me, but agents so kind and at the same time so able in administering the benefits and advantages of that institution, sustained and supported at the public expense, commanded then, as I repeat will always command, my profoundest admiration and regard. To that school, and to the beneficent people who established it, am I indebted, in great part, to say the least, for all that I am, be it little or much, to-day. Hence, sir, when the question of public schools—of free schools—in which the children of all may be educated without price, without distinction of class, of wealth, or of politics or religious opinions, is involved, it is no wonder that I should feel a deep interest in that question. Next to the unity and the continued and happy prosperity of this glorious country that we live in and are all common citizens of—next to its continued and prosperous existence, I owe all allegiance, all love, all admiration, and all effort, to the public schools of our country.

* * * * * *

I am aware that those who advocate this measure profess that they have no purpose in view but the perfection, completeness and extension of educational conditions and advantages; but I would recommend those persons to begin in another way. I object to the manner in which they propose to begin to carry out such an end. Some of them say that the schools of California, or those of a portion of the State, are dens of infamy, are pestiferous in their character, are but sowing the seeds of immorality and death where they exist. But, as a remedy for these great abuses, for this great curse in our land, if it exists, do they propose to renew their efforts to obtain the passage of such laws or enforce such restrictions as will bring about a better condition of things? I think not. What, then, do they propose? If I understand them, and I think I do, they propose to withdraw a portion of the children of the State from what are now known as the common schools of the State. The proposition or purpose in view is better stated to me outside of this hall by citizens of distinction, who are interested in passing this act which we are now discussing, than by the gentlemen who have discussed it here. Their proposition to me is plainly stated—so plainly that he who runs may read and understand it. They say, first, that the schools are now unfit for the reception of their children, or the children of their people. They say they are common contributors to the funds that are consumed in the support of the schools, and that as the schools are unfit for their children, therefore they have a right to withdraw their children from those schools. That part of the proposition I admit, but I deny that it follows as a necessity, in common honesty and fairness, that they should also be entitled to receive a *pro rata* proportion of the common school moneys of the State, to be used under their direction for the support of such schools as they may establish. They say that this right exists in nature. Who, they ask, is so well entitled to the care, custody and training of a child as its natural parent? They invoke the social faculties of mankind to aid them in this argument, because they draw a contrast between the system they propose and the one that now exists, by showing you that on the one hand the government of the State claims the control and jurisdiction of the children of the State, for the purpose of public education, while on the other hand they assert that no such relation should be permitted or authorized while the parent lives who gave existence to his offspring, and whose greatest care is for his advancement and happiness.

* * * * * *

We are here with common objects, and the only question that is presented in connection with this bill now before us is plainly this: Shall we continue, by and through the agency of the State to support and carry out a system of public education in the State, or shall we not? For one, I am in favor of the affirmative of this proposition; I am in favor of renewing effort; of bringing up the standard of education, and the moral condition of our schools, until they shall not only be fit for the reception of the children of our people, but shall also by their superior excellence attract to our State parents and children from other lands. Adopt the proposition that is made in this bill; let every private school that may be established by the parents of children or by their religious teachers, or for profit by teachers, have a *pro rata* share of the school money, and what will be the result? In a very short time the State of California will be engaged in the interesting business of collecting moneys from various sources for the purpose of education, and disbursing and distributing those moneys amongst private parties, to be by them applied in such a way as they see fit for the purposes of education. Inaugurate this system, drive home this wedge that is now pointed at your common school system, and you will have schools exclusively under the control and direction of sects and parties, as well as by persons engaged as educators for profit.

* * * * * *

I have heard nothing to convince me that this bill should pass, and that our system of education should be changed. I have heard no argument within this chamber, because I do not recognize as argument on that point all that is said about the condition of the schools as they now exist. Our public school system in the United States of America is one of the proudest evidences of the greatness of our people, as it furnishes the basis and substratum of our institutions. Let religionists, of whatever class or kind, teach their doctrines and dogmas. They have their organizations for that especial purpose, and they contribute their means, and judiciously and carefully apply them to these ends. It is our business, by law and constitutional sanction, to preserve each in its own particular career, without interference from its neighboring organization. It is that preservation and defense against assault upon any, by either, that has marked our land and made it what it proudly is—the asylum of freedom in the world. No greater means of its continuance, no surer or more certain mode for its preservation can be found, I assert, than in the preservation of our common school system. While we denominate our schools public and common schools, let that not, as is the case now in the interior of our State, be a misnomer any longer. Let them be free, and furnish the means of education to the poor of the land. Your future members of the legislature, congressmen, governors, and presidents, are to be found among these classes, for nature has baptized the child of poverty with the blessing of energy. All the history of our country and of every free country conclusively proves this proposition, for the great men of every free land have sprung from the common people. Education is particularly for them; it is due to them from our hands and the hands of the great body of the people. I would gladly vote for a law that would compel the attendance of all children of a certain age at some school, for a certain length of time each year; but let us first furnish the means before we undertake to apply such a restriction. * * * *

I have heard it intimated more than once that this question was to be made a political question; that the position that men would take here would be carefully written down and noted, and that their political status hereafter would be determined by the position they took. I have regretted this exceedingly; but if there were any reason why I should speak at all upon this subject, so as to be incapable of being misunderstood, the latter would furnish the strongest one. Whenever any portion of the people of this State, or my fellow-citizens, see fit to object to me, because of the opinions I entertain, or the efforts I make in the line and direction of duty, let them object, and let them act. I ask no favors. Whenever any portion of the people cannot find in my acts something to approve, let them condemn; it may be that I can do as well without them as they can without me. I have no high admiration for that class popularly denominated politicians—those whose opinions hang loosely about them; those changelings, who simply seek office that they may get bread. Our country has been cursed; its lamentable throes to-day are the legitimate and logical sequence of the action of these detestable creatures. My doctrine and instincts alike demand that upon any and all occasions I should speak out, and let what I say be tried upon its merits. I have no fear though, that this question will be made a political one. I do not think that there are within the limits of this State a sufficient number of men vain and foolish enough to undertake to erect as a standard of political action any form of supposed religious opinions. I do not believe there are any considerable number of men who will make it a condition of their suffrages hereafter, that the vote to be cast here shall be cast in a particular direction. I trust in God, sir, that we will be spared such a condition of things. But if it should come, and there must be a war of opinions, all I have to say is, that I am prepared to bear my part in it. I would not, to-day, for the concentration of all the offices in the country into one, and my enjoyment of that one, sacrifice the opinions that I have, or the action that my conscience demands of me in connection with this subject.

24. ELEVENTH ANNUAL REPORT, 1861.

In this report Mr. Moulder argued the necessity of more money to make the schools effective; asked for an appropriation of $5000 for a State Normal School, and published the report of the Committee on Normal Schools, appointed by the State Institute, of May, 1861; reported that the State Institute had been largely attended; that the transfer of the power of examining teachers from Trustees to State and County Boards of Examination was driving the quacks out of the occupation; touched upon the subject of schoolhouses; stated that the law authorizing the adoption of a State series of text-books had been suddenly repealed near the close of the session of the Legislature of 1861, and asked for the passage of another; asked the Legislature to make some provision for school libraries; stated that within eight months after the passage of the act of April 22, 1861, 165,463 acres of township lands had been, or were about to be sold; and closed by referring to his previous reports relating to a State Military Institute.

25. SCHOOL LEGISLATION, 1862.

The Legislature of this session passed an act establishing a State Normal School in the city of San Francisco, and made an appropriation for that purpose of $3000. The State Normal

School was subsequently opened during the same year, and Mr. Ahira Holmes was appointed principal.

26. TWELFTH ANNUAL REPORT, 1862.

In his last report, Mr. Moulder recommended a plan for funding the indebtedness of the State to the School Fund; that Trustees be required to report the amount of interest, if any, which they received from Township School Funds; that power be conferred on Trustees to collect rate bills by law; that the State Board of Education be empowered to adopt a uniform series of text-books; stated that the State Normal School had been successfully organized, and asked an appropriation of $6000; alluded to a State Agricultural School under the act of Congress granting lands to the same; and closed by publishing his correspondence with State Controller Warren, who had declined to pay the semi-annual interest on the State indebtedness to the School Fund.

27. SCHOOL LEGISLATION, 1863.

During this session of the Legislature, the Senate Committee on Education referred the subject of revising and codifying the school laws to the Superintendent of Public Instruction, John Swett.

Public opinion was not yet sufficiently awakened to secure any very liberal taxation for support of schools, but some good provisions were incorporated into the law.

The following are some of the leading provisions:

1. A provision requiring the Superintendent, at the expense of the State, to furnish a State school register to each school.
2. Requiring the State Superintendent to visit schools, to attend County Institutes, and to address public assemblies on subjects relating to public schools, and providing for the payment of actual traveling expenses, not to exceed $1000.
3. Provision for the annual appropriation of $150 out of the County General Fund for the County Teachers' Institute.
4. Making the term of office of School Trustees three years, instead of one, and providing for the election of one Trustee annually.
5. Providing a stringent law for the assessment and collec-

tion of district taxes for building purposes, or for the support of free schools.

6. Providing for the assessment and collection of rate bills.

7. Authorizing the State Board of Examination to issue State educational diplomas, valid for six years; State certificates of the first grade, valid for four years; and second and third grade certificates, valid for two years.

An act, framed and introduced by Hon. E. F. Dunne, was passed requiring all teachers, under penalty of being illegally employed, and of forfeiting their salaries, to take an oath of allegiance.

SCHOOL FUND.

An act, prepared by Governor Low and Hon. D. R. Ashley, was passed providing for the gradual funding of the indebtedness of the State to the School Fund, which amounted at that time to $475,520.

Under authority of an act, approved May 3, 1852, providing for the disposal of the 500,000 acres granted to this State by act of Congress for the purpose of internal improvements, and reserved by the State Constitution for school purposes, it was made the duty of the State Treasurer to convert the proceeds "into bonds of the civil funded debt of the State, bearing seven per cent. interest per annum, and to keep such bonds as a special deposit in his custody, marked 'School Fund,' to the credit of said School Fund."

This provision was never complied with, for payments were made in depreciated scrip, or Controller's warrants; the scrip paid in was canceled, and to this extent the School Fund was used by the State to defray the ordinary expenses of government. The State, therefore, owed to the School Fund the sum of $475,520, derived from the sale of 237,760 acres of land, sold prior to April 23, 1858.

The State had always recognized this debt by appropriating annually for school purposes a sum equal to the interest at seven per cent. per annum upon the amount of this indebtedness. But the school department was placed completely at the mercy of the annual general appropriation bill, and if no appropriation was made, as was the case in 1861 and 1862, there was no redress.

This act, approved April 14, 1863, provided for the gradual funding of this unfunded debt to the School Fund, by requiring that whenever State bonds were redeemed, such bonds to such amount as should thus be redeemed with the sum of $475,520 should not be canceled, but should be kept as a special deposit in the custody of the Treasurer, marked "School Fund," in the same manner and for the same purposes as are the bonds directly purchased for said School Fund.

This was an important measure. Under its provisions the entire indebtedness of the State to the School Fund has been converted into State bonds at seven per cent.

28. THIRTEENTH ANNUAL REPORT, 1863.

The constitutional amendments adopted in 1862, provided for the election of the Superintendent of Public Instruction at the Special Judicial Election, instead of at the general election, and for a term of four years. Superintendent Swett's first term of office—three years—was thus cut short to a term of eleven months. He was renominated and re-elected in October, 1863.

The following are some of the main topics treated of in Mr. Swett's first report.

Receipts and Expenditures;
Schools;
School Children;
Attendance;
Teachers' Wages;
Change of Teachers;
County Institutes;
Errors in Reports of County Superintendents;
Reports of Teachers and Trustees;
District School Trustees;
Proceedings of State Teachers' Institute;
Convention of County Superintendents;
State Board of Examination;
State Certificates and Diplomas;
State Educational Society;
County Teachers' Certificates;
Reports and Blanks;
School Registers;
Order Books;
State Normal School;
The California Teacher;
District School Libraries;
Schoolhouses and School Architecture;
State Agricultural School;
University Fund;
Condition of the School Fund;
Department of Public Instruction;
State School Tax;
The Schools and the State;
Public Schools and Patriotism;
Military Drill in School.

The following is an extract from the argument in favor of a State School Tax:

The most important measure which demands the attention of legislators, is that of a State school tax for the better maintenance of public schools. I believe the time has arrived in the history of our State when the absolute necessity of such action can be fully demonstrated, and when the efficiency of the schools cannot be greatly increased without it. Whenever the question of increased taxation is agitated, it is due to taxpayers and property-holders that good and sufficient reasons should be explicitly set forth, and that it should be clearly shown that the public good requires it. The condition of the public schools, as exhibited by the statistical returns, will be to many minds conclusive evidence of the necessity of a State school tax; but the importance of the question demands that argument should be added to the weight of facts and figures.

Our American system of free schools is based upon two fundamental principles or axioms:

First. That it is the duty of a republican or representative government, as an act of self-preservation, to provide for the education of every child.

Second. That the property of the State should be taxed to pay for that education.

Simple propositions they seem; yet they have been recognized and acted upon in no other country but our own. Other nations, it is true, have their national systems of instruction partially supported by Government, and under Government control; but no nation in the history of the world has ever organized a system of schools like ours, controlled directly by the people, supported by taxation; free to all, without distinction of rank, wealth, or class; and training all children alike, whether foreign or native-born, to an intelligent comprehension of the duties, rights, privileges, and honors of American citizens.

In the minds of the hard-fisted, iron-willed settlers of Massachusetts Bay, where, under the wintry sky of suffering, want, and war, the germs of our American school system struggled into existence, common schools and taxation were as inseparably connected as were taxation and representation.

A few extracts from the old colonial laws will show how early our free school system sprang into existence. A section of the Massachusetts Colony laws of 1642 reads as follows:

"Forasmuch as the good education of children is of singular behoof and benefit to any commonwealth; and whereas, many parents and masters are too indulgent and negligent of their duty in that kind; it is ordered that the Selèctmen of every town shall have a vigilant eye over their brethren and neighbors, to see, first: that none of them shall suffer *so much barbarism in any of their families as not to teach, by themselves, or others, their children and apprentices so much learning as may enable them perfectly to read the English tongue*, upon penalty of twenty shillings for each neglect therein."

In 1647 this law was followed by another, to the end, in the words of the statute, "*that learning may not be buried in the graves of our fathers in the Church and the Commonwealth*," which required every town of fifty families to provide a teacher to instruct all the children of the town in reading and writing, and every town of a hundred families to set up a grammar school, with a teacher competent to fit young men for the university; the expense of these schools to be borne by the town, or by the parents, as the town should determine.

In 1692 the law provided that these schools should be supported *exclusively by tax levied on all the property of the town.*

In 1785, an ordinance respecting the disposition of the public lands was introduced into the old Congress, referred to a committee, and passed on the 20th of May, which provided that the sixteenth section of every township should be reserved "for the maintenance of public schools."

The celebrated ordinance of 1787, which confirmed the provisions of the land ordinance of 1785, further declared, that "*general morality and knowledge being necessary to good government and the happiness of mankind, schools, and the means of education, shall be forever encouraged.*"

As the results of this noble policy, more than fifty millions of acres of the public lands have been set apart for the purposes of education.

* * * * * *

It is said—leave the question of taxation to the citizens of each district? The fact that only eighteen districts voted a tax last year is good evidence that the districts will fail to do their duty. If it is argued that the Boards of Supervisors of the different counties will assess a county tax sufficient to maintain good schools, the statistical exhibit of the condition of the schools proves the contrary. Only four counties in the State assess the maximum rate allowed by law.

Shall we rely on the interest of the School Fund for the support of our public schools? Our School Fund amounts to less than a million of dollars, and it will not be largely increased for many years to come. The annual apportionment from that source amounts to only one dollar per child; is that sufficient to properly educate the children?

Can it be said, in view of facts, that California is doing her full duty in maintaining public schools? She raises by taxation only $4.42 per child, and the total amount raised from all sources, rate bills included, is only $7. Massachusetts raised by tax, last year, $6.44 per child; and as the cost of educating in California is at least four times as great as in that State, to make as liberal a provision we ought to raise $25 per child. The cost of educating a child in the public schools for ten months in the year, in San Francisco, where it is made economical in consequence of classification and the concentration of large numbers, is $21 per year. Is an average of $7 per child sufficient for the State at large? San Francisco derives from all sources an average of $13.70 per child; and yet, with this liberal provision, the public schools are crowded to their utmost capacity, and one thousand children more would attend were room provided.

Is it wise for legislators to fold their arms in apathetic indifference, when twenty thousand children of school age, or twenty-five and one half per cent., are reported as "not attending any school?" Is this recognizing the principle "that it is the bounden duty of Government to provide for the instruction of all youth?" When the average length of time school is continued is only six months in the year, is it probable that the children will be more than half educated? When the percentage of daily attendance on the public schools is only twenty-five per cent. of the whole number of children in the State of school age, and the percentage of attendance on the whole number enrolled is only fifty-five per cent., can the State be said to educate her children?

When California has only 219 free schools out of 754 public

schools, can she boast of her liberality in the presence of the other loyal States, whose schools are all free schools?

If one State in the Union needs a system of free schools more than any other, that State is California. Her population is drawn from all nations. The next generation will be a composite one, made up of the heterogeneous atoms of all nationalities. Nothing can Americanize these chaotic elements and breathe into them the spirit of our institutions but the public schools.

STATE TAX.

As the first step towards the organization of a system of free schools, and the better maintenance of the public schools, a special State school tax of half a mill on the dollar ought to be levied on the assessable property of the State. This would yield a revenue of at least $75,000, or about one dollar per child—and two dollars per child on the number enrolled in the public schools. True, this would not make the schools free, neither would it continue them ten months in the year; but it would give a fresh stimulus to county and district taxation, and, in four years, would, I believe, give the State a system of schools virtually free.

The public opinion of the State is in advance of legislation. After traveling extensively through the State, addressing public assemblies, with every facility for careful observation, it is my opinion that the people would indorse this measure, were it submitted to a popular vote, by an overwhelming majority.

The following petition, prepared by the State Superintendent, has been extensively circulated in the various school districts throughout the State:

"PETITION FOR STATE SCHOOL TAX.

"*To the Honorable the Members of the*
Legislature of the State of California:

"WHEREAS, We believe that it is the duty of a representative government to maintain public schools as an act of self-preservation, and that the property of the State should be taxed to educate the children of the State; and whereas, the present School Fund is wholly inadequate to sustain a system of FREE SCHOOLS; we, the undersigned, qualified electors of the State of California, respectfully ask your honorable body to levy a SPECIAL STATE TAX of half a mill on the dollar, during the fiscal years eighteen hundred and sixty-four and eighteen hundred and sixty-five, the proceeds of the same to be disbursed in the same manner as the present State School Fund."

All these petitions have not yet been returned to the Department of Public Instruction, and it is impossible to estimate the number of signatures obtained.

In the districts where they have been circulated, teachers and school officers report that it was a rare exception to find a man declining to sign them, and that the only objection raised was that the petition did not ask for a higher tax.

The names attached to this petition will be entitled to the serious consideration of legislators. They will represent the substantial citizens of the State; men of families, men of property, men who, in attaching their names, consider it equivalent to voting the tax and paying it.

A State tax of half a mill on the dollar was levied last year and is to be levied annually for carrying on the work of building the State Capitol; shall the work of building schoolhouses cease? By the time the Capitol is finished, it will have cost as much as all the schoolhouses in the State built up to that time. Is it not quite as essential that houses should be erected for educating a hundred thousand electors as that a costly pile should be built for the accommodation of a hundred and fifty legislators?

Are we taxed more heavily than the States which have borne the burden of the war? Are we so tax-ridden and so poor that we cannot raise one-fourth as much for educating our children as Illinois or Michigan or Massachusetts? California stands to-day the most peaceful and the most prosperous State in the Union. When the people of other States, staggering under taxation, their sources of prosperity dried up, their able-bodied laborers more than decimated by the calls of the army—when they declare that not a dollar less shall be raised for schools, that not a schoolhouse shall be closed—shall California, of all the States, alone shrink back from the duty of educating her children? Shall all our inexhaustible resources of mineral wealth be expended on "feet," and the brains of the children be left undeveloped? Shall millions be expended in constructing a Pacific Railroad, and the State fail to lay the solid foundations of character and intelligence on which rest the permanent prosperity of the generation which will reap the benefits of that great highway of the world? Shall we make every sacrifice of men and money to maintain the Union, for a generation unfitted, through want of education, to appreciate either our sacrifices or the value of the inheritance we leave them?

The real wealth of the State lies not in mines of silver, or gold, or copper; not in productive fields and fertile valleys, but in her educated men and intelligent free laborers. Educated mind has made the world rich by its creative power. The intelligent minds which have invented the hundreds of labor-saving machines in every department of industry, have created a wealth greater than the total product of the mines of Mexico, California and Australia combined. All these inventions were once dim ideas in the busy brains of educated men; ignorance found out none of them.

How many dollars is the electric telegraph worth? How many cattle and horses and copper mines the invention of sewing machines? What influence is so mighty in developing this creative power of society as the intelligence imparted in the public schools? Go to the Patent Office, and find out how many inventions come from the land of common schools, and how many from the States that have failed to establish them.

The machinery brought into use since eighteen hundred and sixteen is estimated to be equal to the labor of five hundred millions of men.

Ignorance never invented a machine to save the labor of a single man.

The life of the nation lies not in a few great men, not in a few brilliant minds, but is made up of the men who drive the plow, who build the ships, who run the mills, and fill the machine-shops, who build the locomotives and steam engines, who construct the railroads, who delve in the mines, who cast the cannon, who man the ironclads and gunboats, who shoulder the musket, and who do the fighting; these constitute the life and strength of the nation; and it is with all these men that the public schools have done and are now doing their beneficent work. The nation will not be saved by any one "great man;" the bone and muscle of intelligent laboring men must work out its salvation. Blundering statesmen may mar the fortunes of the war; general after general may show up his own incompetence; the concentrated and consolidated intelligence of the workingmen and fighting men will, in the end, prove victorious. When the bayonet has done its work, the ballot-box must protect the freedom won on the battle-field. When every ballot represents an idea, and falls electrified with intelligence to "execute a freeman's will," the States will revolve harmoniously around the central sun of a consolidated Union; no star will shoot off in eccentric orbit into the chaos of disunion, or the cometary darkness and desolation of secession.

29. SCHOOL LEGISLATION, 1864.

The supplementary and amendatory bill prepared by the Superintendent of Public Instruction, and introduced by the Committee on Education in the Assembly, Mr. J. J. Owen, Chairman, contained the following provisions:

1. Levying an annual State school tax of five cents on each $100 of taxable property in the State, to be apportioned in the same manner as the interest of the State School Fund.

2. Requiring each county to levy a minimum county school tax equal to two dollars for each child between 4 and 18 years of age.

3. Raising the maximum rate of county tax allowed by law from twenty-five cents to thirty cents on each $100.

4. Making it the imperative duty of Public School Trustees to levy a direct property tax sufficient to maintain a public school five months in each year, whenever the State and county school money shall be insufficient for that purpose.

5. Authorizing County Superintendents to subscribe for a sufficient number of copies of some State educational journal to furnish each Board of School Trustees in the State with one copy, at an expense not exceeding one dollar a year.

6. Allowing County Superintendents a sum for postage and expressage equal to two dollars for each school district.

7. Requiring history of the United States, and physiology and hygiene, to be studied in all the schools above the grade of primary.

This bill passed the Assembly without opposition, but in the Senate a determined fight was made to defeat it. The following is the Senate vote on this bill, which was one of the greatest advances ever made in school legislation in the State:

AYES—Benton, Burnell, Crane, Cunningham, Foulke, Hall, Haswell, Kutz, Maddox, McMurtry, Moyle, Porter, Roberts, Shepard, Tuttle, and Wright—18.

NOES—Buckley, Dodge, Evans, Freeman, Gaskill, Hamilton, Hawes, Montgomery, Pearce, Redington, Rush, and Shafter —12.

30. FIRST BIENNIAL REPORT, 1864-65.

The change of the sessions of the Legislature from annual to biennial required *biennial* school reports instead of annual.

The *First Biennial Report* was the most elaborate of Mr. Swett's reports. It opened as follows:

At the opening of this report, I take pleasure in stating that the criticisms of 1863 no longer apply to our school system, and that the hope expressed in 1864 has been more than realized.

Notwithstanding the school year closed before the bountiful harvests of the autumn were gathered, and while the State was still suffering from its previous financial prostration, the statistical returns exhibit an educational progress of which all Californians may well be proud.

While the increase of taxable property in the State from 1863 to 1864 was only three and seven-tenths per cent., the increase of school money raised by taxation alone, of 1865 over 1864, on the assessment-roll of 1864, was ninety-one and seven-tenths per cent.

The average length of schools has been increased, since 1863, nearly one month. While the number of teachers has increased only fifteen per cent. during the last year, the amount paid for teachers' salaries has increased sixty per cent.

The amount of school revenue from all sources has been increased, since 1863, $2.58 per census child.

The amount expended for schoolhouses shows an increase over 1863 of $164,000.

While the number of children between 4 and 18 years of age has increased 26 per cent. since 1863, the average number belonging to public schools has increased in the same time 46 per cent. During the last year the increase of census children was 9½ per cent., and of public school attendance 16 per cent.

The number of free schools has been increased seventy-eight in two years, and more than half the public school children are now relieved from rate bills, while the remainder pay an average tuition fee of twenty-five cents a month.

A careful examination of the full statistical tables submitted in this report, will show a great advance in all that relates to the material progress of the schools.

But there is a vital and intangible aspect which no statistics can exhibit.

The stronger hold which the schools have taken on public opinion; the greater skill, earnestness, and ability of teachers; the improvement in methods of instruction and classification; the greater interest and enthusiasm of pupils, consequent upon the introduction of better books; the greater interest of parents; the civilizing agency of well-conducted schools in all the little communities of the State—these cannot be expressed in figures nor conveyed in words.

California has taken her place in the front rank with those States whose material prosperity has been the result of public schools; and it is the duty of every legislator and every statesman to strengthen and perfect a system of schools which shall educate a race of men and women for the next generation that shall inherit, with the boundless resources of the Golden State, something of the energy, enterprise, talent, character and intelligence which have settled and civilized it.

The following are some of the main topics treated of in this report:

What our Public Schools have Cost.
School Property.
Comparative Cost of Public and Private Schools.
Comparison with other States.
Cities and Rural Districts.
School Children.
Length of Schools.
Teachers' Wages.
Amendments to the School Law.
Course of Study.
Boards of Examination.
School Libraries.
Teachers and Trustees.
National Bureau of Education.
State Agricultural College.
County School Tax.
County Institutes.
School Visits.
State Institutes.
Methods of Teaching.
Course of Study for Ungraded Schools.
Common Sense in Teaching.
Physical Training.
Moral Training.
The Bible in the Schools.
School Discipline.
Corporal Punishment.
State Normal School.
Public Schools and Taxation.

This report closed as follows:

I am reluctant to close this long and complicated report of details and statistics, necessary to be made, and yet from their character, tiresome to most except school officers and teachers, without a final appeal to the legislators who will be called upon to act on its suggestions and recommendations.

Previous to the lessons taught us by the great war just closed—in suffering, and doubt, and blood, and tears—the great fundamental truths of our school system had grown to be glittering generalities for gracing political speeches or governors' messages. These truths are now felt as a solid reality by the States on the other side of the continent; and under all the burdens of their debts, incurred in saving the nation, they are striving to make their public schools more effective by more liberal provisions for their support. I am painfully conscious that our schools, while accomplishing something, fall far short of the great work which is pressing upon them. They need both judicious legislation for their government and liberal taxation for their support. It is a matter of deep regret to all thinking men, that some of our citizens who represent the greatest wealth of the community are engaged in a crusade against taxation for the support of schools, and are waging their warfare under the hue and cry of extravagance, for the purpose of exciting the prejudices of the people.

LIBERALITY IS ECONOMY.

Liberality in educating the people is the true economy of States. What would be extravagance in one individual, whose life is limited to a few years, is economy in the life of a State or nation; what would be economy in a single man, is meanness in a State. This generation is not living for itself alone, but for future generations and for the future greatness of the nation. We have those among us who, to save from each dollar they call their own, a tax of one one-hundredth of one per cent., would make serfs of the next generation by leaving the children to grow up in ignorance; who think intelligence, cultivation, refinement, honor, integrity, morality, religion and patriotism among common people—the working classes—are myths; that the only thing tangible is real estate, and the great object of life is to escape taxation. Public schools are synonymous with taxation; they represent taxation, and the sooner the "common people" understand this democratic-republican doctrine the better for the State, the better for property, the better for mankind, the better for the nation. There is altogether too much of this whining about taxation for the support of schools. Where would the nation have been to-day but for public schools? Who fought our battles in the last war, but the men who were drilled into patriots in public schools supported by taxation? Last year the nation paid $22,000,000 for the support of schools; what true statesman wishes it had been less? The public schools are the educators of the working men and women of the nation, and they are the producers of all the wealth which is protected by law. The schools mold the characters of the men whose will, expressed through the ballot-box, makes and unmakes constitutions, and breathes life into all laws.

I appeal to legislators, when the school bill comes before them, to bear in mind that in providing for schools, a liberal expenditure is, in the end, the truest economy; and when the cry of taxation is urged against any reasonable and necessary appropriations, to remember this great truth, so well expressed by Horace Mann: "In our country and in our times no man is worthy the honored name of statesman who does not include the highest practicable education of the people in all his plans of administration. He may have eloquence, he may have a knowledge of all history, diplomacy, jurisprudence—and by these he might claim in other countries the elevated rank of statesman; but, unless he speaks, plans and labors, at all times and in all places, for the culture and edification of the whole people, he is not, he cannot be, an American statesman.

31. SECOND BIENNIAL REPORT, 1866-67.

This report opens with the following statement of progress:

The school year ending June 30, 1867, marks the transition period of California from rate-bill common schools to an American free school system.

For the first time in the history of the State, every public school was made entirely free for every child to enter.

In the smaller districts, having less than 100 children and less than $200,000 taxable property, *free* schools were maintained three months; in the larger districts, having more than 100 children and $200,000 taxable property, *free* schools were kept open *five months.*

More than 21,000 pupils attended *free* schools during the entire school year of ten months.

FREE SCHOOLS AT LAST.

I am glad that in this, my last official report, I can say that a system of *free schools*, supported by taxation, is an accomplished fact.

When I assumed the duties of this office, five years ago, I saw clearly that it was useless to expect to improve the character of the public schools to any considerable extent without a largely increased school revenue, derived from direct taxation on property.

At the session of the Legislature in 1863, I secured a revision of the School Law, and a State school tax of five cents on the hundred dollars, which gave an additional revenue to the State Fund of $75,000 a year. A bill was also passed providing for the gradual funding of the indebtedness of the State to the School Department, then amounting to $600,000. At the next session, in 1864, an additional school revenue was secured by providing that the minimum county school tax should be equal to $2 per census child. This little clause gave an additional county school revenue of $75,000.

In 1866, by the passage of the "Revised School Law," the State school tax was raised to eight cents on the hundred dollars, and the minimum county tax was raised equal to $3 per census child, both provisions together increasing the school revenue by at least $125,000 a year. I need not say that to secure an additional school revenue of $300,000 per annum, in the face of the high county, State, and National taxation, during a period of civil war, was no holiday task.

During each successive session of the Legislature I became a persistent member of the "Third House," arguing, soliciting, meeting committees, and patiently waiting, with a determination to secure for every child in California a right guaranteed by law to an education in a system of free schools based upon the proposition that the *property* of the State ought to be taxed to educate the *children* of the State.

I saw clearly at the outset that even after the revenue was provided, the schools would be to some extent a failure, unless protected from incompetent teachers by a thorough system of State examinations and certificates, for the schools cannot rise higher than the teachers.

PROFESSIONAL TEACHERS.

The second leading object of my administration has been to secure a *corps* of professional teachers, and to elevate the occupation of teaching. How far this has been accomplished, the list of professional teachers, and the graduates of the Normal School, found in this report, will show.

One third of the teachers in the State hold State diplomas and certificates, and one twelfth of the teachers are graduates of the California State Normal School.

A State Board of Education, of Examination, of Normal School Trustees; a uniform series of text-books, a course of study, rules and regulations, an educational journal—all constitute a *system* of education, in place of the irregular and unsystematized half public and half rate-bill schools of five years ago.

THE REVISED SCHOOL LAW.

Early in the session of 1865–66, the State Superintendent submitted a series of amendments to the Senate Committee on Education.

The amendments were so extensive that the committee referred the entire law to the Superintendent for revision. The law, as drafted by me, was submitted to the committee and adopted, with a few slight changes.

The more important improvements effected in the School Law by the first revision in 1863, and the second revision in 1865, may be briefly summed up as follows:

1. Organizing a State Board of Education of nine members.
2. Organizing a Board of State Normal School Trustees of eight members.
3. Authorizing the State Board of Education to adopt rules and regulations and a course of study for public schools.
4. Authorizing the State Board to adopt a uniform State series of text-books.
5. Providing each school with a State School Register.
6. Providing for the binding and preservation of school documents in the State and county departments of instruction.
7. Providing that the Legislature shall furnish the State Superintendent with at least two thousand copies of each biennial report for distribution among school officers and libraries.
8. Requiring the State Superintendent of Public Instruction to visit schools and lecture at least three months each year, and providing for the payment of actual traveling expenses.
9. Establishing County Teachers' Institutes, and providing for the payment of necessary expenses out of the County School Fund.
10. Funding the debt of the State to the School Fund.

11. Enlarging the powers and duties of County Superintendents, in details too numerous to mention.
12. Payment of County Boards of Examination.
13. Postage and Expressage Fund for County Superintendents.
14. Increasing the salaries of County Superintendents.
15. Authorizing County Superintendents to equalize district boundaries.
16. The election of Trustees for a term of three years instead of one.
17. Requiring the District Clerk to furnish the schools with pens, ink, stationery, and school incidentals, at the expense of the district.
18. The establishment of graded schools.
19. Providing for the legal establishment of separate schools for children other than white children.
20. Limiting the school time of children under eight years of age to four hours a day, exclusive of intermissions.
21. Establishing a system of school libraries by the reservation of ten per cent. of the State School Apportionment.
22. Authorizing a State subscription for an educational journal—two copies for each school district, one for the District Clerk, and one for the school library.
23. Life diplomas for teachers.
24. State educational diplomas, valid for six years; and first, second and third grade State certificates.
25. Establishing City Boards of Examination.
26. Authorizing the State Board to issue State certificates on county examinations with the State series of questions.
27. Authorizing the State Board to recognize the Normal School diplomas of other States.
28. Requiring all Boards of Examination, whether State, city or county, to be composed exclusively of professional teachers who are holders of State diplomas, or first grade city or county certificates.
29. A State tax of eight cents on each $100 of taxable property.
30. Requiring a minimum county school tax of $3 per census child, and increasing the maximum tax to 35 cents on each $100.
31. Authorizing and requiring School Trustees to levy a district school tax sufficient to keep a free school five months in a year.
32. Changing the school year to correspond with the State fiscal year, July 1 to June 30.

AVERAGE LENGTH OF SCHOOLS.

The average length of time during which public schools are maintained during the year is 7.2 months. Last year, for the first time in the history of the State, *all* the schools were kept *free* to all pupils for a period of from 3 to 5 months, according to the number of children and the taxable property in the district.

It marks an epoch in the school history of the State. Had rate bills been levied as before, during the entire year, the average length of the term of tuition in the schools would doubtless have been increased.

The death-blow to rate bills has been given, and they will soon be among the things of the past.

Last year 21,200 pupils attended schools which were kept open and entirely free for 9 and 10 months in the year.

10,000 more attended schools which were entirely free, but were kept open less than 9 months.

The number of schools maintained from 3 to 6 months was 387; from 6 to 9 months, 281; and from 9 to 10 months, including San Francisco as 208 schools of 60 children each, 422.

SALARIES OF TEACHERS.

The average monthly salaries of males teachers is $77; of female teachers, $64.

As the average length of schools is 7.2 months, the average annual salary of male teachers is $554; of female teachers, $460.

Even if teachers were employed for the whole school year of 10 months, which is the case only in the city schools, the average annual salary of a male teacher would be only $770 a year, from which deduct $300 for twelve months' board at $25 per month, and there would remain only $470 as the net proceeds of a year's work. Deduct from this $100 for clothing, and the salary stands at $370.

Trustees in some parts of the State who complain that the salaries of teachers are too high, and that school expenditures are extravagant, will do well to consider these figures.

The admission of teachers into the occupation is virtually in the hands of the teachers in this State now engaged in teaching. Elevate the standard of admission, and the occupation will soon become a respectable business. It will soon be better paid than brute labor. No occupation is more laborious; none wears out muscle and brain faster. It is only in the vigor of early manhood that a man can follow his profession. Shall he, then, be paid no more than the mechanic, or the day-laborer who shovels sand on the streets? The brain labor of the skillful teacher ought to be as well paid as the brain labor of the lawyer, the physician, the clergyman, the editor. He ought to dress as well and live as well. His profession ought to cost him, and often does, as much time and money as other professions. He ought to be paid a salary sufficient to enable him to supply himself with a library, and the periodical literature of the day. He should have a salary sufficient to enable him to live respectably, dress neatly, and move in the intelligent circles of society like other educated men. He should be paid enough to support a family. Teachers well paid can devote all their time and energies to the schools. They are not greater philanthropists than their neighbors whose children they educate. None of them teach from pure love of teaching. They do their duty, and expect their pay for it; it is the way in which they earn their living. They ought not to be expected to break mental bread to the children of others and feed their own with stones. Good teachers are not to be estimated by their daily salary of five dollars. Persons enough could be found in the State at half the present rates, but the people would be the losers. It is the teachers who give character and efficiency to the schools. The State may legislate, the people may vote taxes, and build schoolhouses, but the teachers build schools, and mold character, and act on mind. High salaries will attract talent and skill, and hold them both in the schools. Low wages will fill the schools with bunglers, and waste the public money. If the people of California desire to lay well the foundations of the State for all future time, they must employ skilled master-masons to hew the corner-stones.

SCHOOL LIBRARIES.

The school library system provided by the School Law of 1866 is in successful operation.

It was established in accordance with my recommendation in the biennial report for 1865, as follows:

After studying the plans of other States, and considering the subject in every possible relation, I have come to the conclusion that the following plan is the most practicable one which can at present be carried into effect in this State:

It should be made the duty of the County Superintendent in each county to annually set apart ten per cent. of the State apportionment of school moneys to each district, provided ten per cent. does not exceed fifty dollars, and to cause it to be held by the County Treasurer, as a District School Library Fund; and it should be the duty of Trustees to expend this fund for library books, provided that when the amount is less than ten dollars the sum may remain in the treasury until, together with subsequent apportionments, it shall amount to that sum.

It should be made the duty of the State Board of Education to prepare an extended list of books suitable for school libraries, and from the published list Trustees should make all their selections for purchase. Such a provision would protect the libraries from trash literature and useless books. The Trustees should be made librarians, with power to make the teacher a deputy.

RELIGIOUS EXERCISES IN SCHOOL.

The report treats at length on the vexed question of religious exercises, and Bible-reading in school. A few items read as follows:

The Constitution of California (Art. 1, Sec. 4) provides that "the free exercise and enjoyment of religious profession and worship, without discrimination or preference, shall forever be allowed in this State."

Section 60 of the Revised School Law, reads as follows:

"No books, tracts, papers, catechisms, or other publications of a sectarian or denominational character, shall be used or distributed in any school, or shall be made a part of any school library; neither shall any sectarian or denominational doctrine be taught therein; and any school district, town or city, the officers of which shall knowingly allow any schools to be taught in violation of these provisions, shall forfeit all right to any State or county apportionment of school moneys; and upon satisfactory evidence of such violation, the State Superintendent and County Superintendent shall withhold both State and county apportionment."

Section 70 reads as follows:

"It shall be the duty of teachers to endeavor to impress on the minds of their pupils the principles of morality, truth, justice, and patriotism; to teach them to avoid idleness, profanity, and falsehood; to instruct them in the principles of a free government, and to train them up to a true comprehension of the rights, duties, and dignity of American citizenship."

The School Law, then, is silent as to whether or not a public school shall be opened by the reading of the Bible or by prayer. It does not exclude the Bible; it does not make the use of it compulsory; it does not forbid the teacher from opening school with prayer; it does not compel him to do it. It leaves the whole question to be decided by Boards of Education, Trustees, teachers, and the people, as their judgment may dictate.

The present is an age of the largest and broadest personal liberty of religious opinion; the children of all classes are found in the common schools; and school officers and teachers should manifest a tender regard for the religious scruples of both Jew and Gentile, Protestant and Catholic, and hold the schools free from any violation of the great principles guaranteed by the National and State Constitutions, that every man be left free to worship God as he pleases, and to teach his children his own religious faith.

The great purpose of the common school is intellectual culture, as a foundation of moral and religious education; for without intelligence, religion degenerates into bigotry. It is left for the home, the Sunday-school, and the church, to teach forms of religious faith and worship. If each does its work without interference with the other, the result will be harmonious. If the church attempts to make the public school both a church school and a Sunday school, the result will be disastrous.

CO-EDUCATION OF THE SEXES.

I believe that the presence of boys and girls in the same school, far from being injurious to either sex, exerts a mutually beneficial influence. My belief is based on many years' experience in public school teaching, on an extended observation of schools, and on the opinion of the most enlightened and progressive educators.

CONCLUSION.

Since 1863, our public schools have been quietly and peacefully revolutionized. In the grand events of national history, in the building of cities, the construction of roads, the settlement of land titles, and the excitement of life incident to a new State, the progress of schools is hardly noticed except by those who are most directly interested in them. *Then*, we had little to be proud of in our educational record; *now*, California will not suffer by comparison with the most progressive educational States in the Union.

Then, the annual amount of money raised for public schools was $480,000; *now*, it is $1,287,000, or nearly three times as much.

Then, there was no direct State tax for the support of schools; *now*, the State tax is 8 cents on the $100, giving an annual revenue from this source alone of $120,000.

Then, the State apportionment was $130,000; *now*, it is $260,000.

Then, the amount raised by county and city school taxes was $294,000; *now*, it is nearly $600,000.

Then, the amount raised by district taxes, voted by the people, was $7000; last year the amount was $73,000, or more than ten times the amount raised in 1862.

Then, the maximum county school tax allowed by law was 25 cents, and the minimum required to be levied, *nothing at all; now*, the maximum tax is 35 cents, and the minimum tax must be equal to $3 per census child, which in many counties requires the maximum rate of 35 cents.

Then, the amount raised by rate bills of tuition was $130,000; *now*, it is only $79,000, showing a rapid approximation to a free school system. Three-fourths of the pupils now attend free schools during the year, and all are secured by law the right of a free school, either for three months or five months, in proportion to the size of district.

Then, the total expenditure for schools amounted to a percentage on the assessment-roll of the State, of 30 cents on each $100; *now*, it amounts to $58\frac{1}{10}$ cents on the $100.

In 1862 the amount expended per census child was $6.15; last year it was $12.61.

In 1862 the amount expended for schoolhouses was $49,000; in 1865 it was $257,000.

Then, the average length of the schools was less than six months in the year; *now*, it is seven and four-tenths months—an average length of schools which is exceeded only by Massachusetts and Nevada, of all the States in the Union.

Since then, while the number of census children has increased twenty-six per cent., the average number attending the public schools has increased more than fifty per cent.

The stronger hold which the schools have taken on public opinion, the greater skill, earnestness and enthusiasm of teachers, the consequent improvement in methods of instruction and classification, the use of better text-books, the deeper personal interest of parents, the neater and more commodious houses—all these together constitute an advancement which cannot be expressed by a contrast of statistics.

Then, we had no system of professional examinations, no educational society, no organization, and little professional pride; in fact, a man generally apologized for being forced to resort to teaching until he could find something else to do.

EXAMINATION OF TEACHERS.

Then, the "old schoolmasters" of San Francisco were examined every year by doctors, lawyers, dentists, contractors and business men, to "see if they were fit to teach the common school" they had been teaching years in succession. There was no standard of qualification, except the caprice of "accidental boards." Throughout the State, examinations were oral, and in most cases resulted in issuing to everybody who applied a certificate "to teach school one year;" *now*, a new order of things prevails. Every Board of Examination, whether State, city or county, must be composed of professional teachers exclusively; all examinations must be in writing, and in certain specified studies; and certificates are issued for life, or for a length of time proportioned to the grade of certificate issued.

California is the only State in the Union in which teachers have gained the legal right to be examined exclusively by the members of their own profession, and we have just cause to be proud of the fact. It has already done much to make the occupation of teaching respectable. It has relieved good teachers from useless annoyance and humiliation; it has increased their self-respect, stimulated their ambition, and guarded the schools against quacks and pretenders.

Our School Law is the only one in the United States which has taken broad, professional ground, by providing that the diplomas of State Normal Schools in other States shall entitle the holders to legal recognition as teachers in this State.

Strange to say, this new system of professional examinations was violently opposed four years ago, and by none so vehemently as by some common school teachers.

The world moves. Is there a single teacher here who would desire to have the old order of things re-established? But I never doubted that, once established, it would remain a part of our school system as long as schools were maintained.

It was my sanguine hope, for many years, that in this new State teaching might aspire to the dignity of a profession; that teachers might learn to combine their strength, respect themselves, command the respect of others, and honor their occupation. I have lived already to see the promise of the future. It has been and is my highest ambition to elevate the profession of teaching; for I well know that in no other way can the public schools be made the great educators of the State and the nation. If the citizens of this State desire to have good schools, they must pay professionally trained teachers high salaries.

It is only by raising the standard of attainments that the occupation can become well paid and well respected. Set the standard high, and high wages will follow; set the standard high, and good schools will be the result; set the standard high, and teachers will be content to remain in the schools.

Let all teachers who act on County, City or State Boards of Examination, discharge their duty faithfully, without reference to the pressure of friends, or the complaints of unsuccessful applicants, ever bearing in mind the duty they owe to the schools, the people, and the profession of teaching.

Professionally trained teachers, well paid for their work, will bring the schools up to their fullest measure of usefulness, and will secure from the people the most liberal support.

STATISTICS AND REPORTS.

Four years ago there was not a teachers' library in the State, except a few odd volumes in San Francisco.

Now all the large counties have begun a central library, and some of them have quite extensive ones.

We have a course of study, established by law, by means of which teachers are enabled to pursue an intelligent system of instruction, in spite of the prejudices of those parents who are too ignorant to comprehend the purpose of a school.

We have judicious rules and regulations, established by law, to aid teachers in enforcing discipline and order. In no other State is the authority of the teacher so well established and defined by law. Every district school in the State is placed under a judicious system of general rules and regulations.

Four years ago school statistics were notoriously unreliable; the records were kept without system, in old blank books or on scraps of paper, and often were not kept at all; now, every school is supplied with a State School Register, so simple in its style of book-keeping that the most careless teacher can hardly fail to keep a reliable record.

Then, Trustees wrote their orders to County Superintendents on scraps of paper, without much regard to business forms, and often without keeping any accounts; *now*, the neat order-books, in the style of bank check books, furnished by the Department of Instruction, allow of no excuse for failing to keep a financial record of money paid out.

In 1862, 150 copies of the report of the Superintendent were allowed to the office of the State Superintendent for distribution; now, 4,000 copies are published, and the law requires that a copy shall be sent to each Board of Trustees, each school library, each County Superintendent, and that 250 copies shall be bound for distribution to the School Departments of other States.

SCHOOL LIBRARIES.

Then, there were no school libraries; now, a library is begun in every school district, and a liberal provision is made for their enlargement by a reservation of ten per cent. of the State School Fund annually.

The influence of a library in school is second only to that of the teacher; and, in many instances, the information self-gleaned by the pupils from books, is the most valuable part of their common school education. Books will give them a taste for reading, make them *alive* to knowledge, and start them on a plan of self-culture through life. A teacher may fail in the discharge of his duty, but the influence of good books is sure and lasting.

Then, most of the county schools were destitute of maps, charts, and globes; now, most of them are supplied.

Then, all school incidentals, such as pens, pencils, ink, and stationery, were furnished by the pupils themselves, and as a consequence, half of the children were generally without these indispensable articles; now, they are furnished by the district to the pupils, free of expense.

PROGRESS.

When we consider the generally depressed condition of business in the State during the past four years; the heavy losses during the mining stock mania; the losses by flood and drought; the gradual working out of placer mines, and the consequent depreciation of property in many places; the falling off in the trade of many mining towns; the unsettled condition of land titles in many of the agricultural sections, and consequently the unsettled condition of the people; the slow increase of population from immigration, and at times its actual decrease in consequence of attractive mines in neighboring territories, and the slow increase of taxable property—we have reason to be proud of the unexampled progress of our common schools.

In the great work of settling and civilizing a new State—in the building of cities, the construction of railroads, the cultivation of farms, the development of quartz mines, the beginning of manufactures, and all the varied branches of industry—the influence of schools is lost sight of in the figures of material statistics; and it is only when we consider that the 50,000 children now in the schools, during the next twenty years will take their place in society as the workers and producers, that we begin to realize the latent power of the schools. They are silently weaving the network of mental and moral influences which underlie civilization; and when the children shall become the masters of the material wealth of the State, the influence of the schools will begin to be evident.

We are apt to consider immediate results rather than their remote causes; and hence the power of the public schools is seldom fully realized.

Light, heat, and electricity build up the material life of the globe out of inorganic matter, yet so slowly and silently that we hardly observe the workings of their subtle agencies. So the schools act upon society, and organize its life out of the atoms of undeveloped humanity attracted to the schoolrooms.

A few weeks since I visited one of the great quartz mills in the interior of the State. I descended the deep shaft, where stalwart men were blasting and delving in solid rock. Above, the magnificent mill, with fifty stamps, like some gigantic monster, was crushing and tearing the white quartz with its iron teeth; and I saw the immediate result of all this work in the heavy bars of pure gold, all ready to be stamped with their commercial value, and to enter into the great channels of trade. Then I entered a public school a few rods distant, where a hundred children were sitting, silently learning their lessons. I realized the relation of the mill and mine to the material prosperity of the State; but the school, what did it yield?

I rode over the line of the Central Pacific Railroad from the springtime of Sacramento into the snowy winter of the Sierra, and I saw the beginning of the great commercial aorta of a continent. On its cuts, and embankments, and rails, and locomotives, more money had already been expended than has been paid for schools since the history of our State began. I could see the tangible results of the labor expended upon the road; but where should I look for the value received to balance the cost of the schools? After thundering down on its iron rails from the mountain summits, I stepped into the Sacramento High School, and I thought to myself: What are these boys and girls doing, compared with the men who are paving the great highway of a nation?

I go out into the streets of this great city; I hear everywhere the hum of industry; I see great blocks of buildings going up under the hands of busy mechanics; I see the smoke of the machine-shops and foundries, where skillful artisans are constructing the marvelous productions of inventive genius; I see the clipper ships discharging their cargoes; drays are thundering over the pavement; the banks are open, and keen-sighted capitalists are on 'Change; and when I go to visit some little schoolroom, where a quiet woman is teaching reading and spelling to the little children, the school seems to be something distinct from the busy life outside.

A short time ago I saw that ocean leviathan, the "Colorado," swing majestically out into the stream, amid the shouts of thousands of assembled spectators, and glide off through the Golden Gate, to weave a network of commercial interests between the Occident and the Orient; and when, a few days after, I stood in the Lincoln Schoolhouse, where a thousand boys were reciting their lessons, I asked: What are they doing for the city in return for $125,000 invested in the house, and $20,000 a year paid to the teachers? The steamship comes back with its passengers and freight, and makes its monthly returns of net profits; but when will the school show its balance-sheet?

But when I pause to remember that the steam engine was once but a dim idea in the brain of a boy; that intelligence is the motive power of trade and commerce; that the great city, with banks and warehouses, and princely residences, has been built up by intelligent labor; that in the construction and navigation of the ocean steamer so many of the principles of art and science must be applied—I see in the public school, with its busy brains, an engine mightier than one of steam; and the narrow aisles of the schoolroom broaden into the wide and thronged streets of the great city. I know that the school-boys will soon become workers; that one will command the steamship, and one will become the engineer; one will be a director of the Central Pacific Railroad, and one will ride over it to take his seat in the Senate of the United States; one will own the quartz mill; another will build the machinery, and another still will invent some improved method of working its ores; one will be the merchant who shall direct the channels of trade; one will be the president of the bank, and another shall frame laws for the protection of all those varied interests—and the teacher, whose occupation seemed so disconnected from the progress of human affairs, becomes a worker on mind which shall hold the mastery over material things.

CONCLUSION.

I sought the office for the purpose of raising the standard of professional teaching and for organizing a State system of free schools. I am willing to leave the verdict to the future.

If, when my present term of office expires, I fall back into the ranks as a private, I shall feel proud of my profession, for I hold none more honorable, and to it I expect to devote my life.

I love the State of my adoption; I am proud of her educational record. I hope to see California as distinguished for her common schools, her colleges, her institutions of learning, as she has been for the enterprise of her people and the mineral wealth of her mountains.

I feel that her future prosperity is closely related to the education of her people, for the solid wealth of any State consists in educated and industrious men and women; and if the common schools are kept up to the full measure of their usefulness, her future glory will be not so much in her mines, her scenery, or her climate, as in the intelligence, integrity, morality, and patriotism of a people that shall make wealth a servant of science, art, literature, and religion.

32. SCHOOL LEGISLATION, 1868-69.

The only change made in the School Law at this session was a slight increase in the *maximum* rate of district tax voted by the people. The law requiring teachers to take the oath of allegiance was repealed. A local bill was passed, providing that the City Superintendent of Common Schools in San Francisco should be appointed by the Supervisors and Board of Education, instead of being elected by the people, to take effect in two years. A bill was passed to provide for organizing a State University.

33. THIRD BIENNIAL REPORT, 1868-69.

Superintendent Fitzgerald's first report opened as follows:

When I entered upon the duties of State Superintendent two years ago, the situation was peculiar. It was just after an exciting political canvass. The wildest surmises and most absurd apprehensions were indulged in on the one hand, and the most extravagant expectations entertained on the other.

My first official utterance reaching the general public was in my address before the State Teachers' Institute, held in San Francisco, June, 1868. In that address I declared that I had no partisan, sectional or sectarian ends to accomplish; that our public schools were not to be considered as either Democratic or Republican, Northern or Southern, Protestant or Catholic; that all parties were taxed alike for their support, and therefore had equal rights and should be treated with equal respect.

This report touched upon the topics of "Objects of Education," "School Trustees," "Examinations," "State Normal

School," "State and County Institutes," "Attendance," "Female Teachers," "Evening Schools," "Politics in the Public Schools," "San Francisco Industrial School," "Uniformity of Text-Books," "*The California Teacher*," "The Institution of the Deaf and Dumb and Blind," "The State University," and "Cosmopolitan Schools."

It closes as follows:

This exhibit cannot fail to inspire every good citizen with pride, gratification, and hope. It gives assurance that, while our State is evidently about to enter upon a fresh career of material development and prosperity, we have abundant reason to hope that it is destined to a progress equally rapid in the development of the higher interests of education. For what has been done, I take no credit to myself. I only claim that I have earnestly tried to do my duty.

34. SCHOOL LEGISLATION, 1870.

The first legislation of this session was the repeal of the law passed in 1868–9, in relation to the appointment of the City Superintendent of Public Schools in San Francisco. The bill continued the former Superintendent, James Denman, in office for one year, and then made the Superintendent elective at the next general election. The original purpose of this law thus repealed was to take the office "out of politics."

The "Revised School Law" was re-enacted under the title of the "California School Law," but was not changed in any of its main features.

The sections relating to rate-bills were stricken out, being no longer needed; the State Normal School was taken from the hands of the State Board of Education and placed under the control of a Board of Normal School Trustees, appointed by the Governor; and a provision was made authorizing the County Superintendents to fix the rate of county school tax, which was carried into effect in only three or four counties, and was afterwards pronounced unconstitutional by the Supreme Court.

TEXT-BOOKS.

The original provision for *uniformity* extended only to country districts, all incorporated cities and towns having special Boards of Education being independent. The law was amended so as to compel San Francisco and other cities to adopt the State series of text-books.

In 1869 the State Board of Education had made a sweeping change of all the school-books in previous use.

The State tax was increased to 10 cents on each hundred dollars.

35. FOURTH BIENNIAL REPORT, 1871-72.

The last report of Superintendent Fitzgerald opened as follows:

During no period in the history of California has more steady and substantial progress been made in popular education than the two years since the last biennial exhibit was made by the Department of Public Instruction. This progress has been realized in spite of an unusual and general depression in business, resulting from various exceptional causes, and a consequent temporary check upon immigration and material prosperity.

Great educational enterprises have been successfully inaugurated, abuses have been corrected, important and necessary reforms have been made, antagonisms have been reconciled, and a course of policy initiated that, with the united and earnest efforts of the true friends of popular education, will at a very early day culminate in the attainment of what every good citizen of California must desire —a public school system that will furnish the fullest advantages of an English education to every child in the State.

The State is growing, and its educational development keeps pace with its growth in wealth and population. The increase in the number of public school children is more than 20 per cent. in two years. The increase in the value of school property is about 20 per cent. for the same period.

This large increase in the number of children attending the public schools is evidence of their growing popularity. A just and liberal administration of public school affairs has won the confidence and elicited the support of all classes to a gratifying extent. This can be claimed by me in behalf of my co-officials in the Department of Public Instruction throughout the State, without any reservation. The friends of education have worked together in perfect harmony, and rapid progress has been the result.

The enormous amount added to the value of school property, let it be noted, is the result of voluntary taxation, voted directly by the people themselves. This fact furnishes the most conclusive proof of the deep interest felt by the citizens of California in the education of their children, and affords a guarantee that they will cordially sustain any judicious measures that may be presented for the further improvement of our school system.

AN INCREASE OF STATE SCHOOL TAX.

While in our centres of wealth and population the children have the advantage of a full school year's instruction, with the best facilities for learning, truth compels the confession that for the more remote and sparsely settled districts of the State our present system is shamefully inadequate, and is but a pretense for popular education. Under the present system, many districts can maintain schools only from three to six months of the year. No one need be told that such fragmentary bits of instruction are only a little better than none at all. During these short school terms, the pupils of such schools only get fairly started in their studies to be turned out for the greater part of the year, forgetting what little they had learned, and then coming back after this long and ruinous interval to commence again at the former starting-place, at the foot of the hill of knowledge, under a new teacher—the old one having sought a new place rather than attempt to live on the hope of another three or six months' school next year. This is but a sham, a waste of the public money, and a flagrant injustice toward a portion of the children of the State. There are very many of these schools thus revolving year after year on the axis of a defective system, making some motion, but scarcely any real progress. In a State system of public instruction should not all the children of the State be treated alike? As a good mother, she should dispense the blessings of education with an equal hand. The remedy for this great evil and injustice is obvious: *Let all the property of the State be taxed to educate all the children of the State.* This is the chief point that should now engage the attention of those intrusted with the management of our public schools. The public mind is prepared to welcome legislation for this purpose. The people are ready to sustain any practical measure that will give them a thorough instead of a partial public school system. The principle involved is already recognized in our present school law. The ten per cent. *ad valorem* State school tax is an unequivocal recognition of the principle that the property of the whole State may be taxed for the benefit of all parts of the State. All that is needed, therefore, is the extension of the practical application of the principle. If it be objected that the taxation of all the property of the State for all the children of the State would be attended with inequality, some localities paying more than their proportion of taxes into the general school fund, the answer is, that according to the theory already adopted, the State is the educational unit, therefore it must act as a whole, and not partially, in disregard of the avowed theory on which our system is based. As a complete organism, the good of each part is the good of the whole State. There is a fallacy in the assumption that the benefits of education are confined to the particular individuals or localities directly affected by the expenditure of the proceeds of local taxation. The benefits resulting from the diffusion of intelligence by means of education in the public schools affect the entire body politic. The dollar contributed by San Francisco judiciously expended in Plumas for education is no less a benefit to the former than to the latter. It is equally evident that the evils resulting from the prevalence of ignorance and vice in any neglected locality cannot be merely local evils. The virus will spread through the whole organism, and the results will be seen in the criminal courts, jails, hospitals, and insane asylums everywhere. If the State has the right to tax all her citizens equally to maintain State prisons, institutions for the insane, the deaf, dumb, and blind, and orphans, where is the wrong in imposing a tax for education for the whole State, that will lessen all those burdens resulting so largely and so directly from crime consequent upon ignorance?

There is another aspect of this question that deserves consideration. The disabilities of the present system fall upon the frontier and thinly settled districts of the State. The result is that our hardy pioneers, who lead the march of American civilization, extend the area of freedom, subdue the wilderness, and incur the hardships and dangers of frontier life, are, as the reward of their enterprise, energy, and courage, compelled to pay the penalty of seeing their children grow up in ignorance. Such disability may in some cases be inevitable and invincible, but there are in California but few of these children of the border who are beyond the reach of the beneficent hand of the State. Justice and sound policy require that the poorest barefoot boy of the humblest citizen in the poorest district of the most impoverished county should have as abundant facilities for a common school education as the son of the richest citizen of the most opulent city in the State. The fundamental purpose of a public school system is to insure the education of all the children of the State. The chief recommendation of such a system is that it secures the advantages of education to those who can be reached in no other way. If it fail in this it fails essentially to accomplish its highest end. Our system, then, is at present a partial failure. It is not the part of wisdom to ignore such a fact, looking only on the bright side of the picture. It is not honest. While singing the usual pæans of praise to our public school system, and rejoicing, as we legitimately may, in its benefits, such facts as these remind us that we still fall far short of a perfect system, and that much work, wisely planned and earnestly executed, remains to be done.

The following are some of the leading topics of this report:

State Text-Book System.
Drawing.
State and County Boards of Examination.
County Teachers' Institutes.
State Normal School.
School District Libraries.
University of California.
Against Compulsory Education.
School Discipline—a New Departure.

The following is the closing section of this report:

During my term of office this department has been happily free from sectional animosities. I have uniformly deprecated the introduction of sectional prejudices into our public school literature and exercises, and I think I can safely appeal to my late official associates to prove that my action has been consistent with my profession. A Southern man by birth and education, I would not be willing to put into our schools any book that would tend to excite or perpetuate hatred or contempt towards the Southern people. An American in feeling and principle, I would not be willing to put into our schools any book that did not inculcate love for our whole country. I would as zealously protect from insult or disparagement any other portion of our land as that in which I happened to be born and reared. My official relation to the teachers of California gave me a better acquaintance with the men and women from different parts of our Republic, and the consequence has been a broadening of my ideas and an enlargement of the circle of my sympathies and attachments. I will never forget these lessons nor lose these sympathies.

Knowing the teachers and school officers of California as I do, I lay aside the responsibilities and arduous labors of State Superintendent with a firm belief that the educational interests of the State are safe in their hands. Leaving all the various departments of our educational work in vigorous operation and healthful development, I trust the next four years will bring uninterrupted progress and increased prosperity.

36. SCHOOL LEGISLATION, 1872.

At this session there was no school legislation worth mentioning.

The Code Commissioners reported the Codified Statutes, including, of course, the School Law. The main features of the Revised School Law of 1866 remained intact, subject only to rearrangement and changes of phraseology.

Among the minor changes was a provision excepting incorporated cities from the action of "State uniformity" of text-books.

An appropriation of $300,000 was made for erecting buildings for the State University.

37. FIFTH BIENNIAL REPORT, 1872-73.

Superintendent Bolander's Report opens with an argument in favor of compulsory education, from which the following points are taken:

To the question, "What is this remedy?" only one answer can be given, or at least only one answer has thus far been found. Admitted that education forms the only secure foundation and bulwark of a *republican* form of government, if not of every form of government; admitted that the universality of education becomes thus of vital importance to the State; and admitted that the exigencies of the case not only empower but compel the State to provide all the facilities necessary to enable every child to acquire at least a common school education, and we are forced to the conclusion that it is not only the privilege, but the duty of the State, to compel every parent to bestow upon his children at least the education which the State places within his reach.

Education is one of the primary conditions necessary to the very existence of a civilized government. This proposition is so well established and universally acknowledged as to have become trite, and any further consideration of it, beyond its mere enunciation, is unnecessary. The extension and intensity of education in a nation will determine the degree of the nation's civilization, and the degree in which a nation's government is a government "for the people and by the people." This latter office of education has received the fullest recognition in the United States, and every State has declared its conviction that "knowledge and learning generally diffused through a community are essential to the preservation of a free government."

The fundamental idea of government is "the protection of society and its members, the security of property and person, the administration of justice therefor, and the united efforts of society to furnish the means to authority to carry out these objects." The first means thus furnished to authority are the powers of prescribing and enforcing "rules of action" or laws, and to punish any infraction of these laws; that is, to punish crime. But a still higher power than the mere defining and punishing of crime has been delegated by society to authority, namely, the power to prevent crime by diminishing, and, if possible, removing altogether the causes of crime. Fear of punishment helps to repress crime, but only as far as detection is quick and sure, and punishment swift and certain. The repressing or removing of the motives or temptations to commit crime not only represses crime, but prevents crime by making its commission impossible from its unreasonableness.

"Illiteracy is incipient crime," or, as Dr. Lyman Beecher expresses it, "Uneducated mind is educated vice." Experience has given this proposition the force of an axiom in sociology. But there is not only a necessary direct relation between illiteracy and crime; there is also a necessary direct relation between illiteracy and pauperism; and as there is no less a necessary direct relation between pauperism and crime, we have crime once more as a resultant—crime as a direct result of illiteracy; crime as an indirect result through the medium of pauperism, but no other ultimate result than crime.

Hence, in every scheme of civilized government education has been recognized as the only force sufficient to diminish and remove the causes of crime. But education has another office. From the loss of supremacy in manufactures to the terrible downfall of a warrior nation before a student nation, history teaches the lesson: Education is the first condition necessary to the prosperity of a nation.

History teaches still another lesson: Education will be generally diffused only under a system of public schools; that is, under a system in which either the State by direct taxation raises the funds necessary to support for a definite length of time the schools needed to give every child a common school education, or the State compels the different municipalities to establish and maintain such schools. The American States have generally chosen the former alternative; thus testifying, in the most emphatic manner, that as the prosperity, nay, the very existence of the State, depends upon education, so education shall be the first and paramount care of the State.

The only time the people have had an opportunity to express their will, they have declared themselves overwhelmingly in favor of compulsory education. Since then the fearful increase of "hoodlumism" has made the question one of vital importance. And to save themselves from the rapidly increasing herd of non-producers, who must be supported by the community at large, to save themselves from the wretches who prey upon society like wild beasts, some demand already that a law for compulsory education be supplemented by a law requiring the State to establish and maintain labor schools, school ships, industrial and technical schools. The times demand not only that children be educated in the common English branches, but, also, that children be educated how to work.

Superintendent Bolander treats at length on the necessity of increasing the State School Tax, and proposes a *minimum* apportionment of $500 for each district, without regard to numbers; of the need of teachers trained in Normal Schools; and closes with the remark that—

These two--long terms and qualified teachers--are the real educational forces of the State; and with them at our command, the prosperity, efficiency and usefulness of our common schools will be insured beyond peradventure.

38. SCHOOL LEGISLATION, 1874.

The only act of school legislation of any importance at this session, was the levying of a State school tax of $7 per school census child, and the apportionment of $500 as a *minimum* to each school or school district; the balance to be apportioned *pro rata* on the census children.

TEXT-BOOKS.

All the incorporated cities except San Francisco were placed under the law of State uniformity of text-books.

39. SIXTH BIENNIAL REPORT, 1874-75.

Superintendent Bolander's last report opens with the following summary of progress:

Since my last report, 29,953 children have been added to our school population; 117 new school districts, supporting 322 schools, have been organized; 274 new schoolhouses have been built and furnished, and old schoolhouses refurnished, at a cost of $613,-746.41; the school expenditures have been increased $544,885.09; the school property has increased in worth $1,011,262.85; the average school terms have been lengthened 1.33 months, being now 7.47 months as against 6.14 months in 1873; 34 districts, as against 464 in 1873, maintained school less than six months; 765 districts, as against 361 in 1873, maintained school more than six months; and 787 districts, as against 637 in 1873, maintained school eight months and over.

In relief to this showing of our educational statistics, I must note a great advance in the number of first grade schools, *i. e.*, high schools, grammar schools, and schools in which high school and grammar grade studies are taught in addition to the lower grade studies; the greater number of teachers holding high grade certificates; in the better salaries paid to lady teachers; in the greater amount of funds spent for school apparatus, one-half of our districts being now supplied, at least partly, with apparatus. Much remains yet to be done, however, in the equipment of schoolhouses; for one-fifth of our districts have not yet even the outhouses demanded by decency; three-fourths of the districts have not suitably improved school grounds; one-half of the districts do not furnish their schools with the necessary apparatus; and nearly one-half of the districts have not furnished their schoolrooms with improved furniture.

From July 1, 1866, to June 30, 1867, for the first time in the history of the State, every public school was made entirely free for every child; and an important transition was thereby marked in popular education. But, though every public school was made free, the ways and means provided for the public schools, and the manner of apportioning these means to the different districts, were for years such that only in the centres of wealth and population the children had sufficient facilities for obtaining a good common school education, whilst in all other sections of the State the school system was but a pretense for popular education. The system went further, for in some cases it even thrust districts from without its pale. Hundreds of districts did not receive sufficient funds to maintain in every year the three months' school guaranteed by the Constitution to every district of the State. Up to June 30, 1874, districts whose number of census children fell below a certain figure—twenty for some counties, up to as high as thirty for others—did not receive for any one school year sufficient funds to maintain a three months' school for that year.

Thanks to the last Legislature, however, for the school year ending June 30, 1875, and for the first time in the history of this State, every district received sufficient funds for not only a three months' school, but for at least a six months' school. The progress thereby made in popular education can hardly be overestimated. Short school terms—which, until last year have been the rule and not the exception in a majority of the districts of the State—place within the reach of our children only such fragmentary bites of instruction which are only a little better than none at all. Every system of popular education which does not insure to every district of the State at least an eight months' school every year, is but a sham. Long school terms are the *sine qua non* without which it is impossible to give our children the full measure of the amount and quality of education needed by them. Happily, the wise action of the last Legislature has secured to our schools this first factor in every successful system of popular education. The results of this action are patent. In 1873, only 43.3 per cent. of all the districts maintained an eight months' school; in 1875, this percentage is raised to 49.53; in 1872, over 464 districts, or 31.74 per cent., did not keep a six months' school; in 1875, the number has diminished to 34, or 2.15 per cent. of all the districts in the State. In other words, all but 34 districts maintained at least a six months' school.

Superintendent Bolander condemned "text-books" in unmeasured terms, spelling-books in particular. He says:

In short, the board, and through it the State, must furnish each teacher with a *Manual of Instruction*. By this means we can dispense with several text-books, and reduce the bulk of the remaining text-books by rigidly excluding therefrom everything which appertains exclusively to the teacher's office. A text-book should be, what its name implies, a "*book of texts*." "The sermons are to be preached by the teacher—the book is to furnish the texts which are to be analyzed, developed, unfolded, explained, enlarged upon by the teacher—texts which need an exegesis to make them understood."

The Manual of Instruction will furthermore point out to teachers the course of culture and technical training needed by them to qualify themselves for their work; in other words, it will prepare teachers for their work. Being no longer able to rely upon the text-book, teachers will be compelled to assimilate some method of teaching, and, in time, will then become real teachers, instead of mere school keepers.

TRAINED TEACHERS.

For the purpose of securing professional teachers he recommended the following plan:

1. That in our State University be established a school or faculty of education with a four years course of study; all students completing and passing a satisfactory examination in the first year's course, to obtain a life certificate entitling them to teach any primary or third grade school in the State; all students completing and passing a satisfactory examination in the second year's course, to obtain a life certificate entitling them to teach any school in the State not above the intermediate or second grade; all students completing and passing a satisfactory examination in the third year's course, to obtain a life certificate entitling them to teach any school not above the grammar or first grade, and to be eligible to the office of City or County School Superintendent; all students completing and passing a satisfactory examination in the four years course, to obtain a life diploma entitling them to teach in any school of the State, including high schools, normal and training schools, and the Educational College of the University, and making them furthermore eligible to the office of State Superintendent and instructors of normal institutes.

2. That the course of study of the State Normal School be conformed to the one just sketched.

3. That any high school or college, private or public, be authorized to establish a normal school department, with a partial or full course of study as prescribed for the Educational College of the University, provided that such department be taught only by graduates of the four years' course; that the course be the same as provided for the State Normal School, and that the students be examined and certificated only by the faculties of the State Normal School and University. If such department be connected with a public institution, tuition to be free.

4. That any City Board of Education, or County Board of Supervisors, be authorized to establish city or county normal schools, teaching partially, or in full, the course above mentioned, but their students to be examined and certificated only by the faculties of the State Normal School and University.

His plan for the establishment of Normal Institutes was as follows:

1. The present Teachers' Institutes and Boards of Examination are replaced by Normal Institutes.

2. Normal institutes are to be held annually in such places as may be determined upon, either by statute or by authority conferred upon the State Superintendent or other officer or board.

3. Every normal institute must be continued in session for not less than four weeks. It must be under the direction of a teacher who is known or proved to be a thorough normal school instructor; such teacher to be appointed by the State Superintendent, or other officer or board, as may be deemed best. Each of the teachers engaged in the State Normal School or the Educational College of the University, must conduct annually at least one normal institute.

4. Every applicant for a teacher's certificate must be present at the beginning of a normal institute; his admission as a member of the institute must be upon an examination like that required of applicants for admission into the State Normal School; he must attend the institute at least one full term; and must pass, at the end of the term, a satisfactory examination in the instruction given during the institute.

5. The expenses of the institute are to be paid direct by the State, or from the unapportioned County School Funds of the counties comprising the district in which the institute is held.

I have thus given the merest sketch of a system of normal institutes which can easily and profitably be introduced into this State. From this sketch an appropriate system can readily be elaborated; but as so much depends upon the temper and view of the Legislature, and its Committees on Education, it is preferable to leave such elaboration till the time when such committees can act upon the matter.

He quoted extensively from various writers on "School

Hygiene," on "Technical Education" and "Kindergartens," and concluded as follows:

I now retire from an office which I entered with a great deal of hesitancy and many forebodings. I brought to it many firm convictions, the growth of a decade spent in the schoolroom; and according to these convictions have I labored to perfect our system of education; and I feel that I need not fear the verdict of the future. I have at least succeeded in equalizing somewhat the educational facilities enjoyed by the districts of the State, and in rationalizing, in some measure, the system of instruction, and bringing it somewhat more in harmony with the "new education."

The appendix contained a manual of suggestions for teaching the State course of study, including an exposition of the "Grube system" of teaching arithmetic to beginners, and a full course of elementary lessons in local geography, and botany. It contained also an explanation of the "Kindergarten," an essay on "The Nervous System as affected by School Life," by Dr. D. F. Lincoln, of Boston; a report of the State Board of Examination, of the State Normal School, of the Institution for the Deaf and Dumb and Blind, and the report of the Regents of the University.

40. SCHOOL LEGISLATION, 1876.

The first school legislation during the first week of the session, was a bill taking from the State Board of Education the power of changing text-books, it being evident that a majority of the board were in favor of throwing out McGuffey's series of Readers, and Monteith's series of Geographies.

Mr. Carpenter, Speaker of the Assembly, introduced a bill providing for a State Board of Education, consisting of the Governor, State Superintendent and eight elective members, two from each congressional district; the board so elected to assume the powers of the State Board of Education, the Board of Regents of the University, and the Trustees of the State Normal School. The bill also provided for abolishing State uniformity of text-books, and for giving boards of education and school trustees the power of local adoption. This bill passed the Assembly, but was defeated in the Senate.

Mr. Hopkins introduced a bill providing for "county uniformity" in text-books, which passed both Houses but was pocketed by the Governor.

The section relating to county certificates was amended so as to authorize county boards to issue second and third grade certificates, on an examination in only the following studies: Arithmetic, Grammar, Geography, History, Reading, Writing, Spelling and Methods of Teaching.

41. LIST OF STATE SUPERINTENDENTS.

John G. Marvin	1851–1854.
Paul K. Hubbs	1854–1857.
Andrew J. Moulder	1857–1863.
John Swett	1863–1868.
Rev. O. P. Fitzgerald	1868–1872.
Henry N. Bolander	1872–1876.
Ezra S. Carr	1876–1880.

DEPUTY SUPERINTENDENTS.

J. H. Eickhoff	1872–1876.
Mrs. E. S. Carr	1876–1880.

SUPERINTENDENTS AND POLITICS.

John G. Marvin and Paul K. Hubbs were elected by the Democrats.

Superintendent Moulder was twice elected on the Democratic ticket. He declined a nomination by the "Breckenridge" wing of the Democracy in 1862.

In the election of 1862 there were three tickets in the field, and the State Superintendent happened to be the only State officer to be elected. The opposing nominees were Col. Jonathan D. Stevenson, by the "Douglas Democrats;" Rev. O. P. Fitzgerald, by the "Breckenridge Democrats;" John Swett, on the "Union Ticket." The vote stood as follows: Swett, 51,238; Stevenson, 21,514; Fitzgerald, 15,514.

Superintendent Swett was re-elected on the Republican ticket in 1863 by about 20,000 majority over Dr. O. M. Wozencraft, the Democratic nominee, and was renominated in 1867. The canvass was a bitter one on both sides. Rev. O. P. Fitzgerald, the Democratic nominee, was elected by a majority of 1401.

Superintendent Fitzgerald was renominated in 1871, his opponent being Henry N. Bolander, nominated by the Republicans. The canvass was quite an exciting one, and resulted in the election of Bolander by 10,000 majority.

In 1875 the opposing candidates were Rev. O. P. Fitzgerald, Democratic nominee, and Dr. Ezra S. Carr, Republican candidate. This was also an abusive canvass. Dr. Carr was elected by a majority of 7000.

It was expected that the office of State Superintendent would be "taken out of politics" by providing for the election at the special judicial election, but this measure only intensified the evil.

SPECIAL HISTORY OF SAN FRANCISCO.

I. SCHOOL REPORTS.

THE first school reports published in pamphlet form by the Board were those of Superintendent O'Grady, 1854 and 1855. The Superintendent reported the average number of pupils to a teacher to be 87; that a uniform series of text-books had been adopted; and that a Teachers' Association had been formed.

Superintendent Theller in 1856 reported the following statistics:

Teachers, 39; Pupils, 3347.

District No. 1, Mr. Swett, Principal	683
District No. 2, Mr. Denman, Principal	580
District No. 3, Mr. Ellis Holmes, Principal	635
District No. 4, Mr. Ahira Holmes, Principal	733
District No. 5, Mr. Carlton, Principal	374
District No. 6, Mr. Morrill, Principal	200
District No. 7, Mr. Macy, Principal	142
	3347

In the Ward Schools there were educated 1421 pupils. The Male Departments of the Ward Schools were taught by male and female instructors, and the Female Department by the ladies of the different religious orders of the city, known as Sisters of Charity, Sisters of Mercy, and Sisters of the Presentation—all of whom had certificates of capability, and were licensed to teach by the late

County Commissioners of Education, and drew their salaries from the city, county and State educational fund.

The school law of 1855 abolished the separation of the school fund, and all these schools have been mingled into one uniform system. Since the 5th of May last there has been no religious, sectarian or denominational doctrine taught in them.

He reported the discipline good, and the instruction satisfactory.

In fusing the "Ward Schools" with the public schools, the following additional teachers were elected:

Principal of District No. 4, Wm. Hammill, *vice* Ahira Holmes; Principal of District No. 5, Mr. T. S. Dunne, *vice* Mr. Carlton; District No. 7, Mr. T. C. Leonard, *vice* Mr. Macy; New School, Thomas S. Myrick; District No. 8, Mr. H. P. Carlton.

By the Consolidation Act, Mr. Pelton, who had been previously elected as County Superintendent, was made, *ex officio*, City and County Superintendent for one year.

His report contained the first full statistical tables of the schools. He recommended the establishment of evening schools; of a Teachers' Institute; the study of History of the United States; and published the "Course of Study."

The reports of Superintendent Janes for 1857 and 1858 were still more complete.

He reported the weekly Normal School a success, teachers being compelled to attend; recommended the establishment of more evening classes, and treated at length of discipline and methods; gave a short historical sketch of the early schools; treated of methods of teaching; complimented his predecessors in office; opposed May festivals; and reported favorably on the City Normal School, Mr. George W. Minns, Principal; Messrs. Myrick and Swett, assistants.

Superintendent Denman's report, 1861, was longer than any preceding report.

He summed up the improvements in 1860 as follows:

1. Better Classification.
2. The grading into Grammar and Primary Schools.
3. Better accommodations and new buildings.
4. New furniture.
5. School Registers furnished by the Board.
6. Monthly Reports of pupils.

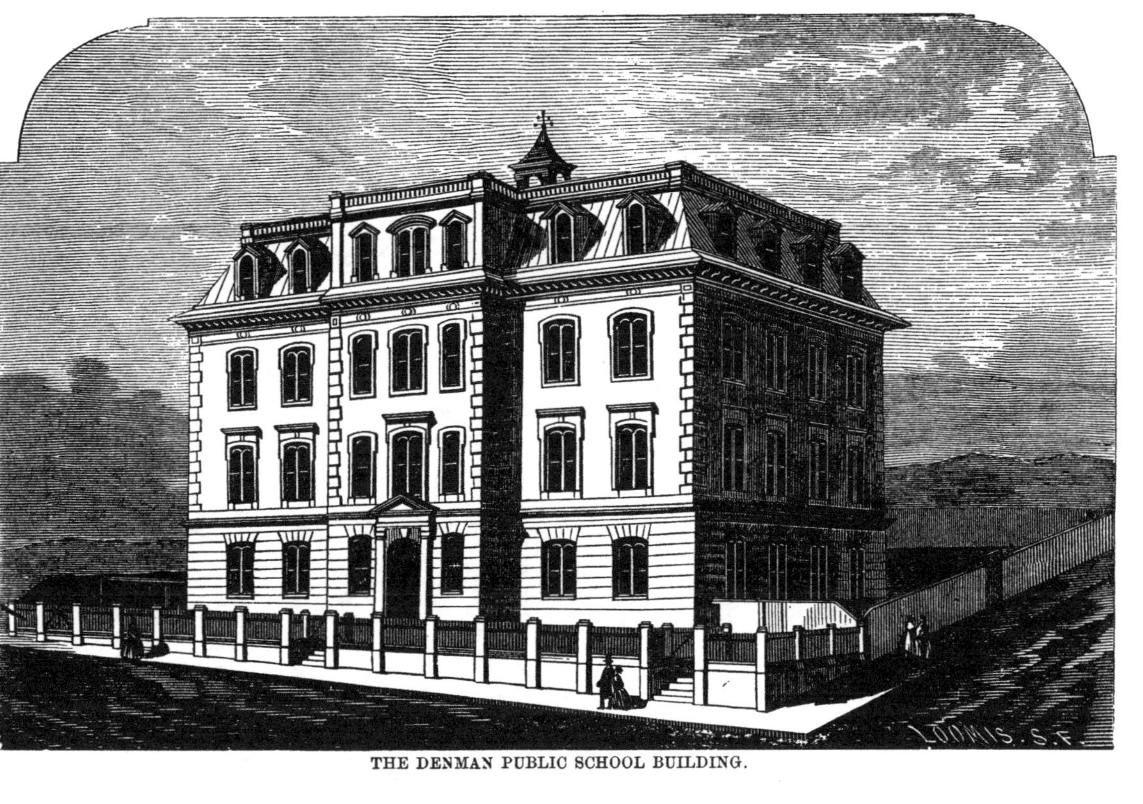

THE DENMAN PUBLIC SCHOOL BUILDING.

The questions used in the examination for admission to the High School were given in this report.

SUPERINTENDENT TAIT'S REPORTS.

The four reports of Superintendent Tait, 1862, '63, '64, and '65, were all creditable documents. In his first report, 1862, Mr. Tait reported a list of graduates of the Minns Evening Normal School—16 for 1861, and 38 for 1862. He recommended that promotions in the primary grades be made semi-annually; that Principals be required to make monthly reports to the board of attendance, etc.; and that no person under 18 years of age should be eligible to teach.

In his last report, 1865, he advocated the reading of the Bible in school.

Superintendent Pelton's report for 1867, recommended an increase of salaries; a simplification of the course of study, and the appointment of a Deputy Superintendent.

COSMOPOLITAN SCHOOLS.

Concerning the school, Mr. Pelton said:

These schools of recent establishment are designed to afford the facilities for acquiring the modern languages—German, French, and Spanish—in connection with the ordinary English course. As elsewhere stated, it has been conceived that the object of our Public School system, its true policy and leading idea, is to meet all reasonable educational demands. A few years since a great number of our citizens, native as well as foreign, were compelled to patronize private institutions, with their less perfect classification, and less thorough instruction, for the sake of the modern languages, which by the more observing and thoughtful of our people are considered of greater importance in the ordinary vocations and positions of society than much, very much else included in the English course, especially in our advanced High School course. And there were many of our best citizens who were unable to meet the expense of private tuition for their children; and yet they were unwilling to permit their sons and daughters to grow up to maturity, and remain forever ignorant of their mother tongue.

Some two years since, to meet this public demand, I recommended the establishment of a single class, now grown to be the Cosmopolitan Schools of this city. This system, though by no means unique, and confined to this city, is here perhaps better organized, and on a more liberal and comprehensive basis, than elsewhere. The plan is European; Germany has multitudes of schools where the French and English are recognized as we recognize the German, French, and Spanish. There are many such schools in the Eastern States.

This system, though at first opposed here, as it had been elsewhere when first proposed and adopted, and before its merits and practicability had been tested, is now exceedingly popular in the community, and enjoys a very intelligent and excellent patronage. Most of its former opponents are now its advocates—some its warmest supporters. These schools now can stand upon their own recognized and admitted merits. I predict that they will more than justify all that has been claimed in their behalf.

SUPERINTENDENT WIDBER'S REPORTS.

The three reports of Mr. Widber, 1871, '72, '73, were models of brevity, containing little except finance and statistics, Deputy Superintendent Swett in his reports made an exhibit of the results of the cramming system as shown by the written examinations; argued against state uniformity of text books; advocated a higher rate of salaries for principals of Grammar Schools; and recommended the adoption of the *Grube system* of teaching Arithmetic to beginners.

MR. DENMAN'S REPORTS.

The last reports of Superintendent Denman, 1874 and 1875, were the longest of the city reports. The report of 1874 treated at length of the new course of study.

The last report of Superintendent Denman, 1875, recommended the establishment of a city Normal School, and treated at length of the course of study. It also contained a valuable historical sketch of schools and teachers.

The report of Deputy Superintendent Leggett recommended the abolishing of annual written examinations for promotion; favored the appointment of a Board of Inspectors and a city Normal School; criticized the methods of teaching modern languages in the Cosmopolitan Schools, and recommended a cutting down of the course of study in the higher grades. The examination questions, in language prepared by Mr. Leggett, were particularly good.

The report of Deputy Superintendent Leggett, on examinations and methods of teaching, was a valuable one. The following extracts illustrate its style:

THE ANNUAL WRITTEN EXAMINATION.

It is curious to observe how hard it is to break the chain in which long habit binds human society, or to get out of the groove of custom. During certain stages of a people's progress no doubt this principle of aversion to change is useful and necessary; but there is also a time (whether we have yet reached it or not) when every practice or custom must make good its claim to future existence or cease to be.

Why should we have annual examinations at all? The question startles most ears, and why? Because we have always had them at the close of the school year. The habit of holding them has become venerable from antiquity, and I know I shall be accused of sacrilegious interference with a time-honored custom in proposing to do away with them. If we ask, why should the annual examinations be kept up, we have for reply: Because we have always had them.

If we ask, why should they be abolished, we have for replies:

First. Because they are not needed.

Second. Because they are expensive, costing the department at least $20,000 a year.

Third. Because they render useless the school work of the last school month of every year, and foster cramming and overwork during that time.

Fourth. Because they tend to produce excitement and lead to over-exertion on the part of pupils at a time when they are wearied by the work of the whole year.

Fifth. Because if they were abolished, many teachers who, under the present system cannot be induced to abandon the practice of cramming for the examination, because they are, as they believe, to be judged by the results of it, could be induced to do some teaching in their classes.

If I am asked how pupils could be promoted without these examinations, I answer, Promote them at any time of the year when their proficiency and the classification of the school would permit. How? I believe it would be best to do it on examination duly made by thoroughly qualified inspectors, such as I recommended the appointment of in my last annual report. But if we are not ready for that, then on the examination of the teacher, the principal and the superintendent or his deputy. There is no one season of the year, so far as my observation goes, at which the minds of children ripen or mature—no particular month out of the twelve in which they become fully ripe and fit for the harvest. I believe the monstrous attempt to put children of widely varying physical and mental powers through the same mill in the same time, has worked infinite and irreparable mischief to many minds.

THE TEACHERS OF OUR PUBLIC SCHOOLS.

The School Department employs more than five hundred teachers at the present time. Most of them are ladies and gentlemen well qualified for the positions which they hold. They are zealous and enthusiastic in their work. They are willing and anxious to do all in their power to further the best interests of the children committed to their care. If they fail to do all that we could wish them to do, it is not because of any lack of desire to do so. It is disheartening to any such body of men and women to be treated with distrust by those who employ them, and I trust that the new Board of Education will extend to the teachers of our schools all the kind consideration, sympathy and aid that it is in their power to do. Young teachers in this city have very meagre opportunities for improvement in the art of teaching. We have no Normal School. We have no teachers' institute, or associations. During the period of my connection with the department there has not been a single lecture on the science of education, or the art of teaching, delivered to the teachers of this city and county. If, therefore, some of our teachers are behind the times, if the ardor of others has slackened, if the professional pride of all has declined a little, is it much to be wondered at? I believe a revival of educational interest is needed in our city, and if the Board of Education can do something to bring about so desirable a result, they will by so doing reflect credit on themselves, and confer a benefit upon the schools under their charge.

A CITY NORMAL SCHOOL.

In my last annual report I tried to call the attention of the Board of Education to the necessity of having a Normal School established for the training of teachers. Up to the present time, however, members of the board have been unable to see the matter in the same light that I do. I think it is a disgrace to our city that we have no school within her limits for preparing young men and women, who wish to devote themselves to the profession of teaching, for their work. I venture to say that there is not on the American continent to-day, a city of 250,000 inhabitants where some sort of a Normal School has not been established. I know that as we are now situated every dollar expended for the support of a really good Normal School would repay the city tenfold in the greater efficiency of the teachers who would be trained in it. Every person who has a particle of educational sense, must see that for lack of Normal School instruction the department is losing every year ten times as much as it would cost to sustain a good Normal School in our city.

The State Normal School at San Jose is, under its present able management, doing a noble work for the cause of education in California. But we need a school of our own in this city for the special training of teachers for our graded schools. I do not think that the Normal School ought to be conducted in the High School, nor taught in connection therewith. I think it would be better to have it in some school in which all the grades are taught. In that case the teacher of the Normal Class could take the teachers in training into the classes of the different grades and there show them how to teach practically, by taking charge of the class himself and showing his pupils how to apply the best methods of instruction. If candidates for the positions of teachers in the public schools were well trained in such a school, we should have much more teaching and much less experimenting done in a large number of our classes.

TOO MANY PUPILS ASSIGNED TO A TEACHER.

I have no reason to change or modify my views on this subject during the past year. I would reiterate my opinion, as expressed in my last report, that not more than forty grammar pupils, nor more than fifty primary pupils, ought to be assigned to any one teacher.

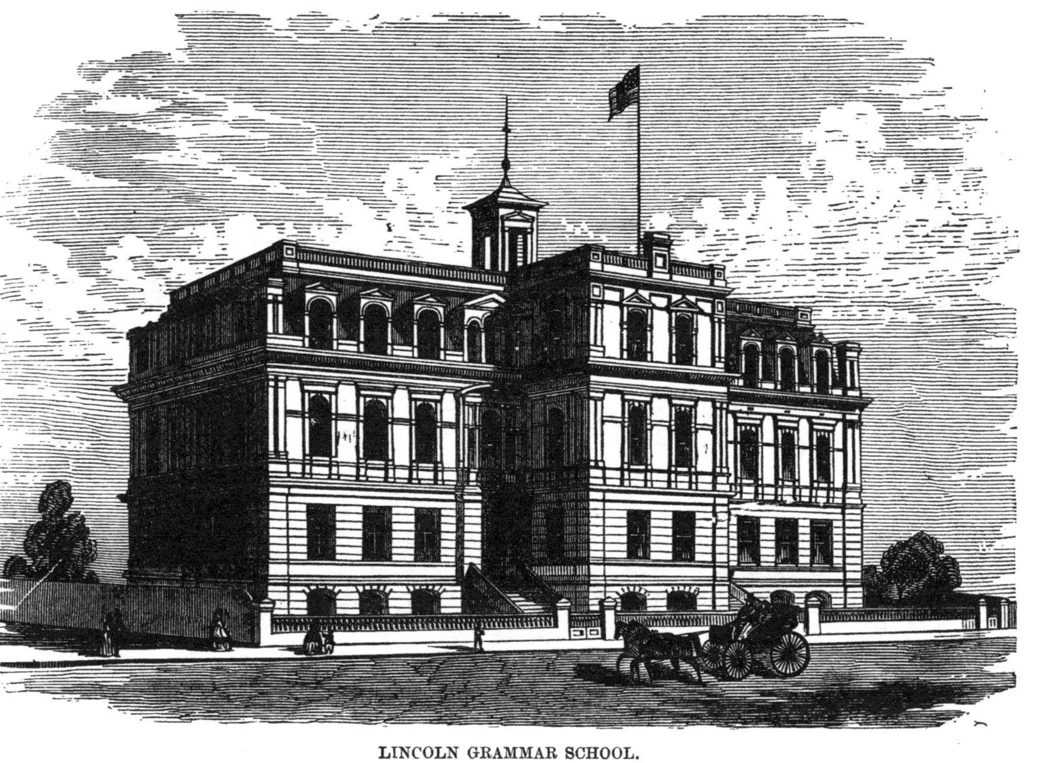

LINCOLN GRAMMAR SCHOOL.

2. MISCELLANEOUS HISTORICAL ITEMS.

1. *Buildings.*—The schools were held in rented rooms up to 1854, when a building on the corner of Bush and Stockton streets was erected for the Denman School; a large brick building for the Union Street School; and a spacious house at North Beach for the Powell Street School. This last building was soon afterward turned into a City Hospital, because it could not be filled with pupils.

The first schoolhouses were arranged on the New York City plan of large session-rooms and small recitation-rooms. Since 1857, the buildings have been arranged on the Boston plan—a separate room for each class of 50 pupils.

2. *Grading.*—The schools were originally classified into Primary, Intermediate, and Grammar Departments, but were not regularly graded on the present plan until late in 1857.

The first printed "course of study" was adopted June 10, 1857, Mr. Pelton, Superintendent, and William Sherman, President of the Board. The High School was organized in 1856, mainly through the efforts of William Sherman, the President of the Board.

3. *Salaries.*—The salary paid Principals in 1852 and 1853 was $150 a month, exclusive of vacations; that is, $1500 a year. In 1854, the salary was increased to $2000 a year; but this was paid in city scrip, worth from 60 to 70 cents on the dollar. From 1854 to 1872, the salaries varied from $1900 to $2100, but in 1873 were raised to $2400.

The salaries of the High School Principals varied from $2300 to $2500 and $3000, until 1874, when the salary of the Principal of the Boys' High School was made $4000.

4. *Certificates.*—Until 1863, teachers were annually examined, to test their "*fitness to teach a common school one year,*" and the pioneer teachers, such as Denman, the Holmeses, Swett, Pelton, and others, were passed through the "examination-mill" a dozen times. The system afforded a fine opportunity for petty officials to browbeat schoolmasters and schoolma'ams.

5. *Annual Elections.*—From 1850 to 1870, at the end of each year, all positions were declared vacant, and there was a general scramble for a "new deal." Occasionally there was the war-cry: "To the victors belong the spoils."

If a "Director" had a spite against some unfortunate pedagogue, vengeance descended when the Board went into star-chamber sessions for the "Annual Election of Teachers."

The doors of the star-chamber were besieged until midnight by anxious teachers, waiting to know their fate.

This senseless annual insult to a whole body of teachers originated in the New England District Schools, when they were kept but a part of the year, and when, of course, a new teacher had to be elected annually. Strange as it may seem, it has been handed down from father to son as a precious heirloom, and is still the law of nearly every city, town, and district in the United States,--San Francisco excepted.

A NEW DEPARTURE.

In 1870, the Board, H. A. Cobb, President, decided to abolish annual elections, and elect teachers "during good behavior." This measure was vigorously supported by most of the city press, but was as vigorously opposed by the Superintendent and a minority of the Board, who tenaciously "held on to the good old way."

6. *Examinations of Schools.*—Up to 1862, the pupils in Grammar and Primary Schools were promoted by the principals and teachers on the records of the scholars' work during the year. Public examinations were conducted orally at the end of the year.

In 1863, the promotion by means of written examinations and percentages was introduced as a system. The result was, that in a few years, the main efforts of teachers were directed to *cramming* for examination. Pupils were made writing-machines. In 1874 and 1875, even the lowest grade primary classes were examined in writing. The evil culminated in a reaction, and in 1876 a committee of principals, with Superintendent Bolander, requested the Committee of Classification, Mr. Tait, Chairman, to abolish the cast-iron system, and allow principals to classify their schools. The permission asked for was granted, and it is to be hoped the cramming system will never be restored.

7. *Secular Schools.*—From 1851 to 1854, it was customary in many schools to open the exercises with prayer and the reading of a passage from the Bible by the teacher. This was authorized by one of the earliest school regulations. The question formed a bone of contention for several years, but by common consent

most of the teachers, after 1856, discontinued the reading of the Bible and prayer. The tendency of public opinion was toward purely secular schools. In his State Reports, Superintendent Swett advocated purely secular schools.

In 1874, for the first time, an official resolution in favor of purely secular education appears on record. The President of the Board, Andrew McF. Davis, ruled that the repeating of the Lord's Prayer was *sectarian*, and in violation of the school law. This decision was sustained by the Board. Public opinion, in most parts of the State, is in accordance with this decision.

8. *Politics and Schools.*—Though nominated and elected by political parties, the Boards of Education have not been, in general, marked by partisan action. From 1856 to 1867, a majority of the members of each Board was elected on the "People's Party Ticket." From 1868 to 1876, there has been a preponderance of members elected on the Democratic Ticket. Superintendent Theller was elected on the Democratic Ticket; Mr. Pelton was twice, and Superintendent Denman three times elected by the Democratic party. All the other Superintendents were elected on the "People's Party" or the Republican Ticket. Under the "Know-Nothing" regime, in 1855, a few teachers were removed on account of "accent." During the war, two or three "secession" teachers were dropped; but, in general, while both political and religious influences have, to some extent, influenced the election of teachers, very few have been proscribed on account of either politics or religion. Protestants, Catholics, Israelites, Democrats and Republicans, work harmoniously together in teaching children of all shades of religious belief and political opinion.

9. *Music and Drawing.*—From the beginning, music and drawing, to the extent of a smattering, were taught in the schools. In 1859, Hubert Burgess was appointed special teacher of drawing, and Mr. F. K. Mitchell, teacher of music. In 1868, Washington Elliott succeeded Mr. Mitchell as music teacher. In 1871, *Mason's Music Readers and Charts* were adopted, with a specific course in the Manual. Real instruction in vocal music dates from this period. In 1874, Smith's System of Drawing was introduced, making the beginning of systematic instruction in this branch.

10. *Changes in Text-Books.*—The changes in text-books, from

1851 to 1876, twenty-five years, may be briefly summed up as follows:

Readers: Swan's, Towne's, Sargent's, Willson's, McGuffey's. Average time of use, five years.

Arithmetics: Thompson's, Colburn's, Robinson's; the last from 1865 to 1876. Average time of use, eight years.

Grammars: Tower's, Weld's, Greene's, Kerl's, Brown's. Average time, five years.

Geographies: Mitchell's, Cornell's, Guyot's, Clarke's, Monteith's. Average time, five years.

Spellers: Towne's, Sargent's, Willson's.

United States History: Parley's, Goodrich's, Lossing's, Anderson's, Swinton's. Average time, five years.

11. *Co-Education.*—Up to 1864, the boys and girls were educated together. When the Denman Grammar School building was completed, only girls were admitted; the Lincoln was made a boys' school, and the Rincon a girls' school. In 1868 the Union and the Washington were made boys' schools, and the Broadway a girls' school. The Boys' High and the Girls' High were formed from the Boys' and Girls' High School in 1864. With these exceptions all the other schools have always been attended by both sexes.

12. *Teachers' Associations and Evening Normal Schools.*—In 1853 the Principals formed a monthly association for the discussion of school questions. This continued until 1857, when a weekly Normal School was established by the Board of Education. Attendance was made compulsory. The school was held at first on Saturdays; afterwards, on Monday evenings. George W. Minns, John Swett, Ellis H. Holmes, and Thomas S. Myrick, were elected teachers. This school continued until 1862. The following is a list of the graduates of what is known as the "Minns Evening Normal School:"

GRADUATES OF 1861.

Miss Ellen Casey,	Miss Lizzie Kennedy,	Miss M. D. Lynde,
" M. A. Casebolt,	" A. B. Kimball,	" Hannah Marks,
" Alice Baker,	" M. A. Wills,	" Beatrice Weed,
" L. E. Field,	" C. L. Hunt,	Mrs. A. E. Du Bois.
" Eliza Hawkhurst,	" D. S. Prescott,	
" Kate Kennedy,	" M. L. Tracy,	

GRADUATES OF 1862.

Miss A. S. Barnard,	Miss Lizzie Macy,	Miss M. C. White,
" C. V. Benjamin,	" W. L. Morgan,	" S. J. White,
" Anna Child,	" A. S. Moses,	" L. A. Humphreys,
" C. A. Coffin,	" H. E. Porter,	" S. M. Hunt,
" L. H. Crocker,	" Geraldine Price,	" Annie Lawrence,
" H. B. Cushing,	" M. E. Scotchler,	Mrs. E. C. Burt,
" E. P. Fernald,	" A. A. Rowe,	" E. S. Forrester,
" E. S. Griffin,	" E. R. Shaw,	" L. A. Morgan,
" H. A. Haneke,	" M. E. Stowell,	" M. S. P. Nichols,
" H. H. Heagan,	" P. M. Stowell,	" H. E. Packer,
" Anna Hill,	" Helen Thompson,	" C. H. Stout,
" M. A. Humphreys,	" E. M. Tiebout,	" S. A. D. Lansingh.
" L. A. Humphreys,	" M. R. Warren,	

The "Minns Normal School" was succeeded for several years by monthly meetings of teachers under the direction of the Board of Education, but these died out in 1869.

In 1872 the Board established another Evening Normal School, which was continued two years, with the following corps of teachers: Principal, John Swett; Assistants, Joseph Leggett, Mrs. Mary W. Kincaid, and Theodore Bradley. Since 1873 there have been no teachers' meetings, associations, or normal schools.

13. *Educational Hobbies.*—In early times *Colburn's Mental Arithmetic* was a favorite hobby, and for many years afterward arithmetic was the leading branch of study to which more than half the school-time of pupils was devoted. In some cases, four hours out of the five were devoted to the favorite hobby of the old-time schoolmaster. Of late years, about one-fourth of the time is given to this study.

The epidemic of self-reporting prevailed from 1859 to 1862. "Map drawing" was fashionable from 1860 to 1871.

In 1868–70 education consisted mainly of "oral instruction."

In early times "exhibitions," "May festivals," and "dancing parties" were in fashion. "Calisthenics and gymnastics" prevailed from 1856 to 1860.

"Written Examinations" and "Percentages" were the rage from 1863 to 1875; they went out of style during the Centennial year.

"Phonography," in the higher grammar grades, was the hobby of 1872 and 1873, but was ridden to death in 1874.

"Mark's Geometry," for the 3d and 4th grammar grades, was the experiment in 1869 and 1870; it failed in 1871.

"Cosmopolitan Schools" became the rage in 1872 and 1873;

there was a reaction in 1874, when French and German were abolished during a revolutionary period of four months. The "restoration" soon followed by act of the Legislature.

The twin hobbies, with Boards of Education from 1854 to 1864, were the annual examination of teachers and the annual elections. Indeed, "annual elections," like bull fights, were in vogue until 1870. "Investigations" raged in 1872 and 1873, while the favorite hobby of the Board of 1874 and 1875 was "rules and regulations."

14. *Merits and Defects.*—The marked merits of the city schools are:

1. Convenient buildings.
2. Good discipline.
3. In general, hard-working teachers.
4. Good instruction in Music and Drawing.
5. The purely secular character of the schools.

The marked defects are:

1. Too many pupils per teacher.
2. Too rigid classification.
3. Too much cramming of text-books.
4. Too many lessons for home study.
5. A complicated system of daily recitation records and monthly reports.
6. A lack of professionally trained teachers.
7. The lack of a City Normal School.
8. A lack of thorough inspection.
9. Short terms of office of Superintendent and School Directors.

15. *Address of President Davis.*—The address of the President of the Board, Andrew McF. Davis, Nov. 14, 1875, sets forth in detail some of the marked features of the city system. The following are extracts:

It is fitting and proper that I should avail myself of this opportunity to say to this audience a few words concerning what this Board, whose term of office is so nearly closed, has done, and also relative to the graded system upon which the schools of the Department are organized.

Under the customs which at present prevail, no report is made by the Board to the people. The only published report concerning the affairs of the Department which reaches the public is the report of the Superintendent. That officer being elected directly by the people, and being only in a measure responsible to the Board, and no report being submitted in published form by the Board, or its

GRAMMAR SCHOOL BUILDING.

Model of three buildings, 1870–71. Cost, $30,000, each. Wood. Capacity 1000 pupils.

Committees, I shall offer no apology for taking advantage of this occasion to say a few words which, under a different organization of affairs, I should have preferred to present elsewhere. * *

The objects and purposes of this school, as originally organized, were substantially what they are to-day. The means at hand to reach these objects and effect these purposes have largely increased, and the school to-day has before it an enlarged field of usefulness, the circle of which not only expands with the increase of the population of the State and City, but the cultivation of which is vastly aided by the generous sympathies of the public.

The necessity of the school is to supplement the graded system of teaching which prevails in the lower divisions of the Department. To accomplish this, the course of study in the school itself must be elastic enough to aid and encourage in their labors:

I. Those who have successfully passed through the Grammar grades and wish to pursue a higher course of study, whether scientific, literary, or classical.

II. Those who have passed through the Grammar grades successfully, and wish to round off their education in a shorter period; to gather in and appropriate what they can, but who are especially desirous of pursuing with diligence for a short space of time certain scientific or mathematical studies.

III. Those whose education has been acquired outside of our city schools, and whose percentages may show a decided falling off in some of the studies, and an unusual prominence in others.

And finally, those who, from some constitutional incapacity, are unable to pursue with success certain studies beyond fixed points, but who are able to reach a certain grade, yet cannot get beyond it, if the inexorable law of percentages is rigidly applied.

For all of these, and perhaps for others, must a place be found in this school.

Because a young man, with a copious diction and a delicate literary taste, can only achieve the *pons asinorum* by memorizing the demonstration, shall we keep him lagging behind the army in its advance, or shall we try him now in this place, now in that, until we find the place where he can do the best work and where we can work him to the best advantage?

Because the graded system demands a certain percentage for promotion, shall we keep a pupil, year after year, in the first grade of the Grammar department, who from some mental deficiency is held back from promotion by absolute failure in some especial study? Is it not better to recognize this as one of the defects of a system, excellent in some respects, which is to be supplemented as far as may be by this school?

In order to realize what the defects are that need to be supplemented, it is essential to look at the organization of our schools and observe of what different materials they are composed. We see, side by side, the children of professional men, merchants and laborers; children whose every step is carefully watched, and those whose normal condition is absolute freedom from restraint; we see the rude and the polished; black and white; rich and poor; all patronizing our schools.

For these children, reared under such different conditions, enjoying such varied advantages, disciplined to such different degrees of obedience, is provided a curriculum, rigid, inelastic, and unconscious of any difference in the characters, the surroundings, or the opportunities of the pupils.

At the age of six years, says the law, you may send your child to the public school, and, continues our course of study, whatever his condition of discipline may then be, he shall pursue the following studies, such and such quantities to be given in stated periods and in definite ways. At the age of six, then, the pupils are launched upon the course of study. But how different are their opportunities! While at home, whether at meals or at play, the one child is under the care of educated and refined parents, who maintain a constant supervising influence over their offspring; who do not neglect discipline in mistaken kindness, and who accomplish far more in the process of leading forward the child than can be possible for any teacher in the lower grades.

Side by side with his little playmate another has to struggle along the path alone. His parents earn their bread by the sweat of their brows. There is no time to waste on refinement or cultivation. Here the case is reversed. The teacher is all in all, and much more is accomplished at school than at home in the process of unfolding the mental faculties and developing the intellectual growth.

Suppose that these two children are of equal mental calibre, will their growth be the same under the graded system? If not, what provision is there for such vast, such inevitable discrepancies? For, in this comparison, I have not drawn the strongest possible, nor even the strongest probable contrast. The law of "hereditary tendency" would assert, as probable, that the child of professional or literary parents would have stronger natural tastes for literary pursuits than the child of the laborer. So that the natural tendency would be to make the contrast even more striking.

How in the world can such grave obstacles to the adjustment of the graded system be overcome? How can any rigid system be made to fit such a variety of minds, from the most brilliant to the positively stupid? How can the same nourishment, in quality and quantity, sustain the giant and the pigmy? These questions seemed to me, when I entered upon my duties as a School Director, incapable of answer.

I have found a partial explanation of the matter in this, that in many schools the promotions are so made that the bright and forward scholars do two years' work in one—actually accomplishing this work with ease. In other words, the course of study, as at present arranged, being adapted as near as may be to the best interests of the *average* intellect under *average* conditions favorable for its development, must necessarily fall below the capacity of a large number of the scholars. To keep these busy, they must either do two years' work in one, which is accomplished by promotions at the end of the first six months (making advance work of what is review to a portion of the grade), or some other means must be devised to keep their minds active during school hours. * * *

This forcing pupils over two years' work in one, is the only source of relief from the rigid demands of the Manual which I have discovered. It is not, of course, capable of extensive application, and the generally inelastic nature of the work in the lower departments remains to be supplemented, and as far as possible compensated for here. We have sought to provide for this by furnishing various parallel branches of study in this school, and it is my hope that the *chevaux de frise* of percentages which bristle upon every avenue of approach to this stronghold of learning may be to some extent removed, and a more liberal view taken of what the school is for. It is true that not every horse can be trained to be a race horse; but it is none the less true that we like to see our coach horses well groomed.

The question has been discussed in public, "What shall we do with our boys?" Orators, lawyers and editors have addressed audiences upon this topic. It interests all classes, and we, who are connected with educational matters, are brought closely in contact with it.

Let those gentlemen who have propounded that question cast their eyes over this audience, and we will show them what we are doing with our boys at this end of the line. But alas! the fruit that we see ripening here to-day is but a small percentage of that which was set in the primary school, and they might still say this does not answer our question.

May I be pardoned at this time, and in this connection, if I throw out a hint of what I believe will help to solve this question in the future. The subject is closely connected with what has gone before, and perhaps these words may fall upon willing ears.

I have alluded to the different planes upon which pupils of the same age stand in the graded system, and the different results that must follow from precisely the same instruction. Apart from all questions of intellectual culture, the habits of discipline and obedience acquired by a child reared in a well-ordered family are probably of more value than any other development. The receptivity of a child who has been taught to move, or to stop when spoken to, must be far greater than that of one whose life has been spent in throwing stones at Chinamen, and building bonfires in the streets.

The generous nature of the climate here is such that the child of a family too poor to maintain constant supervision over it, is turned adrift upon the streets to charge about, committing those minor offenses—promises, and almost certain forerunners of serious difficulty one of these days.

Experience has established, and the law has defined, the proper minimum age for beginning our regular studies in the public schools to be six years, and we all know that practically this is young enough according to our present methods.

But modern German thought has developed a system of amusing children which at the same time prepares their minds for future training, and enables parents to avail themselves of the system while their children are still very young.

If it were possible to erect a few buildings around the city, in those portions where the very young abound so thickly, and gather in the little children between the ages of three and six years, for five or six hours daily, during which time they should be amused and interested; thus removing them from the dangers and temptations of the streets; comforting their mothers with the knowledge of their safety; teaching them little or nothing except methods of thought; I say, if one, two or three such schools could be tried, something could be done for the boy of twelve or fifteen years hence. From the Kindergarten these boys would enter the Primary School upon a par with the boys with whom I have heretofore placed them in contrast; with habits of obedience and methods of thought already acquired. Truancy, that terror of principals, would be reduced, for school by this system is a synonym for pleasure. The little fellows look forward with delight to the hours to be spent there, and leave for home with regret. The wild charms of a nomadic life, the comforts of a night in a dry-goods box or a sugar hogshead—all these can and would be dispelled by continuous kindly effort. The hold that this wild, irresponsible sort of life has upon the unkempt natures of these little fellows is almost incomprehensible, and the necessity for capturing them while young—very young—and molding them to conform more nearly to some recognized social type, is evident to the reflective mind. Further, our knowledge of our pupils and their ways of life would begin earlier, and we should know better what it was essential to do to aid them in the rugged pathways of life.

These, then, are the lessons which my two years' service in the department have taught me:

I. The great evil of our system is its inelasticity.

II. The remedies which can be applied are: The Kindergarten at one end of the course; judicious promotions of exceptionally bright pupils during the course; and a liberal opening up of the opportunities of the High School at the other end.

I entertain the hope that the experiment of the Kindergarten or some kindred school may be tried at an early date. Properly managed it cannot fail. I urge it not so much for its direct educational result (though the experiment elsewhere has proved a success) as for the hold it will give upon the good-will and affections of these nomad children, whose lives are otherwise destined to be lost in the streets. By this means they can be gathered in. They can be kept out of mischief and they can be taught, without knowing it, what obedience is. They can be prepared for the primary work, and the tares of truancy can be weeded out of their desires. This work fairly inaugurated, the effects upon the inelastic graded system could not fail to be realized.

As to the work in the High Schools, I feel sure that all here will give the present Board of Education credit for having labored with great unanimity to improve it, and will join with me in congratulating the teachers and the boys upon the mutual good-will which seems to pervade this school.

I have before stated the purposes of the school. We have shaped our course of study to meet these purposes. In this form we shall hand it over to our successors, our term of office having nearly expired. Its future rests in their hands.

Among the problems which they will have to solve will be the various questions as to what shall entitle a person to admission, and what shall be required of students after admission. In our action we have recognized certain general principles.

It is impossible for us to ignore the fact that after passing beyond the Grammar grades, any course of study which treads beyond certain limits must overtake and lie parallel with that of the University. A due regard for economy will not permit us to retain here, at a great expense, a school simply to traverse ground, which can be gained by crossing the Bay, with little inconvenience to the student and with no expense to the city. Apart from questions of economy we have earnestly labored to maintain harmonious relations with the officers of the University, and have sought to shape our school so that it should prove a feeder and not a rival.

At the same time we have endeavored to enlarge the sphere of usefulness of the school to its greatest possible dimensions. It belongs to the public. It has been carefully provided for, and its dispensations should be made in a liberal spirit and with a liberal hand.

Many questions relating to young men, peculiarly situated, who, under the rules cannot derive any benefit from the school, but who are worthy of our aid and sympathy, will constantly arise. No rule can be laid down that will govern all such cases. The only thing to do is to determine each case on its merits.

What I have said of this school will generally apply to the Girls' High School. We have endeavored to make the course of study there more elastic than it was. The elements with which we have to deal there, differ largely from those composing this school. A majority of the pupils desire to become teachers, and are anxious to pursue a special course of study which shall fit them for that purpose. It is not improbable that the pressure in that direction will at an early day lead to the foundation of a City Normal School. In that case, what will become of the remnant of the school which will be left?

When the school was founded the sexes were together, and I see no objection to an opportunity being afforded them to pursue their studies together now. * * *

I believe this to be the only true policy to pursue with reference to the higher schools. As far as is practicable, give your principals swing and hold them accountable for results. If they fail, depose them, but do not meddle with them any more than can be helped while they are on trial.

In the matter of text-books for the High Schools, fear of popular clamor against new books should not prevent their introduction whenever needed. The world does not stand still, and advanced ideas cannot be obtained from obsolete books. It is nonsense to think of acquiring a higher education without taking advantage of every aid in the way of new books.

15. *Veteran Teachers.*—Ellis H. Holmes ranks as the teacher continuously engaged in teaching in the city schools for the longest period of time—23 years, from February, 1853, to June, 1876. During that time he was never absent a day from school. Mrs. A. E. Dubois, *nee* Miss Anna E. Sandford, ranks next to Mr. Holmes, having begun teaching as an assistant in Mr. Denman's school, April, 1853. She has been continuously in

the schools, with the exception of six months' leave of absence. Mrs. L. A. K. Clappe has taught continuously since November 4, 1854, and Mrs. L. A. Morgan since 1855. Mrs. Margaret Deane has taught since 1854, but not continuously.

James Denman began teaching November 17, 1851, but resigned in 1857, and was elected City Superintendent in 1858. He has taught altogether 13 years, and held the office of Superintendent 7 years.

John C. Pelton taught in San Francisco in 1850; from 1857 to 1860; 1863 to 1870; altogether 11 years. He was City Superintendent 3 years, and County Superintendent 1 year; was Principal of the State Reform School at Marysville, 1860 to 1863, and Superintendent of the San Francisco Industrial School from 1870 to 1872.

Captain Joseph C. Morrill was the popular Principal of the Spring Valley School from 1852 to 1860, when he resigned and soon after entered the volunteer service of the United States, and remained during the war of secession. In 1870, he was appointed Principal of the Industrial School, and soon afterwards Superintendent. During an "investigation" the hue and cry of cruelty was raised against him, and he resigned. He was one of the kindest and most generous of men, and was the most useful teacher ever employed in that institution.

George W. Minns was elected teacher of Natural Sciences in the High School, August, 1856, and Principal of the Boys' High School in 1864, and Principal of the State Normal School, 1866. In 1867, he resigned and went East. Professor Minns was one of the leading educational lecturers in the State.

H. P. Carlton was Principal of a Grammar School from 1854 to 1861; Vice-principal and Principal of the State Normal School from 1863 to 1873; and has been a teacher in San Francisco and Oakland since 1873.

Theodore Bradley was made Principal of the Denman School, 1861, and of the Boys' High School in 1866; in which he remained until 1874.

Thomas S. Myrick was the popular Principal of the Market Street School and the Union Grammar School from 1856 to 1869. He is now teaching at Dutch Flat.

Mrs. E. S. Forrester has been continuously engaged as a primary teacher since May 10, 1856,—20 years.

Miss Kate Kennedy, the first female Principal of a Grammar

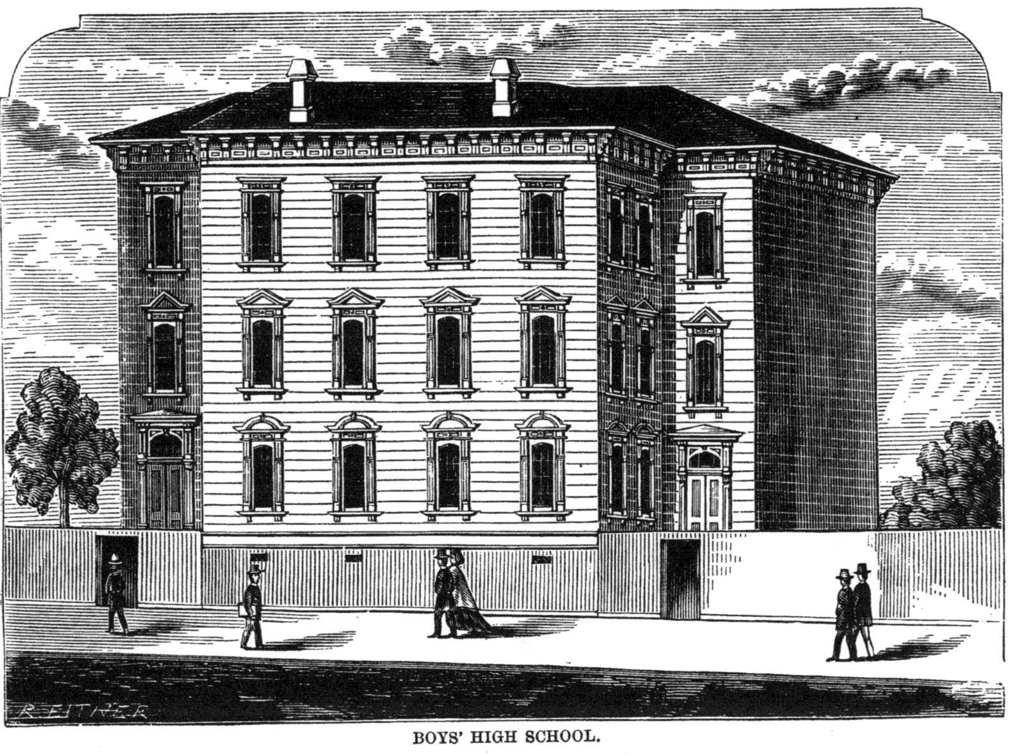

BOYS' HIGH SCHOOL.

School, has been in the Department, without leave of absence, for 19 years.

Miss Dorcas D. S. Prescott, and Mrs. C. V. Gummer, *nee* Benjamin, have taught since 1857,—18 years.

Mrs. E. H. B. Varney has taught school 30 years; one half of that period in this city.

Miss A. E. Slavan, Miss C. L. Hunt, and Mrs. S. N. Joseph, have been teaching since 1859.

Miss P. M. Stowell, Mrs. M. J. Sankey, *nee* Ritchie, Mrs. A. H. Hammill, *nee* Austin, and Miss M. A. Humphreys, have taught for 15 years; Mrs. Mary W. Kincaid, Miss J. M. A. Hurley, Miss Anna A. Hill, 14 years; Miss Helen Thompson, Mrs. E. P. Bradley, Mrs. A. S. Trask, *nee* Duane, Miss Anna Gibbons, 13 years; Mrs. Aurelia Griffith, Miss G. E. Thurton, Miss S. A. Barr, Mrs. C. L. Atwood, and Miss Laura S. Fowler, 12 years.

Hubert Burgess has taught drawing for 16 years, and Washington Elliott has been teaching music for 14 years.

Henry N. Bolander was a teacher in this city for 11 years; he became State Superintendent in 1872, and City Superintendent in 1876.

Ebenezer Knowlton, well known as an Institute elocutionist, was first an assistant in the State Normal School, 1865, afterwards Principal of the Rincon School, and is now an assistant in the Boys' High School.

16. *Ten Years' Teaching.*—The following is a list of teachers continuously engaged in teaching in the city schools for a period of ten years:

Beales, Mrs. C. R.
Bragg, Miss Mary J.
Baumgardner, Mrs. E. M.
Baldwin, Nellie.
Burke, Mrs. L. K.
Cleveland, Miss E. A.
Ciprico, Miss Anita C.
Campbell, Miss Amy T.
Cook, Miss Hannah.
Carusi, Mrs. M. J.
Childs, Miss Katie B.
Campbell, Miss C. E.
Coulon, Miss V.
Castelhun, Miss M. A.
Carter, Mrs. Louisa.
Dore, Miss A. M.
Deetken, Mrs. E. G.
Foster, Mrs. Emily.
Fink, Miss A. P.
Forbes, Miss Jennie.
Flint, Miss A. T.
Grant, Miss Helen A.
Gorman, Mr. W. J.
Humphrey, Mr. E. D.
Hucks, Miss Annie E.
Hoffman, Mrs. M. L.
Harswell, Miss M. A.
Hyman, Miss Deborah.
Jourdan, Miss A. M.
Jordan, Miss M. L.
Jewett, Miss A. S.
Jewett, Miss Lizzie B.
Jones, Mrs. E. B.
Littlefield, Miss Nellie A.
Manning, Miss Agnes M.
Mayborn, Miss M. J.
Marcus, Mrs. E. C.
Malloy, Miss Bessie.
Miller, Miss S. E.
Parker, Miss Jean.
Plunkett, Mrs. C. P.
Reynolds, Mrs. F. E.
Russell, Mrs. L. A.
Rowe, Miss A. A,
Sullivan, Miss Kate M.
Salisbury, Miss M. A.
Shaw, Miss E. A.
Sullivan, Mrs. Therese M,
Stincen, Miss M. A.
Smith, Miss Jessie.
Smith, Miss Jennie.
Smith, Miss M. F.
Stowell, Miss Fannie.
Soule, Miss Fanny L.
White, Miss Elizabeth.
Wood, Mrs. E. A.
Wade, Miss Margaret,
Washburn, Mrs. Georgia.
Winn, Mr. A. T.
White, Silas A.

3. SUPERINTENDENTS OF PUBLIC SCHOOLS, SAN FRANCISCO.

APPOINTED BY THE BOARD OF EDUCATION.

Thomas J. Nevins..........................'52, '53
Wm. H. O'Grady..........................'54, '55

ELECTED BY DIRECT VOTE OF THE PEOPLE.

E. A. Theller..................................'56
John C. Pelton........................'57, '66, '67
Henry B. Janes..........................'58, '59
James Denman..........'60, '61, '68, '69, '70, '74, '75
George Tait........................'62, '63, '64, '65
J. H. Widber........................'71, '72, '73
H. N. Bolander..........................'76–'78

Deputy Superintendents.

[Appointed by the City Superintendent.]

John Swett..........................'71, '72, '73
Joseph Leggett..........................'74, '75
D. C. Stone..........................'76–'78

Secretaries of the Board.

[Appointed by the Superintendent and Confirmed by the Board.]

George Beanston..........................'68–'76

4. PRESIDENTS OF BOARDS OF EDUCATION, SAN FRANCISCO.

[Mayors, *ex-officio*, Presidents of Boards appointed by the Common Council.

C. J. Brenham..................................'52
C. K. Garrison..................................'54
S. P. Webb..................................'55
James Van Ness..................................'56

CHOSEN BY BOARDS ELECTED BY THE PEOPLE.

William Sherman......................'57, '58, '59
William Pierson..........................'60, '61
W. L. Palmer..................................'62
Dr. C. C. Knowles..............................'63
M. Lynch..........................'64, '65
J. W. Winans..........................'66, '67
Thos. H. Holt..................................'68
H. A. Cobb..................................'69
J. M. Burnett..........................'70, 71
Joseph Clement..........................'72, '76
H. J. Tilden..........................'73, '74
Andrew McF. Davis..............................'75

5. HISTORICAL LIST OF PRINCIPALS, SAN FRANCISCO.*

* Taken, mainly, from the Annual Report of Superintendent Denman, '75.

BOYS' HIGH.

E. H. Holmes........Aug. '56.
Geo. W. Minns......June, '64.
Theodore Bradley....June, '65.
W. T. Reed........March, '75.

GIRLS' HIGH.

E. H. Holmes........'64 to '76.
John Swett...........June, '76.

DENMAN.

James Denman.......Nov. '51.
George Tait..........June, '57.
Theodore Bradley....Dec. '61.
James Denman.......July, '64.
John Swett...........Dec. '67.
James Denman........Jan. '71.
John Swett...........Dec. '73.
James Denman.......June, '76.

RINCON.

Silas Weston..........Jan. '52.
Wm. H. O'Grady.....May, '52.
Stillman Holmes.......Oct. '53.
John Swett.............Dec. '53.
John C. Pelton........Jan. '63.
Ira G. Hoitt..........Sept. '64.
Ebenezer Knowlton...June, '65.
Miss E. A. Cleveland...Oct. '74.

WASHINGTON.

F. E. Jones...........Dec. '51.
E. H. Holmes......March, '53.
H. P. Carlton.........Aug. '56.
James Stratton........Jan. '61.
L. D. Allen..........July, '68.
Joseph O'Connor......Dec. '74.

UNION.

Ahira Holmes........June, '52.
Wm. Hammill........Nov. '56.
Ahira Holmes.........Jan. '58.
Thomas S. Myrick.....Jan. '60.
Philip Prior.........June, '69.
Chas. F. True.........Dec. '74.

SPRING VALLEY.

Asa W. Cole ....Feb. '52.
J. C. Morrill..........Oct. '53.
Geo. W. Peck........May, '60.
Geo. W. Bunnell......Jan. '62.
Bernhard Marks........Jan. '74.
Noah F. Flood.......June, '68.
W. J. G. Williams....June, '69.
Silas A. White........Feb. '75.
J. W. Anderson ....Jan. '76.

LINCOLN.

Ira G. Hoitt..........July, '65.
J. C. Pelton..........Dec. '67.
W. T. Luckey.........Dec. '67.
Bernhard Marks......June, '68.
J. K. Wilson..........Nov. '72.

MISSION.

Alfred Rix........... May, '52.
Clara B. Walbridge...Aug. '53.
Thos. C. Leonard.....Nov. '55.
Ahira Holmes........June, '65.
E. D. Humphrey.....June, '67.
Mary J. Bragg........Feb. '71.
Laura T. Fowler......Nov. '74.

BROADWAY.

W. J. G. Williams...June, '68.
Noah F. Flood......June, '69.
Chas. F. True.........Nov. '72.
W. J. G. Williams.....Feb. '75.
C. H. Ham.........March, '76.

SOUTH COSMOPOLITAN.

Mrs. Ulrika Rendsburg..Oct. '65.
H. N. Bolander........Feb. '67.
A. Herbst.............Dec. '71.

NORTH COSMOPOLITAN.

Miss Kate Kennedy.........'67.

EIGHTH STREET.

Wm. J. Gorman.......Jan. '68.
J. Phelps............Sept. '69.
John A. Moore........Sept. '70.

HAYES VALLEY.

E. D. Humphrey......July, '71.

VALENCIA STREET.

Silas A. White..............'71.
J. W. Anderson.......Feb. '75.
Silas A. White........Jan. '76.

MODEL SCHOOL.

Mrs. A. E. Dubois.........'67.

SOUTH SAN FRANCISCO.

W. J. Gorman........Sept. '69.

GEARY STREET.

Wm. A. Robertson....June, '76.

MARKET STREET PRIMARY.

Miss M. D. Lynde...March, '60.
Fred. Elliot...........Jan. '62.
Bernhard Marks......Sept. '62.
Mrs. C. H. Stout......Jan. '64.
Miss Agnes Manning..July, '72.

LINCOLN PRIMARY.

Miss Kate Sullivan.........'66.

TEHAMA PRIMARY.

Mrs. E. C. Burt......June, '65.
Mrs. E. A. Wood......June, '67.

FOURTH STREET.

Mrs. A. E. McGlynn..April, '63.
Mrs. L. A. Morgan....June, '65.

PINE AND LARKIN PRIMARY.

Miss Eliza Hawxhurst..Jan, '62.
Miss J. A. Lyon.....March, '62.
Mrs. C. H. Stout......May, '63.
Mrs. Alice Bunnell....May, '64.
Miss Hannah Cooke...June, '65.

GREENWICH PRIMARY.

Mrs. R. D. Bird.......Jan. '52.
Miss P. M. Stowell.....Dec. '61.
Miss Kate Kennedy...May, '62.
Mrs. W. R. Duane....June, '68.

HAYES VALLEY PRIMARY.

Miss H. B. Cushing....Jan. '63.
Miss L. J. Mastic......May, '64.
Miss P. M. Stowell..March, '68.

UNION PRIMARY.

Mrs. Amelia Griffith........'67.

EIGHTH STREET PRIMARY.

Miss Mary Williams..June, '64.
Miss A. E. Slaven......Oct. '64.

SHOTWELL PRIMARY.

Miss Anna A. Hill.....Feb. '72.

BUSH STREET PRIMARY.

Mrs. C. P. Plunkett....Jan. '72.

BROADWAY PRIMARY.

Miss A. M. Murphy....Feb. '67.
Mrs. L. G. Deetkin....Aug. '70.

SPRING VALLEY PRIMARY.

Miss H. A. Hanecke..March, '66.
Miss P. A. Fink......Sept. '66.
Miss J. M. A. Hurley..Nov. '67.

POWELL STREET PRIMARY.

Mrs. E. C. Burt......June, '61.
Miss Caroline Price...June, '63.
Miss C. V. Benjamin..June, '66.

RINCON PRIMARY.

Miss E. G. Smith......Jan. '67.
Miss Jennie Smith...March, '68.

STOCKTON PRIMARY.

Miss M. D'Arcy............'68.
Miss A. M. Stincen.........'74.

TYLER AND JONES STREET.

Mrs. C. B. Jones...........'70.

SAN BRUNO.

Miss G. Washburn....Sept. '64.
George Pershine......July, '65.
Miss Jennie Sheldon..Sept. '65.
Miss Marion Sears......Oct. '69.
Mrs. M. Dean.........Aug. '72.

TYLER STREET.

Miss A. S. Jewett.....Aug. '66.
Miss S. H. Whitney...Aug. '67.
Miss Mary J. Bragg...June, '68.
Miss E. Cushing.......Feb. '71.

POINT LOBOS.

Wellington Gordon........'71.

WEST END PRIMARY.

Miss A. M. Dore.......Oct. '64.
Mrs. Louisa Carter...June, '65.
Mr. S. A. White.......Oct. '66.
Mr. A. L. Mann......June, '67.
Mr. Robert Desty.....July, '67.
Mr. W. W. Holder ...July, '68.
Mr. J. W. Lannon....Aug. '69.
Mr. Chas. F. True..March, '70.
Mr. C. H. Ham.......Aug. '70.
Mr. W. W. Stone......Feb. '73.
Mr. Selden Sturgess...Sept. '75.

FAIRMOUNT PRIMARY.

Miss M. A. Salisbury..Sept. '64.
Miss A. M. Manning...Jan. '65.
Miss A. C. Bowen....June, '65.
Mr. E. D. Humphrey.June, '66.

FAIRMOUNT PRIMARY—*Continued.*

Mr. Philip Prior .....June, '67.
Mrs. T. J. Nevins.....Aug. '67.
Miss Susie Carey......July, '68.
Mr. Albert Lyser......Oct. '68.
Mr. Geo. B. Robertson.Aug. '70.
Mr. J. W. Lannon.... Oct. '70.
Mr. J. C. Robertson...Nov. '71.
Mr. J. W. Anderson...Oct. '73.
Mr. H. P. Carlton.....Oct. '74.
Mr. W. W. Stone.....Aug. '75.

OCEAN HOUSE.

Mrs. M. McGilvery....July, '66.
Mr. Albert Lyser.....June, '68.
Mr. W. A. Robertson..Nov. '68.
Mr. John Fox........April, '69.
Mr. John A. Moore...June, '69.
Mr. W. Gordon.......Dec. '69.
Miss A. M. Murphy...Sept. '70.
Mr. Jas. Dwyer.......Feb. '73.

NOE AND TEMPLE.

Mrs. E. Foster.............'75.

JACKSON STREET.

Mrs. B. F. Moore ....'75.

Evening Schools.—An evening school was opened, Aug. 1856, Ahira Holmes, principal. James Denman, John Swett, and John Hammill volunteered their services as assistants until the school was established. This school continued with from 100 to 200 pupils until 1869, when John Swett was elected Principal.

The school was then regularly graded, was opened in the Lincoln building, was made free to adults, and in three months the attendance swelled to 900. A commercial class and an industrial drawing class were soon organized. In 1871, Mr. Swett resigned and was succeeded by William A. Robertson, the present Principal.

6. HISTORICAL STATISTICAL TABLE OF THE SAN FRANCISCO SCHOOLS, 1852–76.

YEARS.	TOTAL EXPENSE.	AVERAGE DAILY ATTENDANCE.	NUMBER OF TEACHERS.
1852	$23,125 00	445	15
1853	35,040 00	1,182	16
1854	159,249 00	1,272	19
1855	136,580 00	1,638	29
1856	125,064 00	2,516	61
1857	92,955 00	2,155	60
1858	104,808 00	2,521	67
1859	134,731 00	2,829	75
1860	156,407 00	2,837	68
1861	158,855 00	3,377	73
1862	134,567 00	3,786	82
1863	178,929 00	4,389	94
1864	228,411 00	5,229	108
1865	346,862 00	6,718	138
1866	361,668 00	8,131	206
1867	507,822 00	10,177	253
1868	415,839 00	11,871	285
1869	400,842 00	13,113	326
1870	526,625 90	15,394	371
1871	705,116 00	16,978	416
1872	668,262 00	18,272	480
1873	611,818 00	18,530	506
1874	689,022 00	19,434	510
1875	707,445 36	21,014	552
Total	$7,610,043 36		

7. SPECIAL SCHOOL STATISTICS, SAN FRANCISCO.

Estimated population, 1875 234,000
Number of census children, 5 to 17 37,583
Number of pupils enrolled in public schools 31,128
Average daily attendance 21,014
Number attending private and church schools 6,094
Enrolled in High Schools 702

Enrolled in Grammar Schools 6,055
" " Primary Schools 22,158
" " Evening Schools 2,213
Teachers (men, 63; women, 447)—total 510
Whole number of classes 449
Expenditures $700,147
Tax roll of the city $264,000,000
Estimated value of school property $3,367,000

CLASSES AND TEACHERS.

Number of classes in the High Schools	17
Number of Grammar Classes (average, 50 each)	108
Number of Primary Classes (average, 55 each)	304
Number of Evening Classes (average, 40 each)	20
Total number of classes	449

Total number of Principals of different schools 47
High Schools, 2; Grammar Schools, 12; Mixed Schools, 9; Primary Schools, 24.
Number of Principals of schools not required to teach a class . . 25
Males, 12; Females, 13.
Number of Vice-Principals 16
Males, 8; Females, 8.
Number of teachers in High Schools 22
Males, 10; Females, 12.
Number of teachers in Grammar Schools 129
Males, 27; Females, 102.
Number of teachers in Primary Schools 325
Male, 1; Females, 324.
Number of teachers in Evening Schools 23
Males, 20; Females, 3.
Number of teachers of German and French 22
German, 13; French, 9.
Teacher of Latin and Greek 1
Number of special teachers 11
Music, 6; Drawing, 5.

Total number of teachers 510

PART II.

I. TEACHERS' CONVENTIONS AND INSTITUTES.

1. FIRST STATE TEACHERS' CONVENTION.

THE first State Teachers' Convention, called by State Superintendent Hubbs, was held in the city of San Francisco, Dec. 26–28, 1854, Supt. Hubbs presiding. No roll of members appears on the manuscript minutes, but about 100 teachers, and other persons interested in school matters, from various parts of the State, were in attendance.

Col. E. D. Baker was introduced to the convention, and made an eloquent address on the subject of general education, and painted in glowing language the future of California. Remarks were made by Rev. M. C. Briggs, Rev. John E. Benton, and Dr. Gibbons. Dr. Winslow read an address on the "Use of the Bible in Public Schools," and the Rev. S. V. Blakesly one on "Phonography in School."

On the second day J. M. Buffington, of Stockton, made a report, which was adopted, recommending the appointment of a committee of seven, to make immediate arrangements for organizing a State Institute. John S. Hittell introduced a resolution, which was adopted, providing for the appointment of a committee to memorialize the Legislature on the subject of libraries. Mr. Freeman Gates moved the appointment of a committee to report a State series of text-books. Essays on the management of primary schools were read by Mrs. Hazleton, Mrs. Clapp, Mrs. Williams, Miss Allyn, and Miss Austin. Mr. Wells, of Sacramento, read an essay on the "General Management of Schools," and Mr. Phillips, of Stockton, on the "Free School System." Mr. Buffington, of Stockton, delivered an address on "Education," and Sherman Day spoke on the same subject. John Swett read an address on the subject of "Elocution in the Common Schools," and J. C. Morrill an able address on "Unclassified Schools."

The proceedings of this Convention were characterized by a good degree of interest; the essays and addresses were generally able; but no improvements in school law worth mentioning were recommended, and the convention left no mark on the educational history of the State.

2. SECOND STATE TEACHERS' CONVENTION.

The second State Teachers' Convention met at Benicia, Aug. 12, 1856, Supt. Hubbs presiding.

William Sherman, from the Committee on Text-Books, reported a series recommended for general use.

Gen. Wool being introduced to the meeting, made a brief speech, in which he complimented the ladies, and said that all the greatest men owed their education and the formation of their characters principally to women.

Mr. Morrill offered a resolution in favor of reading the Bible in the public schools, which, after an exciting debate, was tabled by 21 to 16.

Essays were read by Mr. J. C. Morrill, on "Corporal Punishment;" by Mr. Monroe, on "Thorough Training;" by Mr. Wells, on "Course of Studies;" and by Mrs. Hill, on the "Mission of Females as Teachers."

The convention was not largely attended, only 60 members being present. No important measures were acted on, and the convention gave no renewed impulse to the interests of education.

3. FIRST STATE INSTITUTE.

The first State Institute, called by State Superintendent Moulder, met in the city of San Francisco, May 27, 1861, and continued in session five days, with a total attendance of 250 members. The Legislature of the previous year had made an appropriation of $3000 for the purpose of aiding State Institutes.

In his address, Mr. Moulder stated the plan of proceedings, which devoted the morning sessions to regular Institute lectures, and the afternoon sessions to a convention; that the adoption of a State series of text-books was one important measure to be acted upon; recommended the appointment of committees on school laws and State Normal School; and summed up the improvements made in the school laws during a period of four years.

George W. Minns delivered an address on "Methods of Teaching."

Mr. Swett, who was appointed to present the subject of "Object Teaching" and "Gymnastics," introduced first an object lesson, and then a gymnastic class from the Rincon School, which went through with double and single dumb-bell exercises, free gymnastics, calisthenics, wands, and Indian club exercises.

James Denman delivered an address on "School Discipline."

Mr. Sparrow Smith moved that a committee of three teachers be appointed to report on establishing a State Teachers' Journal, and Messrs. Smith, Gates and Minns were appointed.

George W. Minns was made Chairman of a Standing Committee on Text-Books, to report at the next Institute. Mr. Smith, of Sacramento, from the Committee on State school journal, reported in favor of appointing a standing committee to devise ways and means for publishing such a journal, and after the appointment of this committee, the Institute adjourned *sine die*. The proceedings were published in pamphlet form.

4. SECOND STATE INSTITUTE.

The Second State Institute was convened in Sacramento by Superintendent Moulder, September 23, 1862, and continued in session three days, with an attendance of 100 members.

Superintendent Moulder made a brief introductory address. Mr. George W. Bonnell delivered an address on the "Art of Memory," illustrated by a pupil from his school.

Mr. Minns, Chairman of Standing Committee on Text-Books, made a lengthy report on that subject. Union resolutions were unanimously and enthusiastically adopted.

Mr. Pierce, of Yolo, introduced a resolution in favor of a law requiring a uniform State series of text-books, which after a long debate was passed by a vote of 26 to 24.

Mr. Sparrow Smith introduced a resolution, which was adopted, to appoint a standing committee of twelve on State Teachers' Journal.

Mr. Minns delivered a very eloquent and able lecture on "Moral Instruction."

Supt. Moulder then closed the Institute with the following remarks:

Before putting the question to adjourn *sine die*, I desire to express my earnest thanks for the kindness and consideration you have exhibited toward your presiding officer, and more especially for the warm and flattering terms in which you have seen fit to speak of my official action during the past six years.

It is deeply gratifying to find that I have met the approval of those who ought best to know how I have performed the duties of my office, and whose good opinion is therefore most to be desired.

* * * * * * *

My connection with you, fellow-workers in the cause, has always been harmonious and agreeable. In retiring to private life, I shall retain a pleasing recollection of our long association. From the bottom of my heart I wish you all a prosperous and happy career. Thanking you again for your unvarying courtesy and your kind expressions of approval, I bid you farewell, and declare this convention adjourned *sine die*.

The proceedings were published in pamphlet form.

STATE CERTIFICATES.

At this Institute, the State Board of Examination, consisting of the State Superintendent and six County Superintendents, held an oral examination and issued 5 State grammar school certificates and 12 "Mixed School" certificates, valid for two years.

5. THIRD STATE INSTITUTE.

The third State Institute, called by State Superintendent Swett, assembled in San Francisco, May 4, 1863, in the New Music Hall, the largest and finest hall in the city. Four hundred and sixty-three registered members were in attendance. The daily sessions were also attended by hundreds of other persons, and at the evening lectures the hall was filled to its utmost capacity. In the circular announcing this Institute is found the following on the benefits of Institutes:

No argument is needed to prove the great advantages resulting from Teachers' Institutes. They are not intended as substitutes for Normal Schools, nor can they educate teachers to the business of their profession; yet they serve the most admirable purpose of improving those who are only temporarily engaged in the profession, of furnishing those who are not systematically trained, with the best methods of instruction, and of increasing the efficiency of professional teachers.

The exercises of an Institute involve an outline view of subjects relating to the proper mode of imparting instruction, present the latest information regarding the progress of education in our own and in other countries, and afford an occasion for experienced teachers to present practical views, which cannot be obtained from books. The best thoughts and best acquirements of the most original teachers are elicited and thrown into the common stock of professional knowledge. They influence public opinion, by bringing the teacher's labors more prominently before the community, and by promoting a higher estimate of the Common School in its vital relation to society and the State. The routine of a teacher's daily life limits his influence to the narrow sphere of the school-room; but the proceedings of an Institute are carried by the press to thousands of families in the State, and his views become an active element in public opinion. No obstacle to the progress of Free Schools is so formidable as the apathy and indifference of the people. Eloquence the most winning, and logic the most convincing, alike fall dead upon the ears of those who see nothing in the establishment of Common Schools but an increase of the rates of taxation. But let the true relation of schools to property be once clearly seen, let it be generally known that the value of property increases with the excellence of the schools, and real estate cheerfully consents to be taxed, from motives of self-interest. The axiom in our American system of Free Schools, that it is the bounden duty of the property of the State to provide for the education of *all* the children of the State, rich and poor alike, is in accordance with the spirit of our Government, and should be insisted on by the people to the very fullest extent. If the people of our State are indifferent to Public Schools, it is only because more absorbing topics engage their attention, while the educational interests are not urgently and persistently presented to their view.

Association in some form is one of the most powerful agencies of the times. In conventions of industry and arts, mind is dignifying the labor of the artisan. Farmers have their agricultural societies, and hold their annual fairs, in which are exhibited the best stock, the choicest varieties of grain and vegetables, the most approved agricultural implements, and the best labor-saving machines. The inventions, improvements, and discoveries of one, thus become the common property of all.

And while Institutes have accomplished so much in introducing better methods of instruction, they are no less beneficial in their effects on the mental habits of the teachers. Constantly imparting to minds inferior to his own, his faculties exercised in one direction only, his full strength seldom called forth, he needs the stimulus of contact with his equals, or superiors. A vigorous contest in a new arena lessens his self-conceit, and brightens his faculties.

It is a common notion that the occupation of teaching makes a man narrow-minded, or leads him into eccentricities, which stick to him like burs; but it is not true of a teacher who has in him the elements of living scholarship. He may, it is true, run in the grooves of daily habit, until he becomes a machine for dragging the dead weight of a school; but, on the other hand, he may, while imparting to others, himself drink from the perennial fountain of true scholarship.

But no occupation is more exhausting to nervous force and mental energy than teaching; and the teacher needs, above all others, the cheering influences of pleasant social intercourse with those whose tastes and habits are similar to his own.

No wonder, then, that the schoolmaster, buried in some obscure district, surrounded only by the raw material of mind, which he is trying to weave into a finer texture, without access to books, his motives either misunderstood or aspersed, his labors often seemingly barren of results, his services half paid, with no amusement but the collection of delinquent rate bills, and no study but "how to make both ends meet;" no wonder that he sometimes becomes moody and disheartened, loses his enthusiasm, and feels that the very sky above him is one vast blackboard, on which he is condemned to work out the sum total of his existence.

He only needs the social intercourse of institutes, and the cordial sympathy of fellow-teachers, there evoked, to make the heavens glow with hope. There he finds his difficulties are shared by others, his labors are appreciated, and his vocation respected.

The duties of the teacher are not limited to the school-room; his influence should extend to society around him. If teachers fold their arms in listless apathy, it is not strange that public opinion is "dead as a door nail" to their demands. There was a time when a man taught school because he was fit for nothing else; but all such fossils lie buried in the strata of past educational epochs. Now, a living man is asked for, not an abridgment of mathematics.

While a State Institute is designed more especially for the teachers of public schools, professors and instructors in colleges and private institutions of learning are hardly less interested in the success and influence of this educational meeting. The interests of colleges and collegiate institutions are intimately connected with those of the public schools. All those who acquire an elementary education in the common schools, necessarily seek in private institutions of learning to complete a full course of instruction. The better the public schools, the larger will be the number of those whose minds shall be awakened to pursue a course of study beyond the range of the common school. Before our higher institutions can produce disciplined thinkers, and thoroughly trained professional men, the elementary schools must be carried to a corresponding degree of excellence.

As teachers, we are debtors to our profession; and our patriotism ought to incite us to an earnest devotion to the advancement of our system of Free Schools; a system essential to the existence of a free people, and the permanence of a free government.

It is our duty to cultivate in our schools a higher regard for freedom, a sounder faith in the fundamental principles upon which a representative government is based, and a higher estimate of the incalculable blessings conferred by the Constitution—firm in the conviction that our country is working out for the future, amid the present storm, a higher order of civilization and a nobler conception of liberty.

The course of lectures was as follows:

George W. Minns: Physical Geography of the United States. Prof. J. D. Whitney: Character of Humboldt. Rev. Thomas Starr King: James Russell Lowell, or the "Bigelow Papers." John Swett: Duties of the State to Public Schools. Prof. S. I. C. Swezey: State Normal Schools, and how to teach English Composition. Rev. S. H. Wiley: The Place and Relations of the College in our System of Education. H. P. Carlton: Object Teaching. D. C. Stone: Grammar. Bernhard Marks: Waste in School. Supt. Swett: Common Sense applied to Teaching. John E. Benton: Elocution. John S. Hittell: Defects in Teaching. Dr. F. W. Hatch: Need of Good Teachers. Hubert Burgess: Linear Drawing. Ahira Holmes: Report of State Normal School.

The proceedings were published in a neat pamphlet form of 166 pages, and an edition of 2400 copies was distributed among teachers and school officers.

One of the most important results of the Institute was the action taken in favor of a State tax for the support of schools.

The State Superintendent urged this measure in a lengthy address.

The recommendation for a State tax met the approval of the Institute; and the State Superintendent was instructed to prepare a form of petition to the Legislature on the subject, and to circulate it in every school district in the State.

The following form was accordingly prepared, circulated and signed by more than six thousand voters:

PETITION FOR STATE SCHOOL TAX.

To the Honorable the Members of the Legislature of the State of California:

WHEREAS, We believe that it is the duty of a representative government to maintain public schools as an act of self-preservation, and that the property of the State should be taxed to educate the children of the State; and whereas, the present School Fund is wholly inadequate to sustain a system of free schools; we, the undersigned, qualified electors of the State of California, respectfully ask your honorable body to levy a special State tax of half a mill on the dollar during the fiscal years eighteen hundred and sixty-four and eighteen hundred and sixty-five, the proceeds of the same to be disbursed in the same manner as the present State School Fund.

The next important measure was the action relating to a State educational journal.

D. C. Stone, of Marysville, from the standing committee of the previous year, reported against the practicability of starting such a journal.

Sparrow Smith, also of the committee, in a minority report, dissented, and urged an attempt to establish one.

Professor Swezey, J. L. Wilbur, J. C. Pelton, George Tait, James Stratton and Superintendent Swett, spoke in favor of a journal, and Dr. Gibbons and Mr. Rodgers rose in opposition.

A committee, consisting of Messrs. Smith, Tait and Seymour, was appointed, who reported in favor of establishing a State educational journal, called the *California Teacher*, to be published at one dollar per annum, and to be edited by a board of resident editors, consisting of John Swett, George Tait and George W. Minns. Mr. Minns declined to serve, and nominated Mr. Swezey to fill his place. The first number of this journal was issued in July following.

The subject of a State professional society being brought before the Institute, the plan was advocated by Rev. John E. Benton, Theodore Bradley and others.

A committee was appointed, with Mr. Bradley chairman, who made a report, and requested all interested in forming such a society to meet after the final adjournment of the Institute.

A State Educational Society was soon afterwards formed on the plan recommended.

STATE SERIES OF TEXT-BOOKS.

The revised school law having made provision for the adoption and compulsory use of some uniform State series of text-books, no small share of the time of the Institute was taken up in discussing the merits of school-books. The Institute voted to recommend to the State Board of Education the following series, which was afterwards adopted by the State Board with hardly any variation: Willson's Readers and Spellers; Eaton's and Robinson's Arithmetics; Cornell's and Warren's Geographies; Quackenbos' Grammar and History of the United States.

STATE EXAMINATIONS.

One hundred teachers entered the examination for State diplomas and certificates. The examination was conducted in writing, by means of printed questions, and nearly three thousand pages of manuscript were carefully examined and credited by the Board.

State educational diplomas, valid for six years, were granted to the following teachers: T. C. Barker, Stephen G. Nye, Bernhard Marks, T. W. J. Holbrook, Joseph W. Josselyn, Thomas Ewing, William K. Rowell, Cyrus C. Cummings, Edward P. Batchelor.

State certificates were issued as follows:

First grade certificates, valid for four years........	7
Second grade certificates, valid for two years.......	10
Third grade certificates, valid for two years........	20
Whole number, including diplomas...........	46

RESULTS.

Aside from the incidental labors and benefits of the Institute, its practical and solid results may be summed up as follows:

First. A State educational journal;

Second. Action recommending a State school tax;

Third. A State educational and professional society;

Fourth. Adoption of a State series of text-books;

Fifth. The granting of a large number of State diplomas and certificates;

Sixth. The publication of a valuable volume of proceedings and lectures.

6. FOURTH STATE INSTITUTE.

A State Teachers' Institute was held in the city of San Francisco from September 19–24, 1865. No appropriation in aid of such Institutes was granted by the State Legislature in 1863; but owing to the liberality of the Board of Education of San Francisco, which tendered the use of the Lincoln Schoolhouse, and paid the bills for gas, the State Superintendent was enabled to hold one without any expense whatever to the State.

The Institute was convened in September, during the vacation of the city schools, that being the only time in the year when the Lincoln Hall could be used for such a purpose. Notwithstanding the fact that many of the schools in the interior had just opened their new terms for the year, in consequence of which the teachers were unable to attend, three hundred teachers from various parts of the State were present.

The most important purpose for which it was convened was the holding of an examination of applicants for State diplomas and certificates. How well that purpose was accomplished is set forth in another part of this report.

The following lectures were delivered before the Institute: "The State and the School," John E. Benton; "School Law," John Swett; "Geography of California," Charles Russell Clarke; "A Practical Education," Prof. Kellogg; "Physical Training," Ebenezer Knowlton; "Physiology and Hygiene," H. P. Carlton; "Force," Dr. Washington Ayer; "Comparison between the European and American Systems of Education," Bernhard Marks; "Moral Training," Rev. S. H. Willey; "Modern Languages in Public Schools," Ralph Keeler; "Education," Dr. Luckey.

Several of these addresses were published in the *California Teacher*. The subjects of "School Libraries," "Course of Study for Ungraded Schools," and "Teachers' Life Diplomas," were discussed at length.

A committee of all the County Superintendents present at the Institute acted in detail on the sections of a bill of amendments to the school law, and, with a few immaterial changes, approved the provisions submitted to the committee by the Superintendent of Public Instruction.

An evening ticket lecture was delivered by J. Ross Browne, about "Queer People and Queer Places," which netted the sum of $54 for the benefit of the *California Teacher*. Also an evening lecture on "Natural Philosophy," by Professor Minns, of the State Normal School.

The California Steam Navigation Company gave all members of the Institute *free passes to and from San Francisco*, over their several routes of travel, and the railroad lines gave free return passes to Institute members.

7. FIFTH AND SIXTH INSTITUTES.

The Fifth Institute was held in San Francisco May 7-11, 1867, and attended by 500 teachers. Addresses as follows:

Supt. John Swett: "Educational Progress." D. C. Stone: "Self-Improvement." Rev. C. G. Ames: "The Teacher's Motives." Ralph Keeler: "The Oldest Scholar." Rev. John E. Benton: "Readiness." William White: "Teachers and Parents."

The Sixth Institute convened at Lincoln Hall, May 4–7, 1869. Addresses were delivered as follows:

State Supt. Fitzgerald: "Educational Condition." Prof. John Le Conte: "Nebula Hypothesis." Geo. W. Simonton: "True Education." John Swett: "Arithmetic."

The subject of "Text-Books" was discussed and reported upon.

8. SEVENTH AND EIGHTH INSTITUTES.

The Seventh State Institute met in San Francisco, Sept. 13–16, 1870. Addresses and lectures were given by Supt. Fitzgerald; Prof. E. S. Carr, on "Air," and "Industrial Education;" Mr. Marks, on "Mathematics." J. P. Garlick: "Ungraded Schools." Miss Dolliver: A Poem. Dr. Schellhouse: "Grammar." Miss Fowler: "Defects in Education." Dr. Luckey: "State Normal School." Prof. Joseph Le Conte: "Universal Law of Cyclical Movement."

The Eighth and last Institute met in San Francisco, Nov. 7–10, 1871. Supt. Fitzgerald delivered an annual address. Lectures were given as follows:

Dr. Schellhouse: "The Art of Teaching." Dr. Logan: "School Ventilation and Hygiene." Dr. Gibbons: "Hygiene of Dress." Miss Dolliver: "Cobwebs and Brooms." Dr. E. S. Carr: "The Educational Work of Sarmiento."

The discussions were, in general, on unimportant topics. This was the last of the State Institutes, the Legislature of 1872 having cut off the annual appropriation of $250 for expenses.

9. STATE ASSOCIATION.

The State Board of Education called, by resolution, a convention of teachers at San Jose, June, 1875, but the attendance was small.

A State Teachers' Association was organized, but the proceedings were of no special consequence.

II. INSTITUTE ADDRESSES.

1. INDUSTRIAL EDUCATION.*

Mr. President and Teachers: During the past few weeks the world has been watching the sudden, and to the unobservant eye, almost miraculous transfer of power and prestige from one of the great leading European States to another. A quiet, home-loving practical people have suddenly developed a vast amount of latent force, which it puzzles us to name. Is it brains versus bullets, science versus sentiment, that awaits the arbitrament of war, or a territorial question only? Somehow or other, ideas and education have gone up in the scale as they never did before in any ten weeks of human history.

We are all foolish enough to fix our eyes upon the two central figures of the strife; but neither Teuton fox nor Gallic wolf have had very much to do with the results which so astonish and appal the world.

If Prussia, so far victorious, has been busy rearing a nation of soldiers, she has done it openly, in the face of the world. She has made every soldier a fortification by the completeness of an educational system which makes the most of whatever a man is born with. That system is on exhibition, not only of its value for defense, but its moral power, its temperance and self-control. Whatever the final political result may be, it is certain that not one Prussian who has fallen has felt himself a tool or a dupe, played upon by superior cunning and selfishness.

There is not a soldier of that grand army who has had less than ten years' schooling (most of them have had from fifteen to eighteen years); their bodies have been as carefully trained as their minds, and by teachers who make this their life business.

What would you expect from a country that has an army of three million children at school, whether they wish to go or not and whether their parents wish them to go or not, and for a Government that provides for this largely by devoting to it the heaviest outlay of its resources?

Would you expect Prussia to be beaten, when you know that until the year 1831, France had made no provision for the instruction of her millions, had no public elementary schools when Guizot sent Victor Cousin to study the school system of Prussia, with a view to its adoption?

Power is cumulative, and although Napoleon III has nobly fostered education and science, he started at a disadvantage. Poor, beleagured Paris trembles to-day in greater terror of the ignorant and

---

* Abstract of a lecture before the State Teachers' Institute, September, 1870, by Ezra S. Carr, M.D.

therefore brutalized rabble, shut in to watch and wait with her her deliverance or her doom, than the foe outside her gates.

I confess I am anxious that our own Government should keep on the best of terms with those Germans. I should dread a tyranny like that of Wurtemburg, which permits no child to learn a trade, enter any occupation, or receive any pay for any service whatsoever, until he has answered the demands of the school law. Imagine the consternation which the sudden enforcement of such a regulation would cause in America, in low and in high places! As an offset to this terror, imagine what it would be for you, teachers, to be enrolled among the "high mightinesses," to be ranked and considered as the most valuable civil servitors of the State, with honorable compensation and just promotions for your terms of service, and a comfortable pension when you are old.

Do not think I am praising overmuch, and covertly keeping back a part of the truth. Germany has outdone the world in education, and we have outdone Germany in just one respect! We have discovered and put in practice a great natural law of education, viz., that women are better teachers than men. And they only need the higher education from which they have been so long excluded to make their superiority manifest.

The educational creed of Prussia does not take long in the reading.

Article one declares the sacred right of every individual to the best means of development.

Article two, the value to the State, to her wealth, power and civilization, of universal education.

Article three declares the realization of this impossible without the agency of a great profession, acting concertedly, wisely and zealously together, and that the members of this profession must be made to feel their position honorable, secure and independent.

Unless you are dissenters, I ask you to listen patiently to something I have to say about industrial education, for your help is very much needed in creating a desire for it.

On this new field of California, where we have only begun our work, and where there is only a glimmering apprehension on the part of the public of what this business of education is, and what it is worth, the informing and propelling influence must go out from the body of teachers themselves. Let us get a clear idea of the scope and value of our work, and of the wants of the people; let us, with firm and strong convictions of what is essential to the growth and prosperity of the State, be prepared to meet the most uninformed with some practical, tangible knowledge of the things with which they have to deal, and we shall create a public opinion, a demand for education, that will advance quite as fast as we can keep up with it. Our political system is of such a kind as to require this kind of effort. And our public school system, from the university to the primary school, must be a unit in motive and in method, in this respect.

The question has become one of vital importance to the nation, "How shall we educate our youth so that there shall be more farmers and mechanics in the land, and how shall we raise these pursuits to the rank they deserve in the hierarchy of industries?" It is in vain to eulogize a calling whose votaries forsake it with every opportunity, and whose children turn from it with disgust. Congress might give every acre of the public domain to found Agricultural Colleges, making them not only free, but giving a bonus of land as a reward for attendance, and still their halls will remain empty, until the relations of agriculture to human welfare and to human nature are understood and carried into practice—until the farmer, out of his sense of privation, loss, failure and onesidedness, shall resolve that his children be as carefully cultured as his fields; that they shall grow up in pleasant homes, and lay up, if not dollars and cents, capital for after-pleasures of thought and memory.

Let us consider for a little wherein this business of agriculture fails to meet the higher demands of human nature; and why, in California, we are looking to the lower classes of foreigners for the permanent tillers of the soil.

The educational world has been aroused within the last few years to find a remedy for the growing aversion of American youth for pursuits most vital to the public welfare. What are the influences tending to the demoralization of young men by leading them to look to speculative enterprises, instead of steady industry, as a means of support? Is it the monotony of country life, or a want of the right kind of education?

How shall we create in this country, as there is in Europe, a higher attachment to the land than springs from a sordid self-interest, and make our paternal acres represent here, as they do in older lands, social standing, intelligence, leisure and culture?

By educating our youth, boys and girls, into a respect for these pursuits, and by multiplying in every possible way the social enjoyments and embellishments of country life.

The disadvantages of agricultural pursuits were clearly stated, and the remedies by which they can be overcome; social and isolated industries and their results were contrasted, and the methods of uniting the abstract and practical sides of industrial education fully presented. In a rapid survey of European progress, we were shown to what the immense recent development of Prussian power is mainly due.

A concise report of what has been done in America by Michigan and other States, what has been done by Congress, and what California will be able to accomplish for industrial education, if her people appreciate in any just degree the value of that system of free instruction which, from the common school to the university, guarantees to every child the general culture and special training necessary to energize and economize, to lighten and enlighten all labor, until the measure of usefulness shall come to be the measure of greatness.

2. DUTIES OF THE STATE TO PUBLIC SCHOOLS.*

At a time like the present, when the nation is one vast camp of instruction for armed men; when argument has ended in the right of appeal to trial by battle; when the one absorbing topic of each successive day is the brief telegram, telling of victories won, or of

* Read before the State Teachers' Institute, 1863.

hope deferred; when our eyes turn with longing gaze across the Sierras to catch the first breaking of the war clouds which fringe their summits—it might seem, at first thought, that a convention like this, which waives all military and political considerations, and relates only to the peaceful and almost unseen workings of the public schools, would be inopportune, and out of harmony with the spirit of the times.

But when we stop to ponder, and consider the vital relations which public schools hold to our national life; when we consider the agency which they have had in supplying the intelligence and the patriotism of the army; when we begin to feel, amid the terrible realities of war, that the schools have been the nurseries of loyalty, and the lack of them, the right arm of treason; when we begin to fully realize that the trite truism, "The only safety of a Republican Government is in the virtue and intelligence of the people," is no abstraction—there is a deep significance in this meeting, and in all such conventions, as concerning the future stability of the Government, and the integrity, power, glory and unity of the nation. Constitutions and laws may be bequeathed by one generation to its successors; but patriotism, intelligence and morality die with each generation, and involve the necessity of continual culture and education. Public opinion, the sum of the intelligence of the citizens of the nation, constructs and modifies all constitutions, and breathes vitality into all laws by which the people are governed.

Let the public opinion of one generation become demoralized by ignorance, or by passion resulting from ignorance, and any constitution is like gossamer to restrain and bind it.

It is an axiom in education that the great majority of the people can be well educated only by a system of Free Public Schools, supported by law, in which the *property* of the State is taxed to educate the children of the State.

"The first object of a free people," says Daniel Webster, "is the preservation of their liberty." In a government where the people are not only in theory the source of all powers, but in actual practice are called upon to administer the laws, it is evident that some degree of education is indispensably necessary to enable them to discharge their duties, maintain and administer the laws, and to retain their constitutional rights. All nations recognize the necessity of educating the governing classes. In a Government like ours, either we must have officers unqualified for their duties, or we must be ruled by an educated and privileged aristocracy, or we must provide a system of public instruction which shall furnish a supply of intelligent citizens capable of discharging their various official trusts with honesty and efficiency.

If left to their own unaided efforts, a great majority of the people will fail through want of means to properly educate their children; another class, with means at command, will fail through want of interest. The people, then, can be educated only by a system of Free Schools, supported by taxation, and controlled directly by the people.

The early settlers of our country recognized this vital principle by providing by law for Free Schools, and by making schools and taxation as inseparably connected as taxation and representation.

The Puritans of Massachusetts Bay had just escaped from a government which provided only for the education of the higher classes; which declared, in the words of Charles the First, that "the people's right was only to have their life and their goods their own, a share in the government being nothing pertaining to them;" and in nothing does far-seeing sagacity of those self-reliant men appear more conspicuous than in the wise forecast which led them to provide for the general diffusion of the elements of knowledge as the basis of a principle which is expressed in the Constitution of Massachusetts, as opposed to the declaration of Charles the First, in the following words: "The people of this Commonwealth have the sole and exclusive right of governing themselves as a free, sovereign and independent State."

A section of the Massachusetts Colony Laws of 1642 reads as follows:

"Forasmuch as the good education of children is of singular behoof and benefit to any Commonwealth; and whereas, many parents and masters are too indulgent and negligent of their duty in that kind; it is ordered that the Selectmen of every town shall have a vigilant eye over their brethren and neighbors, to see, first: that none of them shall suffer *so much barbarism in any of their families as not to teach, by themselves, or others, their children and apprentices so much learning as may enable them perfectly to read the English tongue*, upon penalty of twenty shillings for each neglect therein."

In 1647, this law was followed by another, to the end, in the words of the statute, "*that learning may not be buried in the grave of our fathers in the Church and the Commonwealth*," which required every town of fifty families to provide a teacher to instruct all the children of the town in reading and writing, and every town of a hundred families to set up a grammar school, with a teacher competent to fit young men for the university; the expense of these schools to be borne by the town, or by the parents, as the town should determine.

In 1692, the law provided that these schools should be supported *exclusively by tax levied on all the property of the town.*

The Colony Laws of New Haven, 1665, provided that the "Deputies of the Court" should have "a vigilant eye" over all parents and masters, "that all their children and apprentices, as they grow capable, may, through God's blessing, obtain at least so much learning as to be able duly to read the Scriptures, and other good and profitable printed books in the English tongue, *being their native language.*"*

If this law was not complied with, the delinquent was fined ten shillings; and if after three months the offender failed to comply, the fine was doubled; and then the magistrates were empowered to take such children and apprentices, and place them till they became of age, "with such others who shall better educate and govern them, *both for the public conveniency*, and for the particular good of said children and apprentices."

In 1669, the Colony of Plymouth passed the following law:

"*Forasmuch as the maintenance of good literature doth much tend to*

---

* Probably the first American compulsory school law.

the advancement of the weal and flourishing state of societies and republics, this Court doth therefore order, that in whatever township in this government, consisting of fifty families or upwards, any meet man shall be obtained to teach a Grammar School, such township shall allow at least twelve pounds, *to be raised by rate on all the inhabitants*."

The following is the old Colonial Connecticut Law for "appointing, encouraging and supporting schools:"

"Be it enacted by the Governor, Council and Representatives, in General Court assembled, and by the Authority of the same: That Every Town within this Colony, wherein there is but one Ecclesiastical Society, and wherein there are Seventy House Holders or Families, or upwards, shall be at least Eleven Months in each Year Provided with and shall Keep and Maintain One good and sufficient School for the Teaching and Instructing of Youth and Children to Read and Write, which School shall be steadily Supplied with, and Kept, by a Master, sufficiently and suitably Qualified for that Service.

"And, also, there shall be a Grammar School Set up, Kept and constantly maintained in every Head or County town of the several Counties, that are, or shall be Made in the Colony, Which shall be steadily Kept by some Discreet Person of good Conversation, and well Skilled in and Acquainted with the Learned Languages, especially Greek and Latin."

For the support of these schools, a tax of "Forty Shillings" upon every "Thousand Pounds in the Lists of the Respective Towns," was levied and collected.

Many of the wealthy counties of California levy, this year, a smaller school tax than was paid by the hard-fisted colonists of Connecticut.

The following preamble to an act shows the germ of our national policy of reserving certain sections of public lands for school purposes:

"And Whereas, the several Towns and Societies in this Colony, by Virtue of an Act of this Court, made in May, in the Year of our Lord One Thousand Seven Hundred and Thirty-Three, Received by their Committees Respectively, for that purpose appointed, considerable Monies, or Bills of Public Credit, Raised by the sale of certain Townships, Laid out in the Western lands, then so Called, to be Let out, and the Interest thereof, Improved for the Support of the Respective Schools aforesaid, for Ever, and to no other Use: Be it enacted," etc.

In 1785 an ordinance respecting the disposition of the public lands was introduced into the old Congress, referred to a committee, and passed May 20, which provided that the sixteenth section of every township should be reserved "for the maintenance of public Schools."

The celebrated ordinance of 1787, which confirmed the provisions of the land ordinance of 1785, further declared that "MORALITY *and* KNOWLEDGE, *being necessary to good government and the happiness of mankind*, SCHOOLS, *and the means of* EDUCATION, *shall be forever encouraged*."

As the results of this noble policy, more than fifty millions of acres of the public lands have been set apart for the purposes of education.

These few references to Colonial laws show how early in the history of our country these two fundamental principles were enunciated and adopted: *That it is the duty of a Republican Government, as an act of self-preservation, to educate all classes of the people, and that the property of the State should be taxed to pay for that education.*

Let us consider the first axiom: *That it is the duty of a Republican Government, as an act of self-preservation, to educate all classes of the people.*

In a representative government all forms of constitutional law spring from the people, and are changed at will by public opinion. If that is demoralized, public officers will be bad, and the Government will be bad. If public opinion is ignorant, demagogues will warp it to suit partisan purposes. The fountain cannot rise higher than its source; and the administration of the laws will not rise above the level of the morality of the masses.

Consider for a moment the various civil duties a citizen of the State may be called upon to perform. First and highest is the duty which is attached to the right of elective franchise. Intelligence must preside at the ballot-box, or it becomes a partisan machine. The elector is virtually a tool and slave just so far as he is ignorant of the questions on which he votes. If ignorant voters elect knaves to office, the State pays the just penalty of neglecting to educate her citizens. Every citizen is liable to be called to the jury-box. Are those light questions which twelve men are called upon to decide? Questions of life or death, of character or reputation, of fortune, of real estate? Can ignorance and prejudice decide those questions legally and equitably? Would the real estate owner, with a hundred thousand dollars at stake, on which, perhaps, he has unwillingly paid a school tax, choose to trust the verdict to an illiterate jury in preference to one educated in the schools which his property has in part maintained?

Consider, again, all the minor official trusts which an ordinary citizen is called upon to fill—district, township, and county offices. Taken together, they make up no small share of the administration of government.

In the legislative department, is it safe to elect men poorly educated to frame the laws? Any citizen may aspire to and reach the place, and the only safeguard is the general education of all citizens. And it must be borne in mind that while laws may remain unchanged, the intellectual and moral qualifications necessary for the discharge of the duties of a citizen of the State cannot be transmitted, like property, from father to son. They are personal, not hereditary, and must be taught anew to each generation. The work of the schools is never done, and property can never escape continual taxation. This general education of the citizens of the State can only be secured by Public Schools. The rich will be educated under any circumstances; education gives power—power, an aristocracy.

But the Public Schools must be of a character which will attract the children of the rich as well as afford an opportunity to the poor. Such schools prevent the formation of castes and classes in society. The only aristocracy which they recognize is that of talent—an aristocracy which always commands respect and wields power. Said a Boston teacher once, to a visitor: "That boy who has just received the first prize for scholarship, is the son of a wood-sawyer; and the boy who has won the second prize is the son of the Governor of Massachusetts."

It is often objected that Public Schools cannot educate high enough. Dr. Bushnell says:

"The chartered privileges of education furnished by our colleges can be more highly valued by no one than myself. But still it should be understood that an educated man is a MAN ALIVE. Many a boy who does not know Latin from Dutch, and has never seen any university but his mother's and the District School, having attained to the distinction of a living soul, is, in the highest sense, educated. Could this, which is the only just view of the case, be once established in the public mind, it would do much to encourage attempts at self-education, and would greatly endear the system of Common Schools.

"Many years ago, in an obscure country school in Massachusetts, an humble, conscientious, but industrious boy was to be seen, and it was evident to all that his soul was beginning to act and thirst for some intellectual good. He was alive to knowledge. Next we see him an apprentice on the shoemaker's bench, with a book spread open before him. Next we see him put forth, on foot, to settle in a remote town in this State, and pursue his fortunes there as a shoemaker, his tools being carefully sent on their way before him. In a short time he is busied in the post of County Surveyor for Litchfield County, being the most accomplished mathematician in that section of the State. Before he is twenty-five years old we find him supplying the astronomical matter of an almanac published in New York. Next he is admitted to the bar, a self-qualified lawyer. Now he is found on the bench of the Superior Court. Next he becomes a member of the Continental Congress. There he is made a member of the Committee of Six to prepare the Declaration of Independence. He continues a member of Congress for nearly twenty years, and is acknowledged to be one of the most useful men and wisest counsellors of the land. At length, having discharged every office with a perfect ability, and honored, in every sphere, the name of a Christian, he dies regretted and loved by his State and Nation. Now this Roger Sherman, I maintain, was an educated man. Do you ask for other examples? I name, then, Washington, who had only a common domestic education. I name Franklin; I name Rittenhouse; I name West; I name Fulton; I name Bowditch; all Common School men, and some of them scarcely that, but yet all *educated men*, because they were MADE ALIVE. Besides these, I know not any other seven names of our countrymen that can weigh against them. These are truly American names, and there are the best of reasons to believe that a generous system of public education would produce many such. Let them appear, and if they shall embody so much force, so much real freshness and sinew of character as to decide for themselves what shall be called an education, or shall even be able to laugh at the dwarfed significance of college learning, I know not that we shall have any reasons for repining."

To this roll of honor we might add a long array of public men and of scholars whose first impulse to self-education was received in the Public Schools: Henry Clay, Andrew Jackson, Stephen A. Douglas, Lewis Cass, Abraham Lincoln, N. P. Banks, Elihu Burritt, Horace Mann, and many others.

The second proposition is, *that the property of the State should be taxed to educate the children of the State.* The only just ground for taking any man's money for a public purpose is that the public good requires it. But, says some stiff-necked taxpayer, "I have educated my children at my own expense;" or, "I have no children to educate; why should I be taxed to pay for educating the children of others?"

But children arrived at the age of maturity belong, not to the parents, but to the State, to society, to the country. Government calls on them for the defense of the Constitution and the laws. Take the half a million of men now in the army; what are they doing but defending the property which has been taxed to educate them? Without them, what would property be worth?

Again: Every able-bodied laborer adds to the wealth of the community; for the real wealth of a State lies in its amount of productive labor. Educated labor is more productive than ignorant labor. The testimony of all the mills, factories and workshops of the world is, that intelligent artisans are far more profitable than ignorant ones. Raise the standard of education among workingmen, and the productive value of property is increased. Ignorance and idleness are companions; vice and ignorance are companions. Experience shows that the education of the masses affords better protection to good morals, and more security to the rights of property, than all the criminal enactments that can be made or the prisons that can be built. Intelligence makes labor respectable and honorable. Brute labor—the labor of the menial—is no more honorable to-day than when the unwilling millions toiled on the Pyramids of Egypt. The intelligent brain gives dignity to the toil-hardened hand. But we may base the necessity for general education on still broader grounds. Every man born into the world to enrich it by his labor, claims an education as an inalienable right, as much as liberty, food, air or light. Civilization is the result of the labors of all generations which have existed upon the earth. Our laws, our institutions, books, arts, sciences and inventions, are mostly the product of generations which have preceded us. What a childlike generation ours would be were the printing-press and steam power swept out of existence! The generation now living strikes its roots deep into the mental strata of the globe, and draws its nutriment from all past generations. As the miners gather the mineral wealth of our State, upheaved by the convulsions of great geological epochs which thrust up the broken ribs of the earth through granite crusts, so do we enrich ourselves with the wealth of past time uplifted by the convulsions of nations. Having been educated by the labors of preceding generations, we cannot escape the responsibility of educating those who are to succeed us. Every man that is indebted to society for an education, is in duty bound to discharge that debt by educating the child who is to succeed him.

EDUCATION IN OTHER COUNTRIES.

Before considering in detail the condition of education in the different States of the Union, let us glance at the national systems of instruction in the countries of the Old World.

Germany may justly claim the credit of first thoroughly organizing a system of public education, under the administration of the civil power. The characteristic features of the German schools are, the power of the Government to compel attendance; provision to make the schools, not free to all, but accessible to all; and excellent methods of instruction, resulting from Normal Schools; and the making of teaching a life profession.

Music is a prominent part of education in Germany, and the strong national pride, love of country, and love of liberty, of the Germans, is born in schools, where the patriotic songs of the nation become as familiar as the alphabet of their mother tongue.

England, with all her time-honored Universities and endowed Public Schools, is far behind Germany in her elementary schools for the common people. Lord Brougham, in 1836, advocated a national system of Public Schools, but the bill failed *on account of the bitter controversies of the religious sects*, and the children were allowed to grow up in ignorance rather than run the risk of an education without the catechisms. In advocating this bill, Lord Brougham said:

"*Let the people be taught*, say I. The school is closed, but the penitentiary yawns day and night to ingulf its victims; the utterly execrable, the altogether abominable hulk lies moored in the face of day, which it darkens, riding on the face of the waters, which it stains with every unnatural excess of infernal pollution, triumphant over mortals."

Macaulay said, in 1847, in the House of Commons:

"*Educate the people*, was the first admonition addressed by Penn to the commonwealth he founded; *educate the people*, was the last legacy of Washington; *educate the people*, was the unceasing exhortation of Jefferson. Yes, of Jefferson himself, and I quote his authority with peculiar favor, for of all public men that the world ever saw, he was the one whose greatest delight it was to pare down the functions of Governments to the lowest possible point, and to leave the freest possible scope for the exercise of individual rights."

CHARLES DICKENS.

Charles Dickens deserves to be classed among English educational reformers, for his caricatures of English schoolmasters, in the character of Squeers, and of boarding schools conducted on the starvation system of that motherly matron, Mrs. Squeers, effected a salutary reform. The merciless wit of Dickens has never spared pompous pretensions to learning, nor pedantic methods of instruction. How capitally he hits off what is termed "practical teaching:"

"'Now, what I want is Facts. Teach these boys and girls nothing but facts. Facts alone are wanted in life. Plant nothing else, and root out everything else. Stick to facts.' The emphasis of the speaker was helped by the speaker's square wall of a forehead, which had his eyebrows for its base; and his eyes found commodious cellarage in two dark caves overhadowed by the wall. The emphasis was helped by the speaker's mouth, which was wide, thin and hard set. The emphasis was helped by the speaker's voice, which was inflexible, dry and dictatorial. The speaker's obstinate carriage, square coat, square legs, square shoulders,—nay, his very neckcloth trained to take him by the throat with an unaccommodating grasp, like a stubborn fact, as it was,—all helped the emphasis. 'In this life we want nothing but Facts, Sir, nothing but Facts.'"

Gradgrind was a teacher with "a rule and a pair of scales, and the multiplication table always in his pocket, Sir, ready to weigh and measure any parcel of human nature, and tell you exactly what it comes to."

Said the visitor, eloquently discoursing "to the little vessels ranged in rows ready to have gallons of facts poured into them until they were full to the brim:"

"We hope to have before long a Board of Fact, composed of commissioners of fact, who will force the people to be a people of fact, and nothing but fact. You are not to have in any object of use or ornament what would be a contradiction in fact. You don't walk upon flowers in fact; you cannot be allowed to walk upon flowers in carpets. You never meet with quadrupeds going up and down walls; you must not have quadrupeds represented on walls. You must use, for all these purposes, combinations and modifications of mathematical figures, which are susceptible of proof and demonstration. This is fact. This is taste."

In the school of facts, Mr. McChoakumchild does the practical work:

"He, and some one hundred and forty other schoolmasters, had been lately turned in the same factory, at the same time, on the same principles, like so many piano forte legs. He had been put through an immense variety of paces, and had answered volumes of head-breaking questions. Orthography, etymology, syntax and prosody, biography, astronomy, geography and general cosmography, the sciences of compound proportion, algebra, land surveying and levelling, vocal music and drawing from models, were all at the ends of his ten chilled fingers.

"He had taken the bloom off the higher branches of mathematics and physical sciences, French, German, Latin and Greek. He knew all about all the watersheds of all the world, and all the histories of all the peoples, and all the names of all the rivers and mountains, and the productions, manners and customs of all the countries, and all their boundaries and bearings on the two and thirty points of the compass.

"If he had only learnt a little less, how infinitely better he might have taught much more!

"There were five young Gradgrinds, and they were models, every one. No little Gradgrind had ever seen a face in the moon; it was up in the moon before it could speak distinctly. No little Gradgrind had ever learnt the silly jingle, 'Twinkle, twinkle, little star; how I wonder what you are!' It had never known wonder on the subject, having at five years dissected the Great Bear like a Professor Owen, and driven Charles' Wain like a locomotive engine driver. No little Gradgrind had ever associated a cow in a field with that famous cow with the crumpled horn who tossed the dog who worried the cat who killed the rat who ate the malt, or with that yet more famous cow who swallowed Tom Thumb. It had never heard of these celebrities, and had only been introduced to a cow as a graminivorous, ruminating quadruped with several stomachs.

"'Bring to me,' says Mr. McChoakumchild, 'yonder baby, just able to walk, and I will engage that he shall never wonder.'

"And Gradgrind, as he surveyed the children, seemed a kind of cannon, loaded to the muzzle with facts, and prepared to blow them clean out of the regions of childhood at one discharge."

DISTINCTIVE FEATURES OF OUR SCHOOLS.

One distinctive feature of our schools is the general education of the sexes together. I believe that the true deference paid to woman, and the chivalric politeness with which she is treated, and the high standard of morality generally prevailing in the United States, are the results, in no small degree, of educating boys and girls together in the same schools.

Another distinctive feature of our schools is their freedom from sectarian instruction. In most European schools direct religious lessons are given by the clergy of both the Catholic and the Protestant churches; in other words, the schools are made the medium of denominational and sectarian teaching of creeds and catechisms.

Happily for their prosperity, and for the best interests of vital religion, our schools are removed from all denominational influences, and the reading of the Bible, without note or comment, affords little occasion for sectarian feeling. All are left free to form their own belief, drawn from the primal source of Christianity.

STATE SCHOOL TAX.

A State tax of half a mill on the dollar has been levied this year for carrying on the work of building up the State Capitol; is it not quite as necessary that the work of building schoolhouses should not be delayed? Of what use will a magnificent State Capitol be, unless educated legislators are sent there to fill it? The State is to be placed on a military footing. It is equally necessary that it should be placed on an educational footing, for educated and intelligent men are a stronger defense than Monitors, Columbiads, or field batteries. During the darkest hour of our national adversity the work upon the dome of the Capitol, at Washington, was carried on without cessation, even under the roar of the enemy's cannon—a fitting type of the faith of the people in the permanence of our Government and the stability of our institutions. Our public schools are not the dome of the Republic, but the solid and everlasting foundations on which is based the permanence and integrity of the nation.

We, of this generation, fall back upon the sword and the bayonet to sustain the laws; but if we expect our children to be capable of self-government, if we have not utterly lost our faith in representative institutions, let us not stultify ourselves by failing to educate our children.

We sprang at once into a high degree of civilization; our mines yield immediate and rich returns for labor, and we are unworthy the fairest inheritance the sun shines upon if we do not provide a system of free schools which shall furnish the means of education to every child as liberally as nature has bestowed her mineral wealth upon our land. Shall California, just entering on a renewed career of prosperity from the recent discoveries of fabulous mineral wealth, contribute less for schools than the States where ice and granite take the place of silver and gold? Is the table of ten mills one cent—ten cents one dime—ten dimes one dollar—ten dollars one eagle—the only ten commandments our children shall be taught? Is the national ensign of the Republic, like the calf of molten gold the children of Israel worshiped in the wilderness, to be made a great golden buzzard? Is metal to be valued more than mind, and "feet" more than the little brain engines that fill the schoolhouses?

Shall we pay thousands of dollars annually for blooded stock, and let the children run wild, like Spanish cattle? Shall we sink costly artesian wells through all our valleys, and keep the living well-springs of knowledge sealed to the thirsty children? Shall we send to Europe for choice foreign wines, and leave the children to grow up like the wild mustard which covers our fertile lands with its rank growth? Shall millions be expended in constructing a Pacific Railroad, and the State fail to lay the solid foundations of character and intelligence on which rest the permanent prosperity of the generation which will reap the benefits of that great highway of the world? Shall we make every sacrifice of men and money to maintain the Union for a generation unfitted, through want of education, to appreciate either our sacrifices, or the value of the inheritance we leave them?

The effect of our abundant wealth, unless its possessors shall be educated and trained to use it in intellectual pleasures and refined enjoyments, will be to sweep us into the rankest and grossest forms of materialism.

The real wealth of the State must ever be her educated men and intelligent laborers. Educated mind has made the world rich by its creative power. The intelligent minds which invented the steamship, the cotton-gin, and the spinning-jenny, created for the world a wealth greater than the products of the gold mines of Australia and California together. How many millions of dollars is Ericsson's invention of the Monitor worth to the nation? How much the invention of the electric telegraph? How much the hundreds of labor-saving machines in every department of industry? Ignorance invents none of these. What influence, tell me, is so mighty in developing the intellect of society as the common school? One single great mind, inspired in the public school with a love for learning—without which it might have slumbered forever—may prove of more value to the State than the entire cost of schools for half a century.

What influence is so mighty in developing this creative power of society, as the intelligence imparted in the public schools? Go to the Patent Office and find out how many inventions come from the land of common schools, and how many from the States that have failed to establish them.

Not many years ago, a member of the British Parliament urged, as a reason against a system of national instruction, "that if they deprived the farmers of the labor of the children, agriculture could not be carried on, because there was no machinery to get the weeds out of the land."

The policy of New England always has been to send the children to school, and let Yankee ingenuity invent machines "to get the weeds out of the land."

She has "saved" enough by the invention of "machines," contrived by laboring men educated in her schools, to pay for the whole cost of her schools twice told.

An agricultural report says:

"The saving to the country from the improvements in plows alone, within the last twenty-five years, has been estimated at no less than ten millions of dollars a year in the work of teams, and one million in the price of plows, while the aggregate of the crops is supposed to have been increased by many millions of bushels."

The machinery brought into use, since 1816, is estimated to be equal to the labor of five hundred millions of men.

Ignorance never invented a machine to save the labor of a single man.

The life of the nation lies not in a few great men, not in a few brilliant minds, but is made up of the men who drive the plow, who build the ships, who run the mills, and fill the machine shops, who build the locomotives and steam-engines, who construct the railroads, who delve in the mines, who cast the cannon, who man the ironclads and gunboats, who shoulder the musket, and who do the fighting; these constitute the life and strength of the nation, and it is with all these men that the public schools have done and are now doing their beneficent work. The nation will not be saved by any one "great man;" the bone and muscle of intelligent laboring men must work out its salvation. Blundering statesmen may mar the fortunes of the war; general after general may show up his own incompetence; the concentrated and consolidated intelligence of the working men and fighting men will, in the end, prove victorious. When the bayonet has done its work, the ballot-box must protect the freedom won on the battle-field. When every ballot represents an idea, and falls electrified with intelligence to "execute a freeman's will," the States will revolve harmoniously around the central sun of a consolidated Union; no star will shoot off in eccentric orbit into the chaos of disunion, or the cometary darkness and desolation of secession.

* * * * * * * *

Intelligent free laborers are working out the great problem of civilizing this continent; intelligent fighting men are consolidating its Government; and, underlying all, the public schools are silently forming a sound national character. Free as air, vital as electricity and vivifying as the sunlight, they act on the organic forces of the nation, as these three physical agents build up the life of the globe out of inorganic matter.

The insurrection will be put down by the sword and the bayonet; but even then the only strength of the Union will be in a public opinion based on an intelligent comprehension of national affairs by the people of the whole nation.

The number of legal voters in the United States who cannot read and write is greater than the ordinary majority by which a President is elected.

It is seldom the Governor of any State is elected by a majority larger than the number of "illiterate voters of the State." What avails the Constitution at the mercy of men who cannot read it? Unless the laws of the several States are administered by rulers chosen by electors whose ballots fall vitalized by intelligence, no standing armies, no Constitutions, can hold them in harmonious spheres around the central sun of a Representative Government. They will shoot off in eccentric orbits into the unfathomable darkness of dissolution and chaos, never to return.

It is a Prussian maxim. "Whatever you would have appear in the life of the nation you must put into the schools."

If the schools inculcate with intellectual training love of country, cordial submission to lawful authority, moral rectitude, some knowledge of the theory and organic structure of our Government, and a true spirit of patriotism, then shall our citizens be truly MEN, and our electors princes indeed.

When I consider the power of the public schools, how they have disseminated intelligence in every village, and hamlet, and log-house in the nation, how they are molding the plastic elements of the next generation into the symmetry of modern civilization, I cannot think that our country is to be included in the long list

"Of nations scattered like the chaff
Blown from the threshing-floor of God."

I hold nothing in common with those fainthearted patriots who are beginning to despair of the future of our country. The latent powers of the nation are just coming into healthful and energetic action, and in spite of treason, are moving the Republic onward and upward to a higher standpoint of liberty.

The Anglo-Saxon race, even in its ruder years, always possessed an inherent power of self-government. Tell me not that now, when this stubborn vitality and surplus energy, expended so long in overrunning the world, are guided by intelligence and refined by Christianity, this same race is to be stricken with the palsy, because of a two years' war.

Long before the completion of the Pacific Railroad, these new recruits, drilled in the public schools, will push their way across the continent, as the Saxons set out from their northern hives, a vast army of occupation, cultivating the "National Homestead," and fortifying the whole line of communication by a *cordon* of schoolhouses that shall hold it forever as the heritage of free labor, free men and a free nation.

"So shall the Northern pioneer go joyful on his way,
To wed Penobscot's waters to San Francisco's Bay!
To make the rugged places smooth, to sow the vales with grain,
And bear, with Liberty and Law, the Bible in his train;
The mighty West shall bless the East, and sea shall answer sea,
And mountain unto mountain call, PRAISE GOD, FOR WE ARE FREE!"

3. METHODS OF TEACHING.*

The common schools are established by law, for the purpose of affording to all the children in the State the means of obtaining a good education, at the public expense. Their design is to have knowledge as common among the people, as are water, air, and the sunlight. They are planted deep in the affections of the people. Their importance cannot be overstated. Any attempt to improve them, or to render them more useful, deserves the encouragement of every good citizen. I understand that the object of this Institute, composed of teachers from various parts of the State, is to interchange views in relation to the great cause of education, in order to assist one another in the practice of their profession.

So much has been written upon the subject of education, that it would seem to have been exhausted long ago. Yet it is, in fact, as inexhaustible as human nature. It comprehends and applies to all men, from the cradle to the grave, under all circumstances, and with all their varieties and peculiarities of character. It endeavors to ascertain the true and philosophical system of human culture, to point out the best methods of teaching, of maintaining good order, of preserving the health, and of developing all the faculties in the natural order, so as to produce the best results for the individual and the community.

The object of the present meeting is more specifically to improve, in every possible manner, the condition of the common schools of this State. We wish to render these fountains, at which the great mass of the people drink, as pure and invigorating as possible.

My purpose is then to take some of the ordinary branches taught in the common schools, and to state what I think the best methods of giving instruction in them. Before doing so, however, let me present a few general considerations.

Although the practice of teaching must have begun in Paradise (indeed, according to the pious legends of the Rabbins, Adam was not only the first man, but also the first schoolmaster, aided by Enoch, I suppose, as his first assistant), yet it is nearly certain that no great improvements were generally effected in the art of teaching, and that there never was known such a thing as the philosophy of teaching, until the institution of common schools, and, in point

* Read before the State Teachers' Institute, 1861, by George W. Minns.

of fact, not even till long after they were known. We owe our fathers a debt of gratitude for the establishment of the first free schools, supported at the public expense, for the education of the whole people. Yet they were very imperfect in many particulars, and the change for the better was very slow and not made without much opposition. There was for a long time great imperfection in the construction of schoolhouses. The Hon. Horace Mann, while he was Secretary of the Massachusetts Board of Education, described schoolhouses in central districts of rich and populous towns, where each seat was a stump, without side-arms or back-board; some of them so high that the feet of the children in vain sought after the floor, and on the hard top of which they were obliged to balance themselves as well as they could, for some six hours in a day.

Mr. Mann says: "I have reason to remember one of another class of schoolhouses, of the wicker-work order of architecture—summer-houses for winter residences—where there was never a severely cold day without the ink's freezing in the pens of the scholars while they were writing, and the teacher was obliged to compromise between the sufferings of those who were exposed to the cold of the windows, and those exposed to the heat of the fire, by not raising the thermometer near the latter above ninety degrees, until that near the window fell below thirty. It was an excellent place for the teacher to illustrate one of the facts in geography, for five steps would have carried him through the five zones. Just before my present circuit," he writes, "I passed a schoolhouse, the roof of which, on one side, was trough-like, and down towards the eaves there was a large hole, so that the whole operated like a tunnel, to catch the rain, and pour it into the school-room. At first, I did not know but it might be some apparatus to illustrate the deluge. I called, and inquired of the mistress if she and her little ones were not sometimes drowned out. She said she should be, only that the floor leaked as badly as the roof, and drained off the water."

I myself have seen a schoolhouse in which an old hat was shown to be a pronoun, by being used instead of the noun, glass.

It is of great importance to provide healthful and comfortable schoolhouses for the young. Let them be placed in the most pleasant locations; let the seats be convenient for children of all ages, and let an abundance be furnished of that prime necessary of life, fresh air.

More improvements have been made in the last twenty-five years, in relation to the structure and management of schoolhouses, and in reference to the modes of teaching the various branches pursued therein, than had been accomplished during the preceding two centuries. I well remember the first grammar-school which I attended. It was a very long room, with a smoke-pipe extending the whole length of it, into which, so the master said, all bad boys would go. I was puzzled for some time to find where it led, as it passed through a partition separating us from the next room. The stove was large and grim-looking, with the head of some nondescript monster upon the door, with the snarling mouth wide open; and when the full power of the draught was on, it roared loud enough to devour several bad boys at once. I kept at a safe distance from it. The walls of this apartment were as bare as prison walls. There was not a map, nor an engraving, nor a picture upon them, and no globe belonged to the school. This was certainly wrong. The walls of our school-rooms should be covered and adorned with maps and pictures suited to the progress of the scholars. There are published in the pictorial papers, and in other ways, farm scenes, pictures of domestic animals, birds, and beasts, of flowers, of different kinds of trees, and views of some of the largest cities of the globe, all of which would be useful in this respect. Nor, by any means, would I have omitted some scenes addressed to that sense of the beautiful which exists in children as strongly as it does in us. All this might be done at a trifling expense, and what a contrast would be presented between such a school-room and the cold, lifeless, and dingy walls within which too many children are confined. If I had a school in the country, particularly if it was one for small children, I would, in the proper season, have many of the exercises conducted in the open air, in a grove, or any shady place near by. Every lesson relating to nature should be studied, or read, in the face of nature, with flowers scattered all around, and under the living trees, instead of hanging over the "desk's dead wood." Why should a class read Bryant's glorious poem, "The groves were God's first temples," in a wooden box lined with Lowell sheeting, when at a short distance may be nature's temple itself, with its lofty pillars, its green arches, its majestic roof, and its sweet songsters.

Then, still carrying out this principle of object-teaching, I would avail myself of it wherever I could. For instance, by the use of the numeral frame, or, if that cannot be had, with buttons, or beans, all the fundamental rules and principles of arithmetic can be taught and made palpable to the eye. I would have the length of a yard, foot, and inch, permanently marked upon the upper part of the blackboard. I would have every grammar school provided with the following articles, for use in the various departments, namely: Peck, gallon, quart, pint, and gill, measures; grains, pennyweights, ounces, and pounds, of the different measures; blocks to represent square and solid measures, and, in addition, a pair of scales. The clock can be used to illustrate the divisions of time. I would have every scholar studying arithmetic show himself, by experiment, whether the tables he commits to memory are correct. In this manner, the learning of the tables, which is so often considered a drudgery, would become a pleasant pastime. After this, do you think the pupil would forget them?

So in commencing grammar. Provide a number of different colored wafers, bits of cloth, silk, or cotton. Show them to the scholars, asking them to state the color of each. Let the pupils tell and write upon their slates the object, the color, and the number shown. Will not they very soon learn which is the noun, and which words merely describe the noun—that is, are adjectives?

A similar course may be pursued with the verb, and it may be modified so as to bring the child to understand the office of pronouns, and to apply some of the tenses of the verbs.

Example—I lift a book (doing it). He lifts a book. The book can be lifted. You may rise. They will sit. She is touching the table, etc.

This exercise may be varied indefinitely. Children should go through these exercises together, pronouncing the sentences, and illustrating them by doing the thing mentioned.

In this connection, I will remark that, in my opinion, children pursue the study of grammar at altogether too early an age. Because they can easily be taught what a noun, an adjective, or a verb is, it by no means follows that their minds are in a fit state to understand the principles of grammar, or analysis. There are other studies more suitable for their tender years. A year or two later, they can enter more readily into the spirit and foundation of the rules of grammar, and their minds will be better prepared to grapple with the difficulties of the study. Time is lost by putting children into studies for which their minds are not ripe. "Grammar is not the stepping-stone, but the finishing instrument." As grammar was made after language, so ought it to be taught after language.

When scholars come to study the natural sciences, these are made, as much as possible, matters of experiment and observation. No one supposes a pupil will make any proficiency in the study of chemistry, or of any branch of natural philosophy, without witnessing experiments, or making them for themselves. Is there not good reason, then, for pursuing the same course, as far as possible, with less advanced children? It is true, as has been remarked, that primary and intermediate schools need apparatus as much as a high school, but, of course, of a different character.

The several faculties of the human mind are not simultaneously developed, and in educating an individual we ought to follow the order of nature, and adapt the instruction to the age and mental stature of the pupil. If we reverse this order, and attempt to cultivate faculties which are not sufficiently matured, while we neglect to cultivate those which are, we do the child an irreparable injury. Memory, imitation, imagination, powers of observation, and the faculty of forming mental habits, exist in early life, while the judgment and the reasoning powers are of slower growth. It is well known that the memory may be stored at an early age with valuable rules and precepts which in future life may become the materials of reflection, and the guiding principles of action; that it may be furnished with heroic sentiments and poetic illustrations, with "thoughts which breathe and words that burn," and which, long after, will spring up spontaneously from the depths of the mind, at the proper moment, to embellish and to enforce the truths of the future man.

This period of life, when acquisitions of this kind are most readily made, is not that in which the judgment and reasoning powers can be most properly cultivated. They require a more advanced age, when the mind has become more matured by natural growth, and better furnished with the material of thought.

An important part of elementary mental instruction is that of imparting expertness in the performance of certain processes, such as spelling, reading, penmanship, drawing, composition, expertness in the first rules of arithmetic. I shall by and by consider some of these branches under another aspect. At present I refer only to that promptness and dexterity in going through certain processes, which can be imparted only by laborious drilling on the part of the teacher, and acquired only by attention and frequent practice on the part of the pupil. As merely one illustration of what I mean, I will mention skill in adding long columns of figures with rapidity and correctness. It is only in early life, while the mind is in a pliable condition, that these mental facilities can most readily and most perfectly be acquired. The practice in each case must be so long continued, and the process so often repeated, that it becomes a mental habit, and is at length performed with accuracy and rapidity, almost without thought. I think this drilling is the most irksome part of a Teacher's duty; it is apt to be distasteful to the pupil, but it must be faithfully and resolutely performed. It is an important principle which should be kept in view by the Teacher, that although the practice of an art is at first difficult, and requires at each step an effort of mind, yet, every repetition renders it easier, and at length we come to exercise it not only without effort, but as a pleasurable gratification of a habitual act. Perseverance, therefore, in this cause, will ultimately receive a grateful reward.

We should carefully avoid having too many studies in our schools. *Non multa, sed multum* is a maxim of sound sense. Do a few things well, not many things poorly. It should never be forgotten that correct spelling, reading, writing, arithmetic, geography, grammar, and facility in expressing one's self in good plain English, are indispensable. They are the foundation of all future acquisitions; in fact, without them, there can be no superstructure. They are worth any quantity of heads full of mere smatterings of *ologies* and *osophies*.

"I want to *conjecture* a map to study *antimony*, and to learn *bigotry*," said a girl to her master. "My dear little girl," was the reply, "you may *project* a map, after having studied geography some time longer; *astronomy* you may attend to when you can understand it; and I would advise you never to learn *bigotry* in all your life. Perhaps you mean *botany*."

It is a great evil, I have said, to introduce many studies into a school. It works evil in another way, and that is, children are put into studies for which their minds are not mature enough. It is an important fact that the mind, at a certain time, may be totally unable to comprehend a subject, because it is not sufficiently developed to understand it. The evident course to be followed is, to *wait, wait* until the *mind has grown*, and then what was formerly so difficult becomes perhaps quite easy.

An incident is related in the Autobiography of Dr. Benjamin Franklin, which illustrates this point.

Dr. Franklin states that he was sent by his father to a school for writing and arithmetic, "kept by a then famous man, a Mr. George Brownwell. Under him," says the Doctor, "I learned to write a good hand pretty soon; *but I failed entirely in arithmetic.*"

It is almost incredible that a mind like Franklin's should be incapable, even at the age of nine years, of understanding the rudiments of arithmetic, which he tells us, he mastered a few years after by himself, with ease. His mind, perhaps, was not sufficiently grown for him to take hold of the subject. Another explanation of this fact is to be found also in the character of the text-books used in Franklin's day, and in the method, or, rather, want of any method, of instruction. Every one, at all interested in the cause of Education, knows the vast improvement that has been made within a brief period, both in the books used in schools and in the methods of teaching from them. This improvement has extended to every branch of a school education. It is difficult for us to form an idea how different was the state of things in Franklin's time. I imagine I see the boy—endowed by his Creator with faculties which were to astonish the world by their strength, acuteness, and grasp—that boy, who afterwards made his name immortal by his discoveries in science, and who did more than any man, except Washington, to carry his countrymen successfully through the war of the Revolution—I imagine I see him in a small and, probably, ill-ventilated school-room in School Street, in the town of Boston, resting his distracted head upon his hand, and endeavoring in vain to catch a glimpse of the meaning of the mysterious rules in *Cocker's Arithmetic*. The various studies that now make school life pleasant were entirely out of his reach. At ten years of age he was taken from school to help his father in the business of tallow-chandler and soap-boiler, having learned from that "famous man," Master Brownwell, nothing except a good hand—a statement which every one will admit to be true who looks at his name, signed in clear, round characters, to the Declaration of Independence. One cannot help thinking with what delight Franklin would, even at that early age, have pored over the most elementary treatise on Natural Philosophy; but it was to be his fate, by his brilliant discoveries, to *make* some of the most important *additions* to such a work, instead of merely reading accounts of the achievements of others.

It should be carefully kept in mind that the object is not to pour information into the mind, but to train and discipline it. Hence, we see the absurdity of learning a lesson merely by rote, and of asking, in hearing a recitation, simply the questions which may be in the book. Montaigne says: "To know by heart, is not to know." Self-development should be encouraged to the fullest extent. The pupil should be *told as little as possible*, and induced to *discover as much* as possible. Encourage him to conquer difficulties himself. Every victory so achieved adds to the strength of his mind, and what he acquires in this way he makes permanently his own. The rule that the teacher should follow, is not to do anything for the scholar which the scholar can do for himself; to remove from the road only those obstacles which are insurmountable, and to put the pupil on the right track when he has got on the wrong one. The true object in teaching is, to enable the scholar to do without a teacher, as in assisting a child to walk; it is that he may walk alone. It is true that certain information must be imparted by the teacher, and the best informed man, other things being equal, will be the best teacher. But in imparting information, the same caution should be used as in feeding a child. Give him intellectual food only when he craves it, then only can he digest it. Don't load his stomach when he is not hungry. There is intellectual dyspepsia in schools.

It is implied in what I have said, that the real object of education is to teach how *to think*. If this is not done, the memory may be crammed with knowledge, so called (even this is like the rude and undigested mass with which Virgil's harpies gorged themselves); but what wisdom is there, what development of mind? Emerson says: "When a great thinker is let loose upon the world, look out." How true it is that very few people do think. Many follow in the beaten track, without asking whether there is not a better road. How many are carried away by mere words, names, devices, without once inquiring—What does all this really mean? Let us not be surprised, then, that the power of thinking is not more frequently found among the young. Few grown persons possess it. But it is a source of great gratification to the teacher when he finds in his class any who do *think*, who turn the matter over in their minds, who inquire why this is, or is not, so; in short, who bring mind to bear upon the subject of their lessons. He wishes that that leaven would leaven the whole lump of juvenility before him. Too many learn their lessons by going over them as a mere matter of memory, not as an exercise of the mind. This will be the case as long as teachers insist upon, and are satisfied with, merely the answers in the book, hearing the lesson almost as a mechanical exercise. The remedy for the evil is to cross-examine the scholars closely, and in a variety of ways, in order to ascertain whether they have clear and definite ideas on the subject which they have been studying. In this manner you probe their knowledge. Take all the pains in the world to see that they *understand* what they recite, perhaps, very glibly.

As the foundation of all memory, of all thinking, of progress in learning, of success in any pursuit, *attention* is indispensable. It is the possession, or the want of this faculty, that makes the great difference among men. It is the power of directing and holding the mind closely and fixedly upon any subject until it is contemplated in all its aspects and relations, and thereby fully understood. You remember Newton said if there was a difference between himself and other men, it resulted from his attention to the subject of his thoughts. This ability to fasten and hold the attention cannot be estimated too highly. It must not be disregarded even in the youngest pupil. Whether one or many are to be instructed, undivided attention must be given. Care and judgment are, of course, highly necessary in presenting just such thoughts and lessons as are adapted to their capacity. One thing at a time should claim attention until it is fully mastered. Let that one thing be within the reach of the child's mind, and then impressed upon it until the idea is fully grasped.

A pleasant method of giving a child a lesson in attention may be found in Ogden's "Science of Education." He says: "A little expedient to which I have resorted, on some occasions, may be suggestive of means that may be adopted for correcting these evils, and of fixing the attention. Holding up my watch to the school, I have said: 'How many of these little boys and girls can look at it for one minute at a time?' The idea, perhaps, is a novel one, and their little voices and hands will respond, anxious for the experiment. Some will say, boastingly, 'I can look at it an hour!' '*Two hours!*' responds another little captain, who is anxious to make a display of his prowess. At this juncture, I ask, how many would be willing to make the experiment of one minute continuous looking? There is a shower of hands and a shout of voices raised to the highest pitch. 'Well, let us try; all ready; now!' And their forms straighten up, and all eyes are bent with intense earnestness upon the watch. It grows very quiet, and every one listens and looks. Presently it occurs to half a dozen, or more, of them, that they are doing it about right. 'I wonder if John, or Charles, or Mary, or Ellen, is looking too? Wonder if they all are doing as well as I am?' And their thoughts leave the watch and the promise, and wander after Charles or Ellen, and the temptation to look away becomes so great that in about half a minute, or less, you will see an occasional pair of eyes glance hurriedly to some convenient quarter of the room, and back quick to the watch again; others, still less cautious, will turn the head, and look carelessly away; others, again, will drop off entirely, and cease to look; while some more resolute and determined and careful than the rest, will not remove their eyes for a moment, and, at the expiration of the time, will announce their triumph with evident satisfaction. At the close, some will insist upon a new trial; it may be granted, and then others will succeed: and here it might be well to vary the experiment. The question might be asked: 'If you are capable of holding your eyes fixed upon that watch, can you, with equal success, confine them to a picture or mark, upon the board?'

"'Now, if you can look at a watch, a picture, or a mere chalk mark upon the board, for a given time, can you look at your books as long without change?' The intention here, perhaps, will be discovered by some, and they will begin to see the force of it. Let the experiment be made with the book, without attempting to study during the first few trials. If they succeed well, suggest that if they can look upon one page of the book, they might study that long without looking away; and if they can thus confine the attention for one, two, or three minutes, they can also, by practicing, continue to five and six; but it will be found that young scholars are not able to endure more than three or four minutes, even after months of practice."

Another method is to read sentences selected for the beauty of the thought, or for the admirable manner in which they express some noble sentiment, or convey some moral truth. They are to be suited to the mind of the scholar, and are to be read to the whole class, beginning, of course, with short sentences, and afterwards proceeding to longer and more complicated. Every one in the class must be told to give close attention. The sentence is then read *only once*, slowly and distinctly. All those who can remember it are requested to raise their hands, and some one is called on to repeat it. It is wonderful to what an extent the attention and the memory can be cultivated by such a course as this. Do you suppose that children, who have had the advantage of this practice, will, when they hear a lecture or sermon in after-life, complain that their memories are so wretched that they cannot recollect a word?

Warren Colburn's "Intellectual Arithmetic" (and all mental arithmetics are based upon his plan), besides addressing the reasoning faculty, and leading pupils to understand the principles of arithmetic, is remarkably instrumental in increasing the power of thought, and in enabling the mind to hold and to follow a line of consecutive reasoning.

The object of the Common School is to give the pupil a good knowledge of the fundamental branches of an English education. I shall now remark upon the methods of teaching some of these branches somewhat more in detail.

Edward Everett says, "I hold that to read the English language well—that is, with intelligence, feeling, spirit, and effect; to write, with dispatch, a neat, handsome, *legible* hand (for it is, after all, a great object in writing to have others able to read what we write), and to be master of the four rules of arithmetic, so as to dispose, at once, with accuracy, every question of figures which comes up in practical life—I say, I call this a good education. And, if you add the ability to write pure, grammatical English, I regard it as an excellent education. These are the tools. You can do much with them, but you are helpless without them."

First, let me speak of reading. To read understandingly, naturally, expressively, and feelingly, is a delightful accomplishment; and yet how few possess it? Vocal exercises are excellent for cultivating and developing the powers of the voice; the proper pronunciation and distinct enunciation of words, the different intonations of the voice should be carefully regarded; but the significance of the words, the *meaning* of the author, is indispensable. *A lesson in reading should be studied as thoroughly as any other lesson set in the school.* The teacher should inquire the meaning of every word and every allusion with which he may suppose the pupils to be unacquainted. As their minds become more mature, he should call their attention to the beauties or defects of any comparison employed. He should endeavor to impress them with a proper conception of the beauty, wisdom, or truth of what they read. If a lesson of only a few lines can be learnt in this manner, set that lesson, *and no more.* Do not be discouraged if the progress be slow at first, it will be rapid by and by. At any rate, it is progress, whereas the other course is no progress at all. For surely the uttering of pages of words, day after day, and month after month, without comprehending their meaning, is not at all elevated above the occupation of the parrot. Nor is it sufficient that the pupil understands the meaning of most of the words; he must know them all. If he is ignorant of the meaning of one word, he may lose all the soul of whatever he reads. Let the teacher, in hearing a class read, have perpetually in mind the question addressed by Philip, "Understandest thou what thou readest?"

There can be no good reading if the lesson is not understood. If, upon examining a school, I found the pupils well acquainted with the meaning of what they read, I should feel the best assurance that they had pursued their other studies understandingly.

I wish to caution all against a theatrical tone. Most Professors of Elocution commit this error, and many who attend their instructions imitate them in this respect. Hence, there is so little good reading among us. On the one hand, some who have never received any instruction from a competent teacher, read in a careless, slovenly, and wretched manner, mumbling their words in the same monotone, whatever the subject may be; while, on the other hand, many, taking their cue from some Professor of Elocution, or some *distinguished* public reader, assume an unnatural tone, and, with an air and manner, all affectation and conceit, begin what they consider remarkably *stunning* reading. Heaven preserve me from it. "I had rather be a kitten, and cry mew," than be obliged to listen to it. I pray you avoid it. Of one of these theatrical readers it was said that, at dinner, she stabbed the potatoes instead of taking them, and that she asked for a knife in the same tone in which she would say, "Give me the dagger."

I proceed next to the subject of Geography. This study is often commenced with a series of definitions, which are got by heart, repeated, laid aside, and forgotten; forgotten, for one reason, because not explained or understood, the language being made to precede the ideas; and for another, because the words which the definitions are to explain are new to the pupils. A better way of commencing geography, with all children, is to call their attention to the spot on which they live; to point out surrounding objects, and mark their relative situations on the floor or black board; and thus, to show how a town, its streets or roads, and its prominent features, natural or artificial, may be represented. As their ideas expand, the scale may be reduced, and distant towns, counties, rivers, and mountains, with which the children are acquainted, or of which they may have heard, may be introduced, correct ideas of space and number being gradually acquired. Pupils should be taught, by reference to objects around them, what is the length of a mile; and by questions put to them in relation to places to which they have traveled, they should be enabled to form a correct idea of what the distance fifty, one hundred, or one thousand miles actually is. Point out in which direction North, South, East and West are, and state why a certain direction is fixed upon for the North. Call attention to the pictorial representations of lakes, rivers, &c. (like those introduced into the San Francisco schools); and having already become acquainted with the *thing*, notice how quickly they will learn and how easily they will remember the *name*. Geography ought not to be studied without continual reference to a globe. It should be looked at during every lesson, and it would gradually stamp upon the minds of the scholars such a lively image of the sphericity of the earth and of the relative positions and sizes of continents, islands, oceans, &c., as would never be effaced.

I find in most geographies, lists of questions directing pupils to learn the situations of small towns, or villages, or insignificant rivers or lakes, as: Where is Toudou, Tzentzin, Sewah, &c., &c.? Such places are of no consequence; the scholar has no assistance from the association of ideas in mastering what may be truly called his *task;* and in ascertaining the position of places, which might as well be called by the letters of the alphabet as by the names used in the book. I should request the scholar to find out the localities only of the more important places, and which these are can be easily known from the book. Why should he be called upon to burden his memory with a mass of useless details forgotten as soon as acquired? You do not wish to make of him a Geographical Gazeteer. You cannot expect him to know the locality of every place upon the earth from Borioboloo Gha to London. You must draw the line somewhere; draw it then between those places which are of importance and those which are not. After leaving school, the scholar can easily ascertain the position of any place in which he may happen to be interested.

I make these remarks because pupils, at exhibitions, have been called upon to run through long catalogues of names of rivers, lakes, seas, oceans, capes, islands, mountains, states, cities, towns, &c. It is well that children should know these, to a certain extent, but this is by no means the important part of geography. They should also become familiar with the grand facts and the leading principles; the real and comparative sizes of countries, using their own State as a unit; the comparative population of different countries and large cities, taking the population of California and San Francisco as the units of measure; the grand features of countries, such as the mountain and river systems; the climate of different parts of the world, and the causes affecting it; the various productions of the globe; the extraordinary natural curiosities found upon the earth; the great ocean surrounding the land, and inviting the nations to commerce; the kind of people that live in any land, their religion, their peculiarities, their social and political condition, and many other subjects which will suggest themselves to the competent instructor.

If geography were taught in this manner, should you think it possible for children to consider the top of a map to be up, and the bottom down, and that, consequently, all rivers which flow into the Arctic Ocean must run up hill? Or to state that Cuba and Massachusetts are of about the same size? Answers which have actually been given in schools of considerable reputation.

The elements of composition are almost invariably a stumbling-block to the young—and, strange as the statement may appear, I think the principal reasons for this fact are that it is not commenced early enough, but is put off until the pupil is considerably advanced in his other studies, and that he is then usually told to write a composition upon some subject—perhaps an abstract one—about which he knows nothing, and in which he cannot, of course, feel the slightest interest. Who does not remember the vacuity of mind and vexation of spirit with which, in his youthful days, he addressed himself to the set task of writing an essay upon such a theme as—*Virtue, its own Reward; The Study of History*, &c.? Of what frightful dimensions, and how supernaturally white, looked the blank sheet (blank as our own minds) of foolscap, which we were to fill with our own thoughts (so the master directed) without receiving any assistance from our friends. How frequently we thrust the pen into the inkstand in the vain hope to hook up some idea which might be concealed in that Stygian abyss! How despairingly we scratched our heads, how closely we scrutinized the walls and the ceiling, as if we expected to catch by the tail some stray idea which might be lurking in some corner or crevice of the room! How firmly did we for the time believe in the non-existence of mind, and the existence of nothing but matter throughout the universe! And then, if, after all this cudgeling of our brains, something did come into our heads, whispered, doubtless, by the pitying spirit of some repentant pedagogue, did we not make the most of it? Did we not dilute it, and dilate it, and amplify it, and spread it out, in the largest hand, upon lines ruled at least two inches apart, being very careful to prevent any quarreling between the words, by placing them at such a distance as to make it impossible for them to cross swords with one another!

Now, the remedy for this unfortunate state of things consists in asking children to write upon those subjects only which they understand, or which relate directly to, or spring out of, their studies, or in which they would naturally, as boys and girls, take an interest. A multitude of such questions, drawn from the everyday pursuits, amusements, and occupations of the young, will suggest themselves to the qualified teacher. It is highly important that the exercise of writing out their own thoughts should commence early. Very soon after children begin to think, and are capable of using and writing small words, a slate and pencil should be put into their hands, and they should be brought to express their thoughts in their own language, no matter how short the sentences or the words. In most of the schools for the deaf and dumb, the pupils begin to write exercises of this character after two years' instruction—in some sooner. And, certainly, if this can be done by those unfortunately deprived of speech and hearing, it can be accomplished by those possessing all their faculties. I have known scholars, in other respects excellent, who found great difficulty in expressing themselves either orally or in writing. They were deficient in language. They ought to have been from an early period frequently practised in the use of their mother tongue. The exercises should be made more difficult, as the pupil becomes older; for beginners, they should, of course, be of the simplest character. As soon as a child can write legibly, he should be put to writing short phrases—original or from dictation; and, as a part of this exercise, he should be taught spelling, the dividing of words into syllables, punctuation, the rules for the use of the capital letters, &c. Teachers complain that it is difficult for scholars to learn to spell correctly; and so it is, especially from the use of spelling-books *alone*. To become a very correct speller, is the labor of years on the part of the pupil. It is continual practice in the writing of sentences, not isolated words, that makes the good speller; and pupils cannot learn to spell correctly without being more in the habit of writing than they now are. A man who writes only a letter or two a year is likely to be a poor speller; but one who, from his occupation, writes every day, is rarely faulty in this respect. Consider, too, in practising such simple lessons in composition as I recommend, how many valuable things they are at the same time acquiring. Besides punctuation, spelling, the use of capital letters, &c., they are, or should be, improving their handwriting; they are exercising their minds pleasantly by the invention of sentences, short or long; they are learning the meanings and the right use of words; they are gradually becoming acquainted with their own language, and accustomed to express their thoughts appropriately. Think how desirable an acquisition this last will be to every boy and girl upon entering into life, and how many have regretted the want of it.

I agree to the opinion, that it is a wicked waste of time to confine children, year after year, to copy-books in penmanship. After a certain stage has passed—and that not a very late one—handwriting should be made the common and every-day means of acquiring and reducing to practice a knowledge of orthography, punctuation, the construction of sentences, &c. Children who have been kept in their copy-books until they could write a beautiful hand have, if required to write down sentences of their own composition, produced illegible and disgraceful scrawls, abounding in errors of punctuation and spelling. This statement proves the importance of early combining handwriting, punctuation, and spelling, in one exercise of the pupil's own composition; of departing from the beaten track, and of making, as soon as possible, scholars do the whole work for themselves without pattern or assistance.

Similar remarks to those which I have made are applicable to the subject of Declamations. Let the boys speak only pieces which they fully understand and appreciate, suitable to their age, and expressive of such thoughts, feelings, and interests, as are natural to *boys*, not men. I take no interest in seeing a stripling ascend the rostrum, and, in tones intended to be very impressive, exclaim: "There stands Bunker Hill Monument," with a gesture directed at the stove-pipe. I object to hearing a youthful prodigy shriek, in the shrillest treble, "My voice is still for war." I refuse to lend my ears, although urgently requested to do so, in the well known line, beginning—

"Friends, Romans, countrymen."

I am not at all withered by the tone of contempt with which the embryo orator "hurls back the base insinuation, with scorn and defiance, into the teeth of the contemptible and inefficient member of the opposite party." I have seen, in a California paper, a notice of an exhibition, in which it was stated that the Great Debate between Webster and Hayne was conducted with decorum by the youthful Senators. Well, I am glad it was; I am thankful that no violation of parliamentary propriety occurred, calling for the interference of the Sergeant-at-Arms. But why should boys personate Demosthenes, Cicero, Burke, Webster, Clay, or James Buchanan? Why not simply and naturally be *themselves?*

Who would shorten this blissful period by introducing into it the passions, strifes, and ambition of men? Let boys be *boys* in every sense of the word, while they are such in years, and neither on nor off the stage ape the bearing, passions, or language of men. I do not wish to be understood as saying that appeals to the highest and best feelings of our nature, that the noble and patriotic sentiments of our great orators cannot be appreciated by boys. Far from it. But I wish particular pains to be taken by the teacher to avoid pieces which do not lie within the comprehension or the experience of the pupil; and let those selected be as thoroughly studied and understood as the lessons in reading, to which I have alluded, or any other lessons, in the school.

I cannot condemn too strongly all dramatic exhibitions, conducted by schools, in which scenes from plays are represented with scenery, dresses, music, &c. I do not object to a good dialogue or polylogue, such as is adapted to interest the youthful mind and touch to finer issues the youthful heart, spoken in the usual manner. But I am opposed to dramatic representations, accompanied, to use the technical word, with all the properties. I do not know that any exhibition of this kind has ever occurred in connection with the Free Schools of America, and I hope none such ever will. There is no talent in spouting. Do not boys have too much inclination for the stage already without its being stimulated? And what a waste of time there is in getting up such representations; precious time which might be, and ought to be, spent in familiarizing the pupil with all the fundamental branches of a good, sound, English education, without which they cannot expect to be useful to themselves or to society.

You must perceive of what primary importance I consider it is, that children should know the meaning of every thing they attempt to learn. It is astonishing with what facility they will use words, or give an answer, to which they attach an erroneous meaning, or perhaps, no meaning whatever. This was much more the case formerly than at present, since our fathers did not, in many respects, pursue the natural course in the education of children.

How pleasantly and successfully nature teaches the infant! No sooner has it begun to exercise its senses, first, probably, the touch, in perceiving warmth, to open its eyes, to take food, to perceive odors, to hear sounds, than it begins to acquire knowledge. In the exercise of these powers the infant takes great delight. That during the first months of a child's life, its progress is highly satisfactory, is evident to a very ordinary observer; its first lispings show how much interest it finds in the appearances of surrounding objects; its first observations are listened to and receive that degree of attention which they demand; and it is not till the pressure of other domestic duties, or other inclinations, divide the mother's care, that the inquiries of the infant are neglected, and it is left, often discouraged and disheartened. A child obtains its notions as as we do, by seeing, sounding, feeling, smelling, and tasting objects. "Do not meddle" puts a stop to these processes. In cases of doubt and uncertainty, it asks for information, and is, perhaps. told, "Little children should be seen, and not heard." After a few years, the child is placed at school, where, instead of that natural course being pursued which should turn to account the observations and knowledge he has already stored up, he is often forced upon studies for which he shows no inclination; he is taught *words*, instead of *things*; and his memory is loaded with phrases and rules, which he does not understand.

Thus, his education commences, and thus a path, which might be strewn with flowers to allure, is choked with brambles to impede, his progress. The thorny track is traveled over, and for a long time the pupil has only confused notions floating in his mind, to the exclusion of that precise and distinct knowledge which lies within the grasp of those faculties which nature courts him to exercise. We all know that in many schools children have been taught, nay, are even now taught, as if they had to use only one or two of the senses. A child who possesses in perfection all the senses, should have them all exercised. We are, none of us, perhaps, more than half educated in this respect. The five senses are the means of communication between the outer world and the spirit within. It is through these media that the child for some time receives all its knowledge. A late writer says of the infant of two years old: "He has acquired more knowledge during this short period than he generally does on the present plan of instruction through the eight or ten succeeding years of his life, and it is a striking instance of the benevolence of the Creator, and a prelude of the vast extent of knowledge the child is afterwards capable of acquiring, that all these acquisitions are made, not only without pain, but, in the greater number of instances, are accompanied with the highest enjoyment."

In the school-room, we should imitate as much as possible *the method of nature.* Young children are not reflecting or reasoning beings; they have no appreciation of abstractions; they are for the tangible, the real, the concrete. It is through their senses that nature is acquainting them with the material world, and how fresh, active, and vigilant their senses are, and what untiring pleasure they take in their exercise.

Children should be taught by *things as much as possible, by words as little as possible.* The *latter* may kill any idea, but the *reality* maketh alive. On this account, I consider object-teaching as a decided improvement in our schools. It is an excellent plan, whenever practicable, to show the scholars whatever may be the subject of the lesson, or, if that cannot be done, then a drawing or picture of it. Their interest is thus awakened; every eye is sure to be wide open; the information imparted is correct; there can be no mistake about it. How quickly, also, it is gathered; how much time it takes to convey, by description, through the ear, a full and accurate idea of what may, perhaps, be understood at a glance of the eye, and so impressed upon the mind as never to be forgotten. There are some teachers who should be informed that they do not have under their charge Institutions for the Blind; but that their pupils have eyes, and would rejoice in an opportunity to use them.

The importance of real objects, natural and artificial models, pictorial representations, experimental and other practical elucidations, cannot be too strongly urged on those who have the direction of the young mind. In most of the subjects which form the school business, such illustrations may be introduced. The school-room should be furnished with receptacles for works of art and nature; the pupils themselves would be the most valuable and active contributors to such collections; and those specimens which are apparently the most humble will often be found to be the most useful. Visits to mines, manufactories, to the sea-shore, to fields and woods, would furnish great additions to such a store. Minerals, vegetables, woods, metals, animal substances, insects, shells, &c., are easily obtained. The arrangement and classification of these objects would call into exercise faculties which are now scarcely ever developed. One writer says that he has known boys of twelve years of age who could recognize and refer to their proper class almost every object around them in nature, and gives it as his opinion that a wide range of descriptive natural history may be imparted at that age.

The world around us is fair and beautiful, and full of wonders; it is always speaking to the heart of man, though the cares of life may prevent him from hearing its voice. But it is in the morning of life, when the heart is free from anxiety, when the spirits are light and buoyant, when the senses are the most acute, the curiosity insatiable, and creation fresh and new, that its language finds a willing and a charmed ear.

How do the young enjoy the glories of sunrise, a lovely prospect, a ramble through the woods, or along the sea-shore, and how much quicker than their elders do they notice any little circumstance that may occur! And what a pity it is to close upon them this broad face of nature which God himself has spread before them for their contemplation and delight, and shut them up within four walls, where they are told to keep their eyes on their lessons, which are some pages of a printed book? Cage the lark, tie up the forest deer—and you do not act more against nature than has been done in sentencing children to imprisonment six hours a day within the blank walls of some penitentiary of a school-house.

Now, I know very well that geography, grammar, and arithmetic are indispensable. They must be learnt, and well learnt. The fundamental branches of a good English education must not be neglected. But while I would not have these in the least interfered with, I would urge it upon all connected with schools not to disregard the natural sciences. The study will, I am sure, contribute to the pleasure and improvement of both teachers and scholars, and promote, instead of retarding, the progress of the latter in their other studies. These first books can be understood by any teacher whose "heart is in her vocation;" in fact, such a teacher will be delighted with them; and if she catches the true spirit of observation, she will be continually led to add facts of her own gathering to those which the author has preserved.

It is certainly possible, during the seven or eight years spent in the Grammar Schools, to pay some attention to the natural sciences. Do not shut the children out from them during this the golden period of their lives for studying them. Consider a few of the advantages to the discipline of the pupil's mind in pursuing these sciences. How much are his powers of observation improved by the study of nature! And this is no small thing. How few people see things just as they are! How often do witnesses under oath disagree with regard to material circumstances in relation to events occurring before their eyes, and where all had equal opportunities of seeing! Men are unwilling to trust their own senses in reference to matters a little out of the line of their own business. They will tell you they are no judges in such cases. Have not persons been made believers in spiritualism and animal magnetism, because their observing faculties were not sufficiently awake to see through the deception?

But after things are seen (and it is a very important thing to see them accurately and fully), then comes the exercise of the faculty of comparison. Now this faculty implies a great deal. We compare things, not merely to see their resemblances, but their differences. He who can do this well, is no ordinary person; he who can do it remarkably well, is one out of ten thousand. Men differ greatly in their ability to perceive resemblances and differences. An unfortunate lawyer is compelled to take his seat in mortification, by the Judge's showing him that the cases he had cited are not analogous to that before the Court, and consequently not at all applicable. The great business of buying and selling depends, as one may say, upon comparison. It sometimes happens that the best of friends will get angry in a discussion, when the difference between them is a trifle, a fact of which they may afterwards become aware, much to their astonishment. We consider it a compliment to any one, when we say that he has a *discriminating* mind; he can make *distinctions*. Now, the natural sciences teach *how to observe*, and *how to distinguish things correctly*—which is, in fact, the greater part of education, and that in which people otherwise well educated are sometimes surprisingly deficient.

It must not be forgotten that the course of study in the Grammar Schools should be comprehensive enough to meet the wants and tastes of every mind. Now, the list is by no means small of those who have been pronounced dunces at school, who have afterwards been widely distinguished for their attainments in science. Hugh Miller, who has been mentioned, is an instance in point. Dr. Franklin was probably considered by his teacher as arithmetic proof, and, perhaps, as stupid in other respects; the reason being that there was no study pursued in the school which interested the youthful philosopher, who was born to be an observer of nature. Many other instances to the same effect might be mentioned. Introduce, then, into the Common Schools the study of Nature, and make provision for those whose tastes, perhaps whose *genius*, lies in that direction.

I know that the general impression is, that the study of any branch of natural science is a study of hard words, particularly in the case of natural history. It is surprising to notice how many school-books will commence with pages of hard words and definitions, the purpose of which at that stage is unintelligible. This is not the case, however, with the books I have mentioned. They are simple, and suited to the young. The great and interesting facts are noticed; hard names are explained, and the definitions given only when it becomes necessary in the course of the works, and thus the pupil is not disheartened or disgusted at the very beginning. We must wait until the mind has become more mature before the scholar can attend to classification or to generalization.

It must not be overlooked that, in consequence of the great advances made in the physical sciences, they are much more the objects of attention now than formerly. The great discoveries of modern times, more or less intimately connected with the welfare and the progress of society, are made in these sciences, and the physical arts themselves have received a new impulse. We must keep pace with them in our schools.

The public are little aware how much interest is taken by naturalists the world over in the natural history of California. The State has been visited and explored, in some parts, for that purpose by agents from most of the prominent universities and societies in the world. The distinguished naturalist, Agassiz, states that he has a friend in San Francisco who has sent him an amount of specimens greater than all those collected by all the United States Exploring Expeditions put together.

Is it not high time for the citizens of California to take an interest in this subject, and to introduce it into the Public Schools, so as to give every young man desirous of entering upon these pursuits an opportunity to make some, at least, of the necessary preparations; and is there any country where such studies are more needed, or will be more useful to the public and to the individual?

There is a very strong desire at the East to introduce more extensively into their schools the study of the natural sciences, including natural history. They acknowledge their remissness in this respect, and all concur in the importance and necessity of this change being made.

In a lecture, delivered by Agassiz, are the following remarks:

"Our school system has been developed in a manner which has produced the most admirable results, and is imitated everywhere as the most complete and the most successful; but, while we have attained the highest point in that respect, we are also best prepared by that very position to make any further improvement which may lead to a better future. And I believe that the introduction of the study of natural history, as a branch of the most elementary education, is what can be added to what is already so admirable a system. The difficult art of thinking can be acquired more rapidly by this method than by any other. When we study moral or mental philosophy in text-books, which we commit to memory, it is not the mind we cultivate—it is the memory alone. The mind may come in; but if it does in that method, it is only in an accessory way. But if we learn to think, by unfolding thoughts ourselves, from the examination of objects around us, then we acquire them ourselves, and we acquire the ability of applying our thoughts in life. The teacher who is competent to teach the elements of this science, must, of course, feel a deep interest in it; he must know how to select those topics which are particularly instructive and best adapted to awaken an interest to sustain it, and to lead forward to the understanding of more difficult questions. He should be capable of rendering the subject attractive, interesting, and so pleasant, indeed, that the hour for the school should be welcomed by the scholar instead of being dreaded as bringing something imposed by duty, and not desirable in itself."

It may be added to what has been said by Agassiz, in illustration of the benefits to be derived from the study of natural history, that it is a fact, which every one acquainted with the subject will admit, that our crops are every year injured to the extent of many thousands of dollars by the depredations of insects whose habits are not properly understood. In this way, the Hessian fly, the canker worm, the apple worm, the apple and peach borers, the curculio, the cotton worm, the tobacco worm, the corn borer, the rice weevil, the wheat midge, and other insects not yet known, make way with capital and labor to an enormous extent. There are many insects injurious to the grape-vine, to one of which a volume has been devoted. Investigations into the habits of such insects have been attended with the best results, one of the most useful of which has been to stop the farmer from destroying his friends with his enemies among insects, as he had been in the habit of doing. The best way of finding an effectual remedy for these injuries is to diffuse and cultivate in our schools a taste for natural history.

In a moral point of view, this study, as well as that of all the natural sciences, is of the highest importance. I never heard of a real lover of nature who was a bad man. They exhibit to man the thoughts of the Creator, for all the arrangements which he sees around him are manifestations of the Divine Mind. In the book of nature we can read a portion of the laws and the designs of the Almighty. The more diligently any one pursues these studies the more deeply he is impressed with the abundant evidences of the power, the wisdom, and the benevolence of the Creator. He sees that a drop of water is full of wonders, as well as the starry heavens; that the tiniest insect that sports in the sun-beam is not so insignificant as to be beneath the care of its Maker, nor the Island Universes, scattered through the realms of space, too vast for His power to control. Every creature made by the Divine Hand he sees to be perfect, with an organization exactly suited to its wants, and its place in the scale of being, and adapted to contribute to its happiness. God provided for all His creatures. Now, the youthful heart readily understands and feels the lesson which Nature teaches; it will not rest satisfied merely with Nature and Nature's laws, but willingly and instinctively is led through them up to Nature's God. It is touched by His goodness; it reverences His power and majesty; as the mind expands, it feels that He is the source of all we possess; it begins to feel the need of His aid and protection, and then earnestly to invoke them. In this manner it at length realizes the great truth, that in Him we live and move, and have our being; it does not read these as unmeaning words, but is pervaded with their deep signification. It is impressed with the heartfelt conviction, that there can be no more utter and dreadful ruin than to disobey the commands of this Good and Just Being, and that there is no greater happiness than to do His will and receive His approbation.

I consider it an evil to stimulate the intellect, almost, perhaps, to its utmost exertions, and to neglect the moral training of the scholar, or to treat the latter as if it were of minor consequence, as if the object were to make smart linguists, or mathematicians, or chemists, instead of *complete* men. We have, undoubtedly, too many *smart* men in the world already; that is, *smart* in the bad sense of the word, and yet, perhaps, in a sense by which they feel complimented.

What is wanted more than anything else is true men, men of principle, men fearing God, loving their neighbor, loving their whole country, and cherishing its free institutions; men who stand for the right as immovable as the eternal pyramids; whose word, whose look is truth itself; whose honor can no more be tarnished than a sun-beam can be soiled; in whose breasts the ruling maxim is not "Cotton is king," nor "Gold is king," but everywhere, both in their most secret retirement, as well as in public position, reigns, enthroned in their hearts and obeyed in their lives, the divine principle—DUTY IS KING FOREVER!

Now, the child is not all intellect, any more than it is all conscience; it has a sense of right and wrong, and this sense is silently addressed in a hundred different ways, as the questions arise whether the pupil shall do this thing or not, whether he shall confess or conceal a certain fault, &c. I know that the importance of this subject is adequately felt by the public school teachers of San Francisco, and that much attention is paid by them to moral instruction, and pains taken to impress upon the minds of their pupils the great religious truths in which all are agreed. At the same time, while this is done, all sectarianism is carefully avoided.

I would have this moral sense carefully cherished as the voice of God; I would have it kept sensitive and acute, and properly trained and educated. I would have every part of the nature of the pupil well and proportionately exercised and developed—the physical, the intellectual, and the moral, the body, the mind, and the heart; the last the most carefully of all, since out of it are the issues of life. I would tell the pupil that the acquisition of knowledge is valuable, but that, though his attainments in science and art, and in all learning, were transcendent, though he might "speak with the tongues of men and of angels," and "understand all mysteries and all knowledge," yet, if he had not a good character, sound moral principles, he would be nothing but a miserable failure. With all the energy I possessed, and all the different methods of appeal I could invent, I would enjoin it upon him to strive to become a good, true, and noble man.

And such words, addressed in the spirit of affection to the young, go directly to their hearts. Their impulses can easily be turned into the right channel. They have a desire after excellence in the acquisition of knowledge; but if their sense of right and wrong is properly appealed to, I believe it can be made the ruling power of their lives. When this result is accomplished, how blessed is the work! It is beautiful to look upon the young, with their clear and honest eyes, their frank and beaming countenances, their warm and pure hearts beating high with aspirations after goodness and truth, and desiring that every evening may find them more worthy of the approbation of their teachers, their parents, and of Heaven.

Fellow Teachers! from our connection with the Public Schools, we must take a deep interest in their prosperity and success, and earnestly wish that each revolving year may render them more efficient. The Common School System is the child of the people, in which they take great pride. The Public Schools are emphatically the *People's College*. From them graduate the bone and sinew of the community—men of sound common sense, of good principles, and with stout hearts, who will stand by the Common Schools as the bulwark of their rights and liberties, and who will defend them against bold and open attack, or vile and secret slander. Their crowning glory is, that their doors are open freely to all; that in them the poorest child is the equal of the richest, and may lay the foundation of an education which may lead him to employment, to competence, to respectability, nay, even to high station and to a glorious fame. Many a poor man has denied himself in order that his little ones might attend school decently attired, and has had his last moments cheered by the thoughts that he had faithfully given his children every advantage afforded by the Public Schools—feeling in that fact a strong assurance of their future good conduct and welfare.

The Common Schools can show upon their rolls the names of distinguished men who laid in them the foundation of a world-wide renown. Franklin, of whom I have spoken; Clay, in the log cabin school-house of Peter Deacon, with no floor but the earth, and no window but the door; Webster, in the log school-house kept by Master Tappan in the wilds of New Hampshire; George Stephenson, the founder, and, to a great extent, the inventor, of the present system of locomotion on railroads, commencing at eighteen years of age in a village school to learn his A, B, C, like a little child; Fulton, Bowditch, and hosts of others. They commenced life in poverty. Had not the Common School afforded them an opportunity *to begin* their education free of expense, how few of them might ever have been known to the world? How many of those yet unborn, and destined to immortal renown in their various capacities, would, but for the Free Common School, be lost in eternal night! We have a right, then, to feel an honest pride in this great system with which we are connected.

Our profession is humble, laborious, and exhausting. The services of the teacher are not adequately appreciated in any community. Neither fame nor wealth belongs to him. He is not allowed even the designation—Honorable. He is overworked and underpaid. And yet his life has its compensations. I know nothing more touching and more grateful to the teacher than, at the close of the year, when he is bidding farewell to those who are passing forever from his care, for him to see every countenance turned towards him with affection and gratitude—to know that these minds have received from him wholesome knowledge--that, by his influence and example, good principles have been implanted in their hearts—and that he has troops of friends growing up and becoming every year more numerous, who will voluntarily pay him that honor, love, and obedience, which they feel to be due to the benefactor of their youth.

The faithful teacher has another reward, of which nothing can deprive him. It is the approbation of his own conscience; it is the consciousness that he is humbly imitating the Creator and Preserver of all, in doing good. "Think not," said Sydney Smith to an aged, poverty-stricken master teaching the art of reading or writing to some tattered scholars, "you are teaching that alone; you are protecting life, insuring property, fencing the altar, guarding the government, giving space and liberty to all the fine powers of man, and lifting him up to his own place in the order of creation." This well describes the nature of the teacher's office.

It was the boast of the Emperor Augustus, that he found Rome brick, and left it marble. Let it be the higher praise of the Public School teachers, that California was found a wilderness, but that they have contributed by their exertions to fill its valleys and cities with a virtuous and intelligent population—a richer treasure than all her nodding harvests, than all her mines of gold.

4. CONCERNING COMMON SENSE IN TEACHING.*

It is one of the highest compliments we can pay a man to say that he possesses good common sense. The article in question is certainly one of the most important qualifications of a successful teacher. Call it "tact," or "knack," or "faculty," or "gift," or whatever you please, it implies always a clear conception of things as they exist, and an adaptation of means to the end sought.

In broaching this subject, I feel that I may place myself in the situation of the learned divine, whose third and principal division of his discourse was "concerning that of which we know nothing." I do not propose to treat of a course of instruction for graded schools, where children are presumed to be in regular attendance for a series of years, and where provision is made for a specific course of learning for all the faculties of the mind; but to consider briefly those schools remote from cities, and continued only a part of the year. What are they expected to accomplish, and what view should the common sense teacher take of his field of labor? Many of our public schools, in the sparsely settled districts of the State, are kept less than six months in the year, and even then the attendance is irregular and inconstant. Pupils may be expected to attend school from the age of six to fourteen; and allowing six months attendance in each year—a high average when one-fourth attend only three months of the year—the actual time at school will be reduced to four years. The question propounded by common sense is: What course of instruction will impart the greatest amount of useful information, and best fit the children for the duties of common life?

Now, hardly any course of study or mental exercise can be sought out which shall be utterly useless. The driest and dullest style of memorizing musty text books, and the most parrot-like *verbatim* recitations, involve some thought, and are not without some advantages. The thoughtful man of wealth, who, in order that his son should not grow up in idleness, compelled him to wheel a huge pile of stones from one part of his garden to another, and then wheel them back again, and so kept him wheeling them back and forth each day of the year, was wiser than the parent who allows his son to do nothing. But it would have been more sensible in the man of

*Read before California State Teachers' Institute, 1863.

wealth had he set his boy at work upon some useful labor, which would have interested his attention, instead of keeping him engaged in unprofitable drudgery.

I cannot help thinking that sometimes in our schools we set the boys to wheeling stones, instead of building walls, or clearing fields for future harvests. For instance, keeping a boy for years drilling on the stereotyped forms of solving Mental Arithmetic, committing a great mass of routine verbiage, when he ought to learn the simple forms of Written Arithmetic used in business life, is undoubtedly "wheeling stones." The boy may repeat the "solution," and the "forms," and the "conclusion," and the "therefores," and "wherefores," with a marvelous skill, and yet it is not common-sense teaching. A man was brought before an Eastern king, and extolled by the courtiers for his wonderful powers of endurance, because he could stand on one leg for twenty-four hours. "A goose can stand longer than that," said the king.

When, in school, we teach boys and girls the abstract rules and scientific mysteries and technicalities of grammar, training them skillfully to analyze complex, compound, and involved sentences, but omitting to teach them by daily practice how to express common thoughts in correct English, or how to talk correctly in ordinary conversation, without using provincialisms or cant phrases—what are we doing but keeping them "wheeling stones," and feeding on husks?

When children study for years the columns of uncommon and obsolescent words, piled up in perpendicular obelisks, staring them in the face like huge exclamation marks of wonder and surprise, and then leave school unable to write a list of articles wanted from the corner grocery without exciting the risibilities of the groceryman, or are unable to write a friendly letter without offending the eye by misspelling the commonest words—what have they been doing but "wheeling stones?"

So when scholars are kept forever drilling on elementary principles and minute particulars, it is not in accordance with common sense. "Be thorough," is a good maxim; but there is such a thing as being *too* thorough—of dwelling on *particulars*, to the neglect of *essentials*. A teacher may be *painfully particular*, like a good aunt of mine, years ago, who was so distressingly neat that nobody ever took any comfort in her house.

In Arithmetic, for instance, it is keeping a boy wheeling stones "to discipline his mind" a month in learning to explain in due form the reason of "inverting the divisor in dividing one fraction by another," if thereby he should fail to learn how to write a prommissory note, compute simple interest, or make out a bill. A teacher from a graded city school would fail in an unclassified school, should he attempt to apply the same test of thoroughness, or to pursue the same exact course of study. Certain *results* must be obtained, to the sacrifice of many particulars which are all good in themselves. One great reason why self-educated men are practical workers, is that they learn *nothing they do not want to use*, and so *learn it well*. Concentration gives them strength. Napoleon dispensed with tents and luggage in his great armies, taking only what he wanted to use—the sword and the bayonet.

It seems to me—and the conclusion has been growing stronger each year, during twelve years' experience in public school teaching --that no small part of what children are required to learn might appropriately be headed: "*Things worth forgetting.*" Nature is wiser than we are, and casts off the useless surplus of facts and figures into utter oblivion. Run through an ordinary school geography, and see how many bushels of chaff to a single grain of wheat. Look at the compendious arithmetics, strike out nine-tenths of which, and the remainder would be more than sufficient. Look at the bulky grammar, grown fat by feeding on all other grammars printed since Lindley Murray's, of which, not even the authors could carry in their heads a moiety. Look at the school histories of our country, full to repletion of dates and chronological tables, containing more of details than any grown man in the United States could learn in a lifetime. I allude to these only to show how much a teacher must *omit* in the school text books, and how essential that he should have common sense to guide him in selecting.

A four years' course of study in an unclassified school can neither be very complicated nor very extensive. A matter-of-fact teacher would look at his work in something of this manner: These boys are, most of them, to become farmers, miners, mechanics, and laborers. All the scholastic education they receive will be gained here. These girls will, most of them, become the wives of farmers, miners, mechanics, and laborers. What instruction is absolutely essential to these boys and girls to fit them to grow up respectable men and women? Letting alone the geniuses and the prodigies, they are of average mental capacity. What shall be done with them?

First, they must learn to read, write, and spell the English language. Reading is usually taught well enough for all practical purposes, whether according to elocutionary rules or not; but penmanship and spelling are too often sadly neglected. Almost every man, in whatever occupation engaged, is called upon to write, more or less, every day of his life. Writing involves spelling, and both are unmistakable evidences of culture, or want of it. Teach these three things thoroughly, so that every child fifteen years of age shall be able to read readily, to write legibly, and to spell correctly, the words in the English language most used in common life. Sacrifice everything to this—even let algebra remain a minus quantity, and the higher branches take a back seat. They are of vastly more practical value than arithmetic—the trite and venerable maxim, that the study of arithmetic is the best discipline of the mind, so often quoted by arithmetic-run-mad teachers, to the contrary notwithstanding. A knowledge of arithmetic sufficient to enable men and women to keep accounts correctly, will suffice, letting alone the mental discipline of the reasoning faculties, so often harped about. Ben. Franklin was a dullard in arithmetic; he grew up with pretty tolerable reasoning faculties, because he kept his perceptives wide awake. Don't let arithmetic, then, be the great nightmare of the school to squeeze out all the vitality from the scholars. Most Americans take naturally to reckoning dollars and cents, without the aid of text books.

Some knowledge of the geography of the world is necessary, and particularly that of our own country. But common sense declines to expect that little boys and girls should learn the names and locations of the two thousand little round dots on the map of the United States, called towns and cities, with figures attached representing the population; or the names and length of the five hundred little black lines, drawn like spiders' webs over the map, representing rivers. Neither is it necessary that they should commit to memory the entire returns of the last census. Strike out one half of the questions and answers in any school geography, and the remaining twentieth will be more than most children of average ability can learn and retain. How I wish some of these bookmakers had to learn their own books! Any teacher who would expect or compel his scholars to answer all the "questions in the book" on examination day, ought to be indicted for a lack of common sense; and any committeeman who should find fault because the scholars couldn't answer them, ought to be strapped within an inch of his —collar. How many teachers, after years of study and daily use of the geography, can remember one fifth of the tenth-rate rivers and towns, or one twentieth of the hackneyed descriptions. I would flog a child of mine if he wouldn't *forget* such rubbish.

A general knowledge of the leading events in the history of our own country, they should be expected to acquire; but if, on examination day, they fail to tell the exact day and hour on which every battle of King Philip's war, the French and Indian war, or the Revolution, or the war of eighteen hundred and twelve, and exactly how many were killed, wounded, and missing; or should they forget that wonderful account given by one school history, of two early settlers of New England, who were frightened up a tree by a lion, and remained there in perfect terror, and came safely down the next day!—common sense would not be shocked.

Next in importance, comes a knowledge of language, and of the meaning and use of words. This must be communicated by the teacher, in questions on reading lessons, and in oral lessons. Dictionaries alone cannot impart it. Printed words are valuable only as the medium of ideas; if the medium is opaque, the ideas will be muddy. After a knowledge of language, comes the framework of grammar. And here, I think, common sense steps in and dictates that in order that scholars may learn to speak and write the English language correctly, they should be exercised in writing sentences, and talking sentences, instead of continually tearing to pieces the sentences of others. Exercises on grammar, sufficient to enable them to write a letter, and speak plain English correctly, should be embraced in the course.

Some little knowledge of physiology and hygiene should be imparted, inasmuch as each boy has to take care of his own body, and when he ruins that by ignorance of the laws of health, he will find it very inconvenient to transfer his knowledge of arithmetic and accompanying mental discipline to another *corpus*. And as most of the young girls will become mothers, and consequently the custodians of the constitutions of the next succeeding generation, common sense opens its eyes in astonishment that committeemen and school teachers should ignore all allusion to physiology, anatomy, and the laws of health, and exalt arithmetic, algebra, and the fashionable branches.

A little drawing, a little vocal music, a little calisthenic and gymnastic training, may be introduced as incidental amusements and recreations. Some provision should be made during the whole course for daily exercise of the perceptive and the expressive faculties, as well as for the reasoning powers. Children should be trained to habits of observation. They should be trained to distinguish colors; to tell the properties of the common objects by which they are surrounded; should be taught something of natural history, at least enough to distinguish a dog from a *coyote*, or a grizzly bear from a calf, or potatoes from yams, or cauliflowers from cabbages. A boy instinctively turns to stories of birds, beasts, and fishes.

Herein lies the most grievous deficiency of our schools: that they deal with the abstract instead of the real. I have repeatedly asked classes which could run off pages of questions in geography with marvelous rapidity, to point north, and the direction generally has been perpendicularly up to the zenith; they had no notion whatever of directions, except as the top and bottom of the map. A city was to them a *dot*, nothing more; a river—a crooked line; and a mountain—a definition. How many classes have I seen versed in "the tables," who would estimate the dimensions of a room sixteen feet by twenty, in numbers ranging from five and forty to ten and eighty; how many who could not estimate the weight of an object weighing five pounds, within four pounds of its weight; how many that had no notion of a mile, except as three hundred and twenty rods; how many who could "parse like a book," and yet could not write five consecutive sentences in tolerable English!

If common sense were a school-master, he would look with favor on the system of object training as supplying a basis of actual knowledge, on which the reasoning faculties should afterwards be exercised. He would also endeavor to collect a small school library, well knowing that many a boy who grows dull, listless, and lazy over his set tasks, will absorb general knowledge from readable books, as a thirsty plant drinks in the rain-drops of a summer shower. In governing his school, he would treat scholars like human beings, bearing in mind that children are born to be happy, not miserable; and that school ought to be made a pleasant place.

The teacher must expect to leave much untaught. If he attempts to teach everything, he will fail; for nobody ever succeeded. He must expect to find some dull scholars, some obstinate ones, some vicious ones, some troublesome ones, some negative ones, some good ones; if he is a philosopher, gifted with a sublime common sense, he will go calmly and quietly at work, do his duty faithfully, and not worry about results—bearing in mind that all the stupid boys and dull scholars, somehow or other, generally grow up into respectable average men and women.

5. ADDRESS BY THOMAS STARR KING.*

This audience, representing the mothers and fathers, the official forces and the rising life of this young, strange city, are to be congratulated on the event and occasion that calls us together. We welcome you to the service here with pride and joy.

The corner-stone of any important representative edifice is laid with elaborate ceremonial. It is well to foster public interest in such forms. And it seems to me that it would be as fitting to recognize, with public rejoicing, the *completion* of a noble building, the moment when the workmen lay the last stone of the turret, the apex of the spire, the final tile on the dome. It was when the corner-stone of the earth was laid, that "the morning stars sang together, and all the sons of God shouted for joy." Can we believe—though we have no record or hint of the hallelujahs—that there was less jubilance amongst the holy hosts when "the heavens and the earth were finished, and all the host of them," and "God saw everything that he had made, and behold it was very good?"

We are here to rejoice in this completed work. There is very little in the building itself, though it is commodious and cheerful, to awaken any enthusiasm. But as a school-room—a new structure to befriend civilization, in a State where the forces of good and evil meet in a more open and demonstrative wrestle, probably, than upon any other equal area on the globe—it does invite us to be glad, and to express our joy that it is added to the landscape of the city, and has sprung out of a deepening popular faith in the worth of education.

And yet it is not simply a new schoolhouse that we are to consecrate to its noble offices. It is the symmetry of an educational system in the city that we complete and establish. It is truly the top-stone, the crown, of an ideal edifice, whose co-ordinate parts are the excellent common schools of the city, that we now lift to its place with rejoicing. If there were any influence to be exerted by the establishment of this High School, in drawing away the public interest from the Grammar Schools, the public pride in them, the public readiness to be taxed to sustain them, there would be no occasion for gratitude in the completion of this building. This would be an unfortunate service and hour. The Grammar Schools are the true fountains of health and power in a community. Whatever tends to slight them, or reduce their efficiency, or throw the shadow of public indifference upon them, is to be deplored, and to be strenuously resisted. The city and state are far more deeply interested in the *general* diffusion of the elements of knowledge than in the concentration of learning in a small percentage of the youth of our community. We want to equip tens of thousands for the toils and struggles of life, not to polish a few hundreds for a better chance to seize its prizes and wear its honors. We must never forget this. And if the erection of this High School into perma-

---

* Delivered September 19, 1860, at the dedication of the High School building, Powell street. From *The Bookseller*, the first educational journal published in the State.

nence threatened to abate the importance, or lower the dignity, or drain the energy of the Grammar Schools, this building, though it were a hundred times more elegant, though it were seemly in proportions as the Parthenon of Athens, would be a mistake and a disaster.

I cannot but think, however, that we strengthen the ordinary schools of the city by confirming this one, and leading the community to regard it with more favor and pride. Not only is the standard of a free education raised, but the earlier removal from the Grammar Schools of the scholars who wish to pursue a higher grade of studies, concentrates the interest and energies of the teachers there upon the progress of the average of students. The ordinary schools can hardly fail to give more thorough training in the elements of English education, by relieving the teachers from the responsibility of carrying small upper classes through a range of studies far above the average lessons; and the ambition that is excited to enter the High School must be felt, after awhile, as a very serviceable stimulant throughout the ranks of the scholars below. Wherever the plan has been tried of projecting schools on the system of Primary, Grammar, and High, it has been found that each grade helps the one beneath. No New England cities now, I am sure, could think of parting with their High Schools. They would account it deliberate mutilation of the symmetry of the educational system, and treason against the mental rights of the scholars who can spare two or three extra years for instruction and discipline.

And we must not fail to take into account the needs and rights of the hundred and fifty youths, of both sexes, in our city, who are ready and willing to postpone their entrance into practical life, for the sake of a more generous culture. The free-school system has duties to them as manifest and binding as to the lowest class in a Grammar School. Let us rejoice that we can fulfill them in entire harmony with our duties to the *mass* of the children whose education is intrusted to us. Let us rejoice that we can see that all jealousies are unwise. Let us be glad and grateful, to-day, that we strengthen the whole structure of our teaching organization by this crowning school to which we here devote an excellent building. The masons lay, strong and compact, the stones which make the floor of the porch to an edifice after the Grecian style. They rear column after column along its front. But when the beautiful entablature is lifted aloft, to rest on the pillars, there is not only completed proportion, but more strength. Each column is firmer; the base itself is fortified; and the edifice stands in harmony with the force of gravitation. So, we believe, it is here. We send strength into the important schools below, the pillars and pavement of our public welfare, by the import of this service of dedication. And I believe the whole system of education would attain final symmetry, and be still stronger in all its parts, if we had not only High Schools in our cities and large towns, but a free and largely planned University besides, in every State, in which the sons and daughters of the poorest could obtain the best training which the resources of the State might afford, free of cost. When we get this, we shall have the majestic dome overarching and strengthening our intellectual temple.

But very likely in all this I am speaking needless words. Perhaps

I have done wrong to assume or hint that there can be any question, in any quarter, of the value of the school whose home we consecrate here, or of its advantageous relation to the other schools of which we are justly proud. Let us turn to other considerations that should awaken grateful joy here.

It is now, throughout this State, the time of rejoicing in the harvest. We have been reading in the papers glowing accounts of many district agricultural fairs. This very day the yearly State fair is to be inaugurated in the Capital. What interest is felt, throughout the State, in the improvements of stock, in the new varieties of fruit, in the production of more efficient and economical machinery for planting, reaping, threshing, stacking! The man who refines a breed of sheep; the man who brings from his ranch a calf or colt, perfect according to its type; the man who displays the noblest yoke of steers; the cultivator who offers to view the soundest and sweetest plums, the most lovely and savory peach, the weightiest cluster of grapes, or who can say the wisest word about preventing the curled leaf in peach trees, the rust in wheat, the "foul brood" among bees; yes, the man who produces a mammoth pumpkin, a monstrous sweet potato, a beet that will half fill a barrel, a watermelon as ample as Daniel Lambert in girth, is heard of throughout a county, perhaps throughout the limits of the State.

What interest in education can we bring yet into competition with this scientific enthusiasm for vegetable and animal products? What would the honest answer be, taking the State through, if we should ask which the people of the State were more concerned about, a better type of calves or a higher grade of children; more efficient grazing-grounds or more thorough school training; vineyards that should double their profits, or methods of education that should equip pupils twice as efficiently for noble success in life; the reclaiming of tule lands, or the gathering of twice as many youth, who now receive *no* instruction, into the intellectual folds where they may have a teacher's care? Alas! we know what it would be. If one tithe, or one hundredth part, of the watchful, patient, cultured and strenuous exertion that has been expended by the general community on peach-raising, short-horned cattle, the perfecting of horses and bee-culture, during the last five years, had been devoted to the training of children, and fitting them to be competent masters of their fathers' colts, and meadows, and carrot fields, the State, to-day, would be immeasurably advanced, beyond its present attainment, in civilization. We should not read such sad statistics as are forced upon us now, showing that hardly more than a third of the children of the State attend regularly any school.

There is really some danger that we shall be pulled down, materialized, half-barbarized, by the very advance and splendor of our scientific control of the elements of agricultural opulence. One of our poets tells us that now

"Things are in the saddle,
And ride mankind."

It behooves us to be a little careful lest we cultivate beeves and racers to such superiority over ourselves that they shall get the upper hands, and we find ourselves, after a generation or so, in which animals rise and children sink, yoked and harnessed, owned by our Durhams, and Alderneys, and Morgans, and perhaps fatted for their advanced and dominant appetites.

The spiritual forces must be started soon in States like this, and trained to ten times their present vigor, or we shall be unable to wield the majestic armor and implements of our science and materialistic culture. And this building, which lifts the torch of education higher, as a beacon to the State, which will turn out nobler specimens of young manhood and womanhood, invites us, by peculiar fitness, in this harvest-time, to rejoice in its completion, and to express our gratitude by elaborate ceremonial and reverent prayer.

And we should rejoice also to be here, to-day, in order to pay a conscious and deliberate tribute to the service of teachers in our civilization. Every time I enter a school-building I travel back to the time, twenty years ago (when I was a *young* man), when my name was enrolled in the army of instructors. During the three years of service appointed to me in that department, I learned so much of the difficulties and responsibilities of the office, that the stepping into a pulpit seemed like passing into an easier sphere of duty. It is not on abstract grounds and observation, but on trials which gave me my first knowledge of what serious responsibility is, and of how closely moral forces must be allied with intellectual ones in every successful school, that my own reverence for the teacher's call and duty is based. And from that day to this it has been widening and deepening.

We do not pay our social reverence wisely as yet, even in our most advanced and thoughtful communities. The men who do the most for the world are those who work scientifically upon the land, increasing its productiveness without exhausting its fertility—and the men who increase the mental and moral forces of the State. These classes are the fountains of lasting power, and the true conservators of public health and vigor. In a truly ordered society, these classes would receive the heartiest and most stable honor.

But as yet, alas, even in the most Christian districts of society, the question is scarcely raised, as a condition and gauge of respect, what the relation is between his employment and the permanent benefit of the community—what the moral aroma is of a man's gold and position. And so the best men work with very little recognition. The most useful ministers are those who work through years of quiet fidelity, encouraging good purposes in the village circle, warning with sincere and uneloquent unction, the humble and steady friend of humble people, threading the life of a small community, through more than the years of a generation, with a golden influence of charity, and fortunate in not having to see their names in half the issues of the newspaper press. Some of the purest pages of heroism might be copied from the long careers of country physicians, who spend themselves without the patronage and solace of cultured society, and cross the line of old age without a competence.

In the case of teachers, however, the fact is peculiarly striking. Think what an influence, during the past ten years, has been exerted upon the intellect and character of the best portions of our country, by the ambition of teachers to be more efficient in their work, by the establishment of journals of education, by county, district and

State conventions of instructors, not sunned by public applause, not paid for by the public either, in which the wisest unfold the best results of their experience, and the youngest are stimulated by the contagious enthusiasm of the leading masters of the profession!

"Profession," did I say? No. Here is the injustice; here is the proof of the marvelous infidelity of our public as yet to the service which can hardly be surpassed by any other type. American liberty and hopes are based on comprehensive education—mental and moral—and we do not yet recognize the teacher's calling as one of the "learned professions." There is the degree of M.D., a title of respect for every one who enters the ranks of the healers by the regular door. Every clergyman has his prefix of "Rev.," which floats him sometimes like a cork upon waters where he could not swim. "D.D." is conferred, every year, upon many a man who is no scholar in Christian history or dogmatics. I have known cases where LL.D. has been affixed, by prominent colleges, to the names of men who could not have told what the two L's, with a period after them, were the abbreviation of. But there is no title for teachers. And I am ignorant of the fact if any University or College has yet sought out an eminent, consecrated, thoroughly efficient teacher, to confer upon him or her any title of honor as an acknowledgment of personal service to society, or the rank of the calling to which he or she is pledged.

We must do what we can to repair this injustice—we who know the value of the office, the grand proportion of the gifts that are so often brought to it, and the nobleness of the spirit in which those gifts are frequently dedicated.

Let us make this festival time, in the consecration of this building, a season in which we pledge ourselves to greater interest in the school cause in this city and State. It is not in the structure we are interested, so much as in the edifice of education itself, which has been erected here by faithful, far-seeing men, against the opposition of lazy wealth and skeptical hearts. It is not the porch and hall and seats and roof that we are grateful for, so much as the wise management and skilled instruction, which, so successful in the past, are to have a better inclosure for their operation in years to come.

Would that the services of this day might be more joyous and welcome by the appearance here of the philosophical apparatus that is needed by the teachers, and would be in various ways a benefit to the community! The $3000 which it would cost ought to be contributed by the wealth of San Francisco the next week, and *would* be, if we were not still in our public life so blind to the immense meaning and value of public education. And let us cherish a deeper respect for the office and influence of every good teacher, as we recognize here anew the solid truth of a noble American poet's words:

"The riches of the commonwealth
Are free, strong minds, and hearts of health;
And more to her than gold or grain,
The cunning hand and cultured brain.

She heeds no skeptic's puny hands,
While near her school the church-spire stands;
Nor fears the blinded bigot's rule,
While near her church-spire stands the school."

6. MORAL INSTRUCTION.*

The fervent prayer which every parent offers is, that whatever poverty, destitution, pain or misery, his children may be called upon to bear, God will mercifully grant that they may preserve their purity, and all be found at last worthy to be reunited in that kingdom prepared for the just, beyond the grave.

The faithful teacher, occupying as he does, for a time, the parent's place, must feel a similar anxiety, as he looks round upon those placed under his charge. His situation is inferior in responsibility only to that of the parent. Indeed, since so many parents neglect their duty in this respect, his influence upon those who continue for any length of time under his charge, is probably not surpassed by that of any other class of men in the community. He must often seriously ask what will be the lot of those committed to his trust. Could the veil with which Heaven conceals the future be removed, would he behold this noble and ingenuous boy, with heart full of aspirations after all excellence, still rising higher and higher, or would he behold him descend from the lofty heights of honorable renown, and become dishonored, degraded, and corrupt? This fair girl, with the light of Heaven in her eye, and its purity surrounding her as with an atmosphere of holiness, would she be seen still the same in her spotlessness and innocence, or would the light be extinguished, the glory have departed, and nothing remain but the wreck of what was once so lovely and so promising?

It is related that an Eastern prince once offered a prize to be given to the most beautiful boy in all his dominions. Many were presented for the premium, but it was bestowed, by acclamation, upon one for his transcendent and angelic loveliness. So beautiful a boy had never been seen upon the earth before. Some years after, the same prince again offered a prize—but this time it was for the ugliest man to be found in all his possessions. Diligent search was made; many exhibited themselves to view, of all kinds and degrees of ugliness, but among them it was difficult to make a choice, until one day there was brought into the royal presence a being, if he could be called a man, so hideous, so loathsome, so bestial, that the people shuddered while they gazed upon him. Sin had stamped its polluting mark upon every feature; from every wrinkle in that horrible face stared out a vice. Upon inquiry, it was ascertained that this frightful and disgusting wretch had been the attractive and lovely boy. A life of intemperance, sensuality, and iniquity, had made the awful change. God save our pupils from any and all the causes tending to produce so terrible an alteration.

In view of the great responsibility pressing upon every teacher to do all in his power to train up his pupils to a life of virtue and excellence, I invite your attention to some remarks upon the importance of Moral Instruction. I have a fear that some few teachers (I know they must be very few) may think their duty done if they preserve good order in the school, and give instruction to their scholars in the course of study prescribed. But no teacher, who has an

*Read before the State Teachers' Institute, Sept., 1862.

adequate sense of the responsibilities devolving upon him, can entertain this opinion. His duty is not performed by merely cultivating the intellect. He must also educate the heart. No parent would consider any teacher fit for his post, who not only did not check even the slightest infringement of morality, but who did not endeavor to elevate his whole school to a high standard of moral excellence. To think otherwise is a great mistake—and the popular notion of education falls in with and confirms this mistake. Talk about giving a young man the advantages of education, and the thoughts immediately run on what is taught in schools and colleges. Speak of giving a young lady a finished education, and almost every one wishes to have the seminary pointed out where she can accomplish, in the shortest space of time, botany, French and Italian, music, and drawing, besides a few of the ordinary branches. As if what is taught in schools and seminaries were able, of itself, to make one either great, or good, or happy.

The truth is, my friends, that hitherto, all over the world, the cultivation of the head has been regarded as the principal thing, while the cultivation of the heart comes in only incidentally. Speak of any school, and most probably the conversation will be upon who is the best scholar in the school. Talk about college, and a certain young man is pointed out to you as the first scholar in his class. Ten prizes are offered for intellectual, to one for moral excellence. The student who can make the best Greek verses, or run through a complicated mathematical demonstration, or write the most flowery oration, or deliver it in the most eloquent manner, is the recipient of the honors, while one, perhaps infinitely his superior in moral character, but not possessing his precocity or assurance, is passed by unnoticed. Now this is surely wrong. The heart is of more importance than the head. The essence of greatness, always and everywhere, is a great *spirit*. Acquisitions and attainments are not the man; they are mere additions to him. Intellectual talents are not the man; they are merely the *instruments* he uses. The *man himself* is behind them all, and he may use them either for good or for evil. The spirit with which a man works, the motives which prompt his conduct—these show us and constitute the man, and these are moral qualities, springing from and dwelling in the heart. The character is the man; the life, in its every particular, which one lives, is the man; and what is it that makes life what it is but the man's motives, his moral qualities, his heart. Therefore we are told that God judgeth the heart; that with the heart man believeth unto righteousness; that out of that, and out of that alone, "are the issues of life." And, therefore, I repeat, the heart is more than the head.

Sir Walter Scott says: "We shall never learn, and feel, and respect our real calling and destiny, unless we have taught ourselves to consider everything as moonshine, compared with the education of the heart." When, after his fruitless journey for health, he had returned to Scotland and to Abbotsford, as he was near his end, he said to his son-in-law, "Lockhart, I may have but a minute to speak with you. My dear, be a good man; be virtuous, be religious; be a good man. Nothing else will give you any comfort when you come to lie here."

"Here was a man," remarks a writer, "who had won the highest prizes of life; had gained the most splendid literary reputation; had been honored, flattered and caressed as few men have ever been; and yet, at the last moment, falls back for support on moral and religious faith—that possession which all may earn."

Horace Mann, as the shades of death were gathering around him, was heard to utter the words, "God—man—duty"—and shortly after, bidding all near him "Good night," sank quietly into that last, deep sleep, which knows no waking in this world. But who that witnessed his peaceful and joyful end would not say, with the poet,

> "That *deeper shade* shall fade away,
> That *deeper sleep* shall leave his eyes;
> Thy *light* shall give eternal day,
> Thy *love* the rapture of the skies."

The formation of an honorable, upright, Christian character, is the great business, the great success of life. This must be done, or nothing is accomplished. Do this first; do this at any rate; do this even if everything else is left undone; though that sacrifice is not required of us. What parent would not prefer his child should leave school with good principles, well settled, his heart in the right place, even though he might be deficient in knowledge, to seeing him adorned with all the accomplishments taught in the schools, if, at the same time, he fears that he is compelled to distrust the soundness of his moral character? What man or woman does not demand of his friend that he shall *first* be true, sincere, *hearty*, whether possessed or not of any remarkable intellectual penetration or sagacity?

Now, I am not decrying intellectual attainments—I value them highly—but I am only placing them on their true level, namely, below moral attainments. It is a matter of great importance that the pupils in our schools should be well instructed in the branches taught in them; and any teacher who succeeds in so doing has accomplished a great good. But it is of the highest consequence, it is absolutely necessary, that we should all become good men and good women. For that purpose, infinitely above all others, we were sent into the world. For that purpose, the world and all that belongs to it were created. For that purpose, the sun shines upon man, the winds invigorate his blood, the rains descend upon his fields, society surrounds him with its blessings, and wife and children warm his heart and strengthen his arm to action. For this purpose, above all others, the school-house, as well as the house of God, was reared.

I see no proper use of language in those who speak of the godlike intellect of such a man, or of another as having a gigantic understanding. We have all heard the observation, "Sir, he is the most remarkable man in America." You may be certain that man is not remarkable for moral qualities. A godlike, a gigantic intellect ascribed to a mere creature of an hour! When the more we know only shows us the immensity of our ignorance. How true it is, also, that purely great intellectual achievements cannot be understood by the great majority of mankind! I suppose there are not one thousand persons in the world that can go through the steps of the reasoning by which Leverrier proved the existence of the new planet, and determined its position. But the triumphs of goodness are at once felt and acknowledged by all. We are through them made personally acquainted with the individuals by whom they are accomplished. *Howard* and *Florence Nightingale* are household words. Every deed of true heroism, of self-sacrifice, of devoted patriotism, of love to brother man, thrills the heart of the world. The heart is quicker, and keener, and truer in insight than the head.

"One touch of *goodness* makes the whole world kin."

The best eulogy ever pronounced upon George Washington was that which declared him to be *first* in the hearts of his countrymen.

I do not intend to go into detail upon the best methods of imparting moral instruction to the young. Here again the heart is of more worth than the head. Every teacher who really and earnestly feels the importance of this work, will instinctively select and adopt the best methods. One thing, however, may be said—that moral instruction cannot commence too early. Its essence lies in training children to do right; and they understand the difference between right and wrong even before they can talk. An essayist—commenting on the fact that sometimes a man, characterized by genuine piety during early and late manhood and into old age, has, when he fell into second childhood, broken out into profanity, and manifested evil habits that surprised, if not shocked his friends—says that *second* childhood is but a repetition of *first* childhood, and that the follies, bad habits, and vices, which were allowed to pass unchecked in childhood, will be likely to reappear in dotage. If this is so, it shows us of what great importance is careful and judicious moral instruction in early life. The lessons then received are never entirely obliterated. It is in the morning of life that the seeds of good principles must be planted. Do not be disappointed if you do not meet with immediate or speedy good results. Think how slowly the world is improving. A higher morality, even more than a higher intelligence, is frequently a plant of slow growth. I suppose there is nothing which makes a greater demand upon the parent's or teacher's patience than the slowness with which a wayward and obstinate child improves.

Sometimes, perhaps for years, the course appears to be all down hill. But persevere; still exercise love, patience, and hope. Years after, when the child has long since left your care, when the good seed which you sowed seems to have been lost forever, and the ground choked up with rank and noxious weeds, a tempest of affliction may rush over the place and sweep off the brambles and thistles, and then may appear, "first the blade, then the ear, then the full corn in the ear," until the fields are white with an abundant harvest, fit to be gathered into the granary of the Lord.

Moral instruction is not to be conveyed to the young by preaching or lecturing. It is a work to be performed. "*Train* up a child in the way he should go," says the Good Book. The teacher must be diligent in seeing that the child acquires good habits—habits of obedience, order, punctuality, method, neatness, studiousness, gentleness, courtesy, respect for elders, reverence for the law, and a love and devotion for his country, which knows not and never can know "a shadow of turning." Teach him to check the first symptoms of envy, jealousy, cruelty, arrogance; to be honest in word and deed; to think the truth, to speak the truth, to act the truth, and to shrink from using a profane word as he would from touching his tongue to red-hot iron. Show him that the brave man never brags; that true courage is in daring to do right; that the man of high and noble spirit will forgive an injury rather than avenge it, because he infinitely prefers to suffer rather than to do wrong. And finally, impress him with the conviction that the greatest victory is not over one's enemies, but over one's self; that the sight upon which Heaven smiles is that of the good man relieving and comforting his fellow-man in distress; and that "the fear of God is the beginning of wisdom." * * * * * * *

I have said that the influence of the faithful teacher is not surpassed by that of any other class in the community. Listen to Martin Luther's words:

"The diligent and pious teacher, who properly instructeth and traineth the young, can never be fully rewarded with money. If I were to leave my office as preacher, I would next choose that of schoolmaster, or teacher, for I know that, next to preaching, this is the greatest, best, and most useful vocation; and I am not quite sure which of the two is the better; for it is hard to reform old sinners, with whom the preacher has to do, while the young tree can be made to bend without breaking."

A distinguished educator remarks:

"Next in rank and efficacy to that pure and holy source of moral influence, the mother, is that of the schoolmaster. It is powerful already. What would it be if, in every one of those school districts which we now count by annually-increasing thousands, there was to be found a teacher well-informed, without pedantry; religious, without bigotry; proud and fond of his profession, and honored in the discharge of its duties? How wide would be the intellectual, the moral influence of such a body of men?"

This is the opinion of every enlightened man upon the nature of the teacher's office. Let us endeavor to justify it in every particular, and then we shall elevate our vocation to the true position which it ought to occupy.

In the remarks I have made upon the propriety and necessity of moral instruction, based upon our duty to God, I do not mean that there should be any formality, any affected sanctity, or any pretensions to superior holiness on the part of the teacher. God forbid. I would have him as pleasant, and cheerful, and honest, as a summer's day. I would not have the moral lessons occupy too much time, or crowd out the other indispensable studies of the school. But I would have them receive *all* the share of attention which their importance demands. The judicious teacher will avail himself of the favorable moment for making the right impression upon the minds of his scholars.

I am conscious that I have very imperfectly presented this subject to your consideration. But I do not exaggerate its importance. If I have said anything which is true, anything which really bears upon the most important question which can be submitted to any human being, I urge and entreat you to give it careful thought, to allow it all the weight to which it is fairly entitled. So shall your influence never be lost, but go on, extending and widening. No sincere effort to promote the good of others can be wholly ineffectual. I remember the kindly tones, the pleasant face, the affectionate warning, and the cheering words of encouragement of a teacher under whose care I was placed when a small boy. The influence which he exerted upon me will, I think, be felt forever; and it is an influence always leading to right. I shall never forget him. How often do I see him in imagination! He is living at the present time, and if he knew that I have been thinking and speaking of him to-day to an audience of teachers upon the distant Pacific coast, his first emotion would be that of surprise that I still think of him after the lapse of so many years; the second would be a thrill of joyful gratitude to God that his counsels had made so deep an impression upon the minds of his scholars, that he had been remembered with esteem and affection.

May our efforts be such in relation to all who may be entrusted to our care that hereafter, wherever the lot of our pupils may be cast upon the broad earth, they may look back upon the school-house which they attended, as the place where they received, besides all useful learning, a love for all that is good, pure, and honorable, which has never left them, but exerts an abiding influence on their characters. So shall your memory be ever kept green in their hearts; so shall your faithful efforts be blessed in their lives.

PHYSICAL TRAINING.*

Intellectual training being the main object of the public schools, it is not surprising that the body has too often been remorselessly sacrificed to the brain.

The neglect of physical culture having produced a long train of evils, too serious to be longer evaded by the most stubborn conservatives, the result is, that systematic physical training is beginning to be recognized as a duty in the public schools of the United States.

In some schools, gymnastic and calisthenic exercises form a part of the daily drill of pupils, quite as regularly as the mental exercises in arithmetic and grammar. In some colleges, muscular training in the gymnasium is insisted on quite as strenuously as a knowledge of the classics. They are using their gymnasiums to build up stout bodies, as well as strong minds. A four years' war taught the nation to place a higher value on physical manhood. In many public schools, the elements of military drill have been introduced, and, under the stimulus of the war spirit, successfully carried into effect. But the first great requisites for good soldiers, before which all others sink into insignificance, are sound health, activity, and power of endurance. The rawest recruits can be taught to handle a musket in a few weeks, but muscles of iron and sinews of steel cannot be fastened upon men like knapsacks. The Greek and Roman veterans were trained from boyhood, by gymnastic

*First Biennial Report, 1865.

exercises, and athletic games and sports. To lay a solid foundation for our own military strength as a nation, we must begin with the three millions of boys in our public schools; and, while we breathe into their hearts the spirit of patriotism, we must train them to a muscular power which will give us fit soldiers to fight and win the battles of the republic. Ten years of boy-life in schools where regular gymnastic drill is followed up, and where a fondness for all athletic games and sports is cultivated, will make a good foundation for military drill.

Physical training is important as an efficient aid to mental culture. It comes into school as an amusement, a relaxation from the hard work of mental application. School amusements are a necessity of childhood. One of the greatest defects of our schools, is their failure to recognize the laws of animal life.

In Germany and Prussia, the children are trained in the schools to gymnastic and athletic exercises; and the result is a national trait of fondness for out-of-door life. English schools are noted for rough-and-tumble games, foot-ball, cricket, leaping, running, wrestling, rowing, boxing, and fencing. Pluck is a national trait of English school-boys, and of English men.

Amusement, in all nations and among all people, in some form, comes in to lighten the burden of toil. Labor is a means, not an end; and the true end of life, usefulness and happiness, lies in the golden mean, the alternation of labor, rest, and amusement.

When the only standing recreation of the American people is business, and their lighter amusements billiards and the ball-room, we have little reason to expect great fondness for sports in schools. This distaste for fun and frolic comes down to us as a natural inheritance. The grave old Puritans, who settled New England, and laid in granite the foundation of the nation, had too much hard work to do in clearing farms and hunting Indians, to think much of amusements. They brought with them, too, something of the old Roundhead antipathy to May-poles, dancing, and theatres.

Whatever may be the reason, it is certain that the Americans, as a people, have little fondness for athletic games and out-of-door sports, without which it is hard to keep the muscular system in good condition.

The ancient Greeks carried to the highest perfection the cultivation of the intellect and the training of the body. Their Olympic games, their athletic exercises, their school discipline, their military drill, secured the highest possible degree of physical perfection. Their poets, orators, philosophers, painters, sculptors, and historians, were good fighters. Alcibiades, the sybarite, the fop, the reveler, could live on black broth, and rough it in the camp with the hardiest of the common soldiers.

Socrates was a soldier as well as a philosopher, and would have been less respected had he wanted the attributes common to all citizen soldiers—strength, courage, and endurance.

When, in Greece, a luxurious civilization corrupted the tastes of the citizens, and reduced them to effeminacy, the rude barbarian claimed the land, and won it.

Their severe gymnastic training, it is true, had for its primary object the perfection of military discipline; but it also produced clear heads, strong minds, and the perfect forms which still live in marble.

Its influence was felt in literature, to which it gave a healthy cast. It gave to the nation its immortal sculptors and painters.

It is in the power of the public schools to educate the nation to a more healthful taste for simple amusements, and to raise the standard of manly strength and womanly beauty.

But apart from this, the highest degree of mental culture cannot be attained in violation of the laws of physical life. Childhood is the season or growth, of animal development. It is a mistaken notion that children are born into the world for the purpose of going to school to learn to read and write. Playfulness is, with them, as much an instinct as with kittens. Even in the long, dark winters of the arctic zone, where nature in her savage forms almost freezes out the life of man, Dr. Kane found the stunted little Esquimaux boys playing their games of ball on the snow-banks. Let the children in school have amusements in the form of healthful, muscular exercises. It is absolutely painful to think how most of our primary schools sin against the laws of nature; how they cramp the little bodies, and repress childish emotions and impulses.

Education is the harmonious development of all the faculties of the human mind, and the training of the human body to its greatest strength and highest beauty. Why, then, in our public schools, should not physical training be considered, as well as mental development?

It is evident to all who are in the least familiar with the daily routine of our schools, that the muscular natures of the children are as little regarded as if they were made of gutta percha. Now, I do not suppose that many children are killed outright by the high pressure of mental training. Occasionally some nervous boy, brilliant and ambitious, his vitality all running to brain instead of body, drops out of school into his grave, and his death is attributed to Providence instead of mathematics. But thousands of boys leave school, thin, pale, and weak, or bungling, clumsy, and awkward, when they might as well have left it strong, active, and graceful.

It is not so much the positive harm which the schools inflict of which we complain, but their neglect to accomplish positive good. It might be hard to prove, in court, that delicate girls, of fine nervous organizations, have been killed outright by long lessons, overstimulated ambition, late study hours, and mathematical puzzles; yet all teachers very well know that brain fevers have taken off many promising young girls, and that many more leave school with diplomas and ruined constitutions. All the girls in public schools have neither crooked spines, round shoulders, sunken chests, nor pale faces; but how much more perfect might be their physical development, did their health receive half the attention devoted to music, drawing, and mathematics. Can any mental culture be of greater importance than the health of those who are to become the mothers of the next generation of men? Few girls who are educated in the public schools escape the universal law of labor. Most of them, when they enter homes of their own at an early age, will need strength as well as accomplishments. Many of them must do their own housework, in addition to the care of children; and is the question of physical strength of no consequence to them? Is it of little consequence to the laboring man, with a family to support, whether his wife be strong or feeble, well or sick?

The strong boys, in the long run, come out ahead. When an ox is let into a pasture full of cattle, there is a trial of horns, and the strongest takes the lead. So with the boys of a public school. The strong, the energetic, the active, are the real kings of school, whether they are at the head or foot of the arithmetic class. Give the boy, then, the exercise his nature craves, and which will make him a live boy and a manly man. If he leaves school with a fondness for athletic amusements, he has one of the surest safeguards against expensive and ruinous dissipation.

A judicious union of social, mental, and physical culture, will make our public schools practically adapted to the wants of the people. If parents, through ignorance, neglect the proper training of their children, let the public school take charge of them. Amusements form a part of education, and much excellent gymnastic and calisthenic training may be connected with games, or made delightful by music.

But some will say, leave children to follow their own inclination in plays and sports; it is not natural for boys to climb the ropes and ladders of a gymnasium, to swing clubs, lift weights, and revolve on bars; nor is it desirable that young ladies use wands, swing dumb bells, and romp in the play-ground. Any attempt at systematic and repeated drill will prove irksome, and therefore useless.

Then why not leave the mind to its natural, untrained action? Why submit the brain to regular training? Children's brains are as active as their bodies; why not leave both alike to the ill-regulated laws of impulse and feeling? In mental culture we recognize the great law of nature, that no perfection is attained without repeated and systematic effort. Mental gymnastics of the severest kind are rigidly practised during at least ten years of early life. Strength, readiness, and quickness are the result. Leave the mind to its own aimless action, and its strength all runs to waste.

The same law applies to the muscular system; yet we leave the boy in school, day after day, year after year, cramped over his desk, his muscles weak and relaxed, and his nervous energy, diverted from his growth, to be poured on an already overworked brain. If he have unusual stamina, he comes out in tolerable health, but clumsy and bungling; if of a nervous temperament, he leaves school precociously sharp and quick, but thin, pale, and weak.

Take a class of boys and subject them, from the age of six years to fifteen, to a careful and judicious daily exercise of an hour in such gymnastics as are best adapted to the growing body, and will not their physique be vastly superior to that of a class left to run wild in the yard? And would not such an additional stock of animal vigor and strength stand them in quite as good stead in the world as their limited store of school-book learning? The graduates of West Point can be singled out of a crowd by their straight forms, erect walk, general quickness of movement, and superior physical development. On a small scale, why cannot the elementary schools reach the same results? Any business man knows that sound health and power of endurance are quite as necessary to success as quickness in mathematics, or skill in the use of language. What merchant would not rather have his son come to the counting-room with every muscle strung to its highest tension, quick, active, self-reliant, strong, and proud of his strength, even if he knows a few pages less of a few books, than to see him drag home a thin face and attenuated muscles? Do not mechanics and laborers think it of some importance that their sons, who will take their places and live by manual labor, shall have sinewy frames, as well as intelligent minds? By far the greater number of boys who attend the public schools grow up working men. To all such, power of endurance is the most practical education. The arm to lift a fifty-pound dumb bell is better than the analysis of cube root.

A sound body is the only capital they have to start with in life. Knowledge may be power, but muscular strength is food and clothing. Some men must earn their living by muscular labor, as well as others by their wits. Horace Mann said, and he *knew* the truth of it, "All through the life of a pure-minded but feeble-bodied man, his path is lined with memory's grave-stones, which mark the spots where noble enterprises perished for want of physical vigor to embody them in deeds."

Sound health is a necessary condition of all permanent success, and the greatest drawback to our public school system is the neglect to provide for this necessity. Better illiterate strength than sickly erudition. It is true that sometimes a heroic spirit conquers physical weakness, but such cases are exceptions. Dr. Kane braved the terrors of the arctic regions, and endured more than many physical giants, but died in Cuba. Nature had her revenge.

Many teachers will say, that is all very fine theoretically, but it is utterly impossible to carry it out practically in the school. Yet, it can be done, has been done, and *is* done in a great many public schools.

Connected for a period of ten years with a public school of five hundred children, during five years of that time gymnastic and calisthenic training was made a part of daily education, just as much as arithmetic, or geography, or grammar, and with quite as satisfactory results. Having practiced all that I recommend, I am troubled with no doubts in urging the practicability of physical culture in the public schools. True, it was rather hard in the beginning, to be blamed for innovations, laughed at by conservatives, and found fault with by parents. But persistence and patience overcame all obstacles. Mothers who at first objected to letting their boys exercise in the gymnasium, for fear they would break their necks or tear their clothes, soon grew proud of the strength and agility of their sons.

Delicate girls, who horrified their mammas with accounts of wands and dumb-bells, grew to like both, as they grew stronger under daily drill. Pale, weakly, good-for-nothing boys, who at first only moped around the yard and looked at the other boys, soon became interested and took hold in earnest, until the narrow chest expanded, the round shoulders straightened, and the soft, flabby arm became like knotted whip-cords.

The measurements of many boys' arms showed an increase of circumference of one inch in three months, and an expansion of the chest of two inches in the same time. Some of my most pleasant memories of teaching are connected with my gymnastic classes of athletic boys, who could kick foot-ball, play base-ball, lift dumb-bells, swing clubs, climb ladders, vault the bar, walk the parallel, swing on the rings, foot it twenty miles on Saturday excursions, and box and wrestle with their teacher. I would not give those boys, who have since grown up to be rugged men, rejoicing in their health and strength, for all the arithmetical prodigies in the United States. As I feel the hearty grip of their hands, my only twinge of pain is, that when I went to school my teachers did not have a higher estimate of muscle, and a lower one of books.

One of those "big boys" of my class has been several years the leading gymnast of the Olympic Club Gymnasium of the young men of this city, and I am quite as proud of him as of another boy who has grown to be a scholar. Another strapping fellow, six feet two, straight as an arrow, and strong as Hercules, who has been two years in the army, fighting Indians, is a walking illustration of the benefits of gymnastic drill in a public school. I would not thus allude to my own experience, except that any reference to gymnastics is met by many teachers with one argument, condensed in a single word—*impracticable.*

How shall such exercises be conducted in a public school? The excellent books on the subject render it unnecessary to go into detail. All children have arms, and the will to use them. With or without music, any teacher in any school, graded or ungraded, can give ten minutes a day for free arm movements. A few dollars will buy a set of wands, and some wooden dumb-bells; and the girls can make two dozen "bean bags." With this simple apparatus alone, any teacher with an ordinary amount of ingenuity, tact, or skill, can, with the aid of a book, have a good light gymnastic class.

Half an hour a day can be taken out of the school hours, and the children be all the better for losing so much study time. A vast amount of training can be given, even in the short period of a year. The time for study and recitation ought to be reduced. In years to come, little children will not be confined in school more than three hours a day. Years ago, the good old-time clergymen preached sermons two hours long, and those who could not stand them patiently were held to be weak in the faith. Better sermons are now delivered in thirty minutes, with quite as good results. So it will be with schools. Better teachers than we, when the present six-hour system shall have become obsolete, will teach more in half the time. Not length of time in study, but the quality of thought, and the force of action, is the measure of mental progress.

The light gymnastics are good for the smaller boys and girls; but the "big boys" will generally prefer some out-of-door exercises. The movable horizontal bar is a great favorite with boys, and the exercises on it are among the best of the gymnasium. One can be set in any school-yard for twenty dollars. A few iron dumb bells will be useful. The Indian clubs are excellent for the arms and chest, but boys do not generally "take to them." The swinging rings cost but little, and are liked very much. Leaping is a pleasant yard amusement, and requires only two sticks and a string. Football is a rough and tumble game; but it has the charm of intense excitement, and the more the boys get of it the better. Bruised ankles and sore legs are forgotten in the exultation of winning. Rugby ought not to monopolize it. Base ball is a fine old game, which ought always to be kept before the boys. An occasional Saturday pedestrian excursion of twenty miles is a fine thing if the teacher can stand it. I was reminded of one the other day by a strapping fellow, who exclaimed: "It made my legs ache, but how nice the beefsteaks were that we broiled on sticks over the fire." A set of boxing gloves will make fine fun for the older boys, and yet give them the most vigorous kind of exercise. "Do you box any nowadays," was one of the first salutations of one of my "boys," who has just returned from the army. He was thinking of the half hours after school with the boxing gloves, in the old schoolhouse, and how, with the aid of what he had learned there, he whipped the eyes out of a big "bully" at the West Point Military Academy. Wrestling used to be a favorite amusement, and what New England boy does not remember many a hard tussle on the green sward round the "old schoolhouse."

Teachers who wish to succeed in physical training must study variety in their exercises. Boys are fond of novelty and change, and the same routine day after day will soon tire. Marbles, tops, kites, and ball follow after one another, changing quite as often as the moon. It requires more skill, tact, judgment, and knowledge of boy nature to succeed with a gymnastic class than to teach arithmetic or grammar; one requires a soul and sympathy with boy nature, the other does not. An owl should not mingle with singing birds; and a cold, formal, dignified, melancholy teacher has no business in the boys' playground. If he cannot kick a foot-ball well, the boys will laugh at him.

Every teacher needs gymnastic exercises and amusements. No occupations so drains the nervous power; he must find the "fountain of youth" in the sports of boyhood. What matters it if examinations are a little less "brilliant," children less precocious, and "school phenomenons" less common? The object of school is to train up children to be sensible men and women, and to form tastes and habits which shall follow them through life.

The indirect lessons of the play-ground are often more valuable than the formal teachings of the class-room, and the kind words there spoken will soften the necessary severity of discipline in a public school. In the hours of play, when "off duty," the teacher with a great heart can win the *souls* of children while training their bodies. What teacher would not be remembered by his pupils as a sharer of their sports, a sympathizer with their boyish amusements, as a living man who had a heart, and moulded their character, and formed their tastes, rather than as a mere schoolmaster who only expounded text-books!

III. UNIVERSITY OF CALIFORNIA.

In 1866, Hon. Wm. Holden introduced a bill to organize a State Agricultural School, in order to secure the 150,000 acres of land granted by Congress for that purpose. The bill became a law, but no action was taken under it; and in 1868, Hon. John W. Dwinelle drafted and introduced a bill, which was passed, providing for a State University with an Agricultural College.

The University of California was opened in Oakland, in the College of California buildings, Sept. 23, 1869, with an attendance of about 50 students.

The University was made free, and opened for the admission of young men and women.

The first Board of Regents was composed as follows:

EX-OFFICIO REGENTS.

H. H. Haight	Governor.
Wm. Holden	Lieutenant-Governor.
O. P. Fitzgerald	State Supt. Public Instruction.
C. T. Ryland	Speaker of the Assembly.
Chas. F. Reed	President State Agricultural Society.
A. S. Hallidie	President Mechanics' Institute.

APPOINTED BY THE GOVERNOR.

Samuel Merritt	2 years.	John T. Doyle	4 years.
R. P. Hammond	6 years.	John W. Dwinelle	8 years.
Horatio Stebbins	10 years.	Lawrence Archer	12 years.
Wm. Watt	14 years.	S. B. McKee	16 years.

ELECTED BY THE BOARD.

Isaac Friedlander	2 years.	Edward Tompkins	4 years.
J. Mora Moss	6 years.	S. F. Butterworth	8 years.
A. J. Moulder	10 years.	A. J. Bowie	12 years.
F. F. Low	14 years.	John B. Felton	16 years.

Andrew J. Moulder, having been elected Secretary, resigned his position as Regent.

The College of California, incorporated in 1855, disincorporated, and conveyed its grounds at Berkeley, 5 miles from Oakland, as a site for the State University.

The men chiefly instrumental in this consolidation, were Henry Durant, Gov. F. F. Low, and Horatio Stebbins.

The College of California had its germ in a private school, established in Oakland in 1853, by Henry Durant.

FACULTY OF THE UNIVERSITY.

On the 10th of November, 1868, the Regents elected General Geo. B. McClellan, President, with a salary of $6000. He declined, and Prof. John LeConte was made "Acting President."

In 1869, the following Professors were appointed:

Joseph LeConte....Prof. of Geology, Natural History, and Botany.
John LeConte.........Prof. of Physics and Industrial Mechanics.
Martin Kellogg.....................Prof. of Ancient Languages.
R. C. Fisher.........Prof. of Chemistry, Mining, and Metallurgy.
W. T. Welcker..........................Prof. of Mathematics.
Frank Soulé, Jr......................Ass't Prof. of Mathematics.
Paul Pioda.........................Prof. of Modern Languages.
Ezra S. Carr.....Prof. of Agriculture, Agricultural Chemistry, and Horticulture.
Wm. Swinton.........Prof. of English Language and Literature, History, Rhetoric, and Logic.

Henry Durant was elected President in 1870. In 1872, he resigned, and D. C. Gilman was elected, Sept. 1st. President Gilman resigned in March, 1875, and was succeeded by Prof. John LeConte, as "Acting President." In June, 1876, Prof. John LeConte was elected President.

The Legislature of 1870 appropriated $300,000 for building purposes, and in the Autumn of 1873, the buildings being completed, the University was removed from Oakland to the permanent site at Berkeley.

The resignation of Prof. Fisher was requested by the Regents in '71, and the chair of Chemistry was filled by Prof. Rising. In 1874, the resignation of Prof. Carr was requested by the Regents. He demanded an investigation, which was refused, and his chair was declared vacant. He was nominated and elected Superintendent of Public Instruction, in 1876.

In 1874, Prof. Swinton resigned his professorship to go East, and E. R. Sill was elected to his place.

During the same year, Fred. G. Hesse was elected to the Chair of Industrial Mechanics; John D. Hoffman, Prof. of Industrial Drawing; Wm. Ashburner, Prof. of Mining Engineering; E. W. Hilgard, Prof. of Agriculture; George F. Becker, Instructor in Metallurgy.

A. J. Moulder resigned, and R. E. C. Stearns was elected Secretary.

The Regents and the Faculty, 1876, are as follows:

EX-OFFICIO REGENTS.

William Irwin.........Governor, ex-officio President of the Board.
J. A. Johnson.............................Lieutenant-Governor.
Hon. G. J. Carpenter..................Speaker of the Assembly.
Hon. Ezra S. Carr....... State Superintendent Public Instruction.
R. S. Carey, Esq............President State Agricultural Society.
A. S. Hallidie, Esq....Pres. Mechanics' Institute of San Francisco.
John LeConte.......................President of the University.

APPOINTED REGENTS.

Rev. H. Stebbins, San Francisco.	D. O. Mills.............Millbrae.
Hon. L. Archer.......San Jose.	William Meek....San Leandro.
J. West Martin........Oakland.	Hon. F. M. Pixley, San Francisco.
Hon. Samuel B. McKee, Oakland.	Hon. W. T. Wallace, San Fran'co.
Hon. J. F. Swift, San Francisco.	Hon. E. Casserly..San Francisco.
Joseph Winans...San Francisco.	Hon. J. S. Hager, San Francisco.
J. Mora Moss........ Oakland.	A. J. Bowie......San Francisco.
J. M. Hamilton........Guenoc.	Hon. John B. Felton...Oakland.

ACADEMIC SENATE.

John LeConte, M.D....Pres. and Prof. of Physics and Mechanics.
William Ashburner.............................Prof. of Mining.
Geo. W. Bunnell, A.M....Prof. of Greek Language and Literature.
Geo. Davidson, A.M..Non-Resident Prof. Geodesy and Astronomy.
Stephen J. Field, LL.D..............Non-Resident Prof. of Law.
Frederick G. Hesse...............Prof. of Industrial Mechanics.
E. W. Hilgard, Ph.D..Prof. Agriculture and Agricultural Chemistry.
Martin Kellogg, A.M.....Dean, and Prof. of Ancient Languages.
Joseph LeConte, M.D......Prof. of Geology and Natural History.
Bernard Moses, Ph.D..........................Prof. of History.
Paul Pioda.........................Prof. of Modern Languages.
Willard B. Rising, Ph.D......Prof. of Chemistry and Metallurgy.
Edward R. Sill, A.M....Prof. of English Language and Literature.
Frank Soulé, Jr.......Prof. of Civil Engineering and Astronomy.
William T. Welcker.......................Prof. of Mathematics.
W. A. Barbour, A.B....................Instructor in Chemistry.
Geo. F. Becker, A.B., Ph.D..............Lecturer on Metallurgy.
Samuel R. Christy, Ph.D.................Instructor in Chemistry.
G. C. Edwards, Ph.B..Inst'r in Mathematics, and Com. of Cadets.
Carlos F. Gompertz.......................Instructor in Spanish.
L. L. Hawkins, Ph.B....Instructor in Mathematics and Surveying.
John D. Hoffman..............Instructor in Mechanical Drawing.
Henry B. Jones..................Assistant Instructor in German.
G. de Kersaint-Gily........................Instructor in French.
Robert E. Ogilby...............Instructor in Free-hand Drawing.
Edward A. Parker, Ph.B.....Instructor in Physics and Mechanics.
Jas. M. Phillips, A.B...Instructor in Hebrew and Ancient History.
Albin Putzker...........................Instructor in German.
Ambrose C. Richardson, A.B.......Instructor in Latin and Greek.
Joseph C. Rowell, A.B...............................Librarian.
E. H. Sears, A.B..................Instructor in Latin and Greek.
F. Slate, Jr., S.B......................Instructor in Chemistry.

GRADUATE ASSISTANTS.

John W. Bice, Ph.B....................College of Engineering.
Isaac T. Hinton, Ph.B............................Mathematics.
Wm. Carey Jones, A.B....................Recorder of Faculty.
Franklin P. McLean, Ph.G............................Chemistry.
Frank S. Sutton, Ph.B...................College of Agriculture.

STUDENT ASSISTANTS.

Fred. L. Button..................................Mathematics.
J. B. Clarke..Mathematics.
X. Y. Clark.......................Natural History and Geology.

NUMBER OF STUDENTS.

The number of students from 1870 to 1876 is as follows: 40, 78, 153, 185, 191, 234.

ENDOWMENT.

The 150,000 acres of land granted by Congress for the support of an Agricultural College have been sold, or applied for, at an average price of $5 per acre. If paid up, there would be a fund of $750,000, which, at six per cent., would yield an annual revenue of $45,000. But in selling these lands, only 20 per cent., or $1 an acre, is required in cash, the remainder draws interest at the rate of ten per cent.; so that the income ought to exceed $50,000, or even $60,000.

In addition to this endowment, the State has given from the sale of tide lands an endowment fund sufficient to yield an annual income of $50,000—about $800,000, invested in State bonds. The endowment fund of the University may be set down, in round numbers, at $1,500,000, and its annual income at $128,000.

IV. STATE NORMAL SCHOOL.

Under the appropriation of $3,000, by the Legislature of 1861-2, Ahira Holmes was appointed as Principal by a Board of Trustees, consisting of Superintendent Moulder, George Tait, Superintendent of San Francisco, and Dr. Taylor, Superintendent of Sacramento.

The school was opened in one of the vacant rooms of the San Francisco High School, July 21st, 1862, with 34 pupils, during the first term. The school was soon removed to rented rooms. on Post Street. Henry P. Carlton was elected Vice-Principal, and Miss Helen M. Clark and Miss Kate Sullivan teachers in the Training School.

The first graduating class, December, 1863, consisted of Bertha Comstock, Augusta P. Fink, Nellie Hart, and Louisa Mails.

In July, 1864, Miss E. W. Houghton was elected as an Assistant, and in July, 1865, George W. Minns succeeded Ahira Holmes as Principal. The school was removed to the rear of the Lincoln Grammar School, and Mrs. C. H. Stout was appointed Principal of the Training School.

The number of pupils, October, 1865, was 86. The School Law of 1865-5 made the State Board of Education *ex officio* a Board of Normal School Trustees.

At the first meeting, April 13, 1866, Professor Minns was granted a year's leave of absence, and H. P. Carlton elected Acting Principal. In 1867, Mr. Minns, concluding not to return from the East, resigned. Mr. Carlton continued Principal until July, 1867, when George Tait was elected Principal. Mr. Tait resigned in 1868, and was succeeded by W. T. Luckey.

Under the Act of April 4, 1870, Gov. Haight appointed a Board of Trustees, consisting of James Denman, J. H. Braly, C. T. Ryland, H. O. Weller, and A. J. Moulder, the Governor and State Superintendent being *ex officio* members.

This Board proceeded to erect a building at San Jose, completed in 1872, at a cost of $250,000.

In June, 1873, Charles H. Allen was elected Principal, *vice* W. T. Luckey, and J. H. Braly, Vice-Principal, *vice* H. P. Carlton.

At present, the school is filled to its utmost capacity—350 students—and is, in fact as well as in name, a Normal School.

The Board of Instruction, June, 1876, is as follows:

Charles H. Allen	Principal
J. H. Braly	Vice-Principal.
Henry B. Norton	Natural Science.
Ira Moore	Language.
Miss Eliza W. Houghton	Preceptress.
Mrs. Lucy M. Washburn	Assistant in Junior Class.
Miss Cornelia Walker	Assistant in Junior Class.
Miss Annie E. Chamberlain	Assistant in Junior Class.
Miss Phebe P. Grigsby, Miss Helen C. Wright	Preparatory Department.
Miss Mary J. Titus	Principal of Training School.
Miss Florence Grigsby	Assistant in Training School.

NUMBER OF GRADUATES OF THE STATE NORMAL SCHOOL.

Year.	No.	Year.	No.
'63	4	'70	45
'64	28	'71	21
'65	25	'72	17
'66	22	'73	20
'67	41	'74	33
'68	38	'75	46
'69	29	'76	36

Whole number........414.

V. STATE BOARDS OF EDUCATION.

By the School Law of 1852, the State Board of Education was made to consist of the Governor, State Superintendent, and the Surveyor-General. The Surveyor-General was included because the law originally proposed to entrust the Board with the sales of school lands. This, however, was not done; and the State Board remained, up to 1864, without powers or duties, except to apportion, annually, the State school moneys. In 1864, the State Board was made to consist of the Governor, the State Superintendent, and the County Superintendents of San Francisco, Sacramento, and San Joaquin. The Board was empowered to adopt a uniform series of text-books, for all schools except in incorporated cities; to require a uniform course of study, and to make rules and regulations for the schools. In 1865, the Board was enlarged by the addition of the Principal of the State Normal School, and of two members appointed by the State Superintendent. In 1872, the two appointive members were cut off. In 1864, the State Board was made, *ex officio*, the Board of Normal School Trustees; repealed, 1870.

VI. TEACHERS' CERTIFICATES AND BOARDS OF EXAMINATION.

From 1850 to 1860, the power of examining teachers for certificates was vested in District School Trustees and City Boards of Education. These Boards were authorized to grant certificates "of good moral character and fitness to teach a common school *one year*."

In 1860, Superintendent Moulder secured the passage of a law providing for a State Board of Examination, appointed by the State Superintendent, with power to grant certificates, valid for two years, and for County Boards, appointed by County Superintendents, with power to issue county certificates, valid for one year.

The power of examining teachers was still vested in City Boards of Education, which were not required to recognize State certificates.

At the State Institute, Sacramento, 1862, the first State examination was held by Superintendent Moulder and a Board made up of County Superintendents. The examination was somewhat informal, and mostly oral. The Board granted five Grammar School certificates and twelve "Mixed School" certificates.

From 1851 to 1863, teachers in San Francisco were examined every year. At first, these examinations were oral; but, in 1856, the Board introduced written examinations.

Concerning this annual re-examination of experienced teachers, Superintendent Swett, in his first Report, said:

No one cause has done so much to render the occupation of a public school teacher distasteful as the old system of annual examinations. Teachers were condemned to be tried, not by a jury of their peers, but too often by men who knew little or nothing of practical teaching, and who not unfrequently made the annual examination a guillotine for decapitating any unlucky pedagogue who had fallen under ban of their petty displeasure. A teacher in the public schools, though he might have, added to the finest natural abilities for teaching, a complete professional training in the best normal schools in the United States; though he might be crowned with honors, won by many years of successful experience; though he might be esteemed by the community, and revered by thousands of grateful pupils—at the end of each year, forsooth, he must be "examined" by a committee of lawyers, doctors, dentists, book-binders, contractors, and non-professional men, to ascertain if he were "*fit to teach a Common School!*" After having passed through the examination mill annually, nine years in succession, turned out each time with a "bran new" certificate of "fitness to teach a Common School one year," I can speak feelingly on this subject. These annual examinations of experienced teachers offered an annual insult to intelligence, by lumping character, aptness to teach, moral and social culture, in tabular statements of "percentage" on arithmetic and spelling, in which infinitesimal details counted everything, character and success nothing at all. Actual trial in the school-room is the best test of fitness to teach; and when a teacher has once passed examination, and proved successful in school, subsequent examinations are uncalled for and unnecessary.

I remember more than one successful teacher, arraigned before the Examination Star Chamber, who was decapitated by the official guillotine of "percentage," because he happened to fail "on the best route from Novogorod to Kilimandijaro," or from "Red Dog to You Bet;" or forgot the population of Brandy Gulch, Humbug Canon, or Pompeii; or could not remember the names of all the rivers of the world, from the Amazon down to the brook where he caught "minnows" with pin hooks when a boy; or blundered on some arithmetical shell, hard enough to pierce the hide of a monitor; or chanced to spell traveler with two l's; or happened, finally, to fall one tenth of one credit below nine hundred and ninety-nine, the standard which exactly gauged the moral character and intellectual ability of a man "fit to teach a Common School one year." The new State law, by granting diplomas for six years, relieves teachers from the annoyance of such examinations, and is the first step towards recognizing teaching as a profession. It was my firm conviction from the first, that the end sought would be best attained by vesting the authority to examine candidates in a board of practical teachers, selected for that specific purpose. The future success of this important movement will depend upon retaining this principle as a foundation. Teachers have a right to demand an examination by their peers.

In the State Institute circular, 1863, the subject of teachers' certificates was noticed as follows:

The State Board of Examiners will hold an examination of all applicants who desire to obtain State certificates during the Institute Session. By an amendment to the school law, these certificates remain in force during the term of four years—relieving the holders from all further examination by County Boards. It would be difficult to adduce any reason whatever for the annual examination of teachers, except the natural desire which some seem to entertain for tormenting unlucky applicants for district schools. There are many able teachers in the State whose pride revolts at the humiliation. Under the old law, a teacher in the public schools, though he might have added to the finest natural abilities for teaching, a complete professional training in the best Normal schools in the United States —though he might have grown gray in the service, might be crowned with the well-earned honors of many successful schools, be revered by thousands of grateful pupils—though he had graduated from a university—yet he could not apply for the smallest district school in the remotest corner of the State, without "passing an examination;" and, if he wished to teach another year, he had to travel twenty or thirty miles to pass examination, to satisfy the State that he was "*fit to keep a common school!*" And further, if he wished to remove to another county, he must be examined by another Board, to ascertain his fitness to teach a *common school!* If *examination* imparts fitness to teach, some of the teachers in this State ought to be well fitted for their occupation.

In 1862-3, Superintendent Swett secured important amendments to the law relating to certificates and examining boards; and in 1865-6, the Revised School Law made elaborate provisions for the whole subject.

This law authorized the State Board of Education to issue State Life Diplomas to teachers of at least 10 years' experience, holders of State Educational Diplomas; provided for City Boards of Examination, consisting exclusively of professional teachers; required City Boards of Education to recognize the validity of State certificates; required the percentages obtained in the different studies to be indorsed on the back of the certificate; required the State Board to issue certificates to the holders of State Normal School diplomas, and of State life certificates of all other States in the United States; provided for granting State certificates on the results of county examinations with the State series of questions—in other words, made teaching a legal profession.

These provisions, with slight amendments, are retained in the present school law.

On this subject, Mr. Swett spoke as follows, before the National Educational Association, at Boston, August 6–8, 1872:

By way of introducing my subject, and for the purpose of showing why I entertain radical views on the common methods of examining teachers, and of granting them certificates, I am constrained to offer my own experience as an illustration.

Twenty years ago this very month, moved by the migratory instinct that seems to be hereditary in so many Yankee boys, impelling them to take flight in search of warmer climes and richer feeding-grounds, I sailed out of Boston harbor bound for California, "round the Horn."

My pocket-book was not plethoric with money, but carefully stowed away in its ample folds there were three certificates, every one of which bore the most positive evidence as to my good moral character, and certified to my "ability and fitness to teach a common school for the term of one year." One of these, like its holder, had its birth in the Old Granite State.

It bore the signature of a "*Deestrict School Trustee,*" dear old Deacon Brown, who examined me in the vowel sounds, and the consonant sounds; asked me to pronounce correctly *g-e-w-g-a-w*, and, by way of a clincher, required me to define the four parts of English Grammar according to Lindley Murray, to wit: Orthography, Etymology, Syntax, and Prosody.

The other two certificates were dated in the town of *Timbuctoo*, in the old Bay State, almost in the shadow of Bunker Hill. I was examined in the dingy office of a cobwebbed old lawyer, who was quite as scientific in his style of doing things, as was dear old Deacon Brown.

It is enough to say that every one of these examinations was as great a farce as it would be for Vincent Collier to examine an Apache Indian in mental and moral philosophy and theology, or rather, as absurd as it would be for a green-grocer to examine John Stuart Mill in political economy.

I would not rake up old events that happened so near the cradle of the common-school system, except that on returning, nearly a quarter of a century later, I find that good old way of examining teachers still going on in my native State, and in some other States that I do not now care to mention.

When I reached California, I mined, until I found myself dead-broke; worked as a day-laborer on a ranch; sought in vain for permanent employment, save only the profession of blacking boots;

and, at the end of the year, looked sadly at my certificates, and, as a last desperate resort, "looked round" for a school.

I heard of a school, but my old certificates were not current in California; and the flattering letters of Prof. Russell, who taught me how to teach, availed me nothing. I had to be "examined" before I could be patented to be "fit to teach a common school in the State of California, for one year," and a miserable little school of half-Spanish children at that.

The school trustee, a Yankee minister, a man of huge body and enormous pomposity, did his duty with an awful dignity, which nobody but a little-minded man, in a petty little office, can ever aspire to. It was the same old rigmarole of "readin', 'ritin' and 'rithentic," with never a question to test education, culture, or power to teach.

After a half-day's examination, he gave *me* a certificate, and the school to somebody else.

Then I went to San Francisco. There was a vacancy in the school department. The old examination-mill was still kept running under Yankee management. Fifteen of us, all in a row, like good little boys in school, were questioned "once round" in arithmetic, "once round" in grammar, "once round" in geography, "once round" in spelling, by the Superintendent and the Mayor—the former a Vermont Yankee, and the latter like unto him, except he hailed from a city nigh unto Boston, where they gibbeted witches instead of teachers.

I was told I ranked first of the batch; and of course somebody else, who had "influence with the board," got the place. The successful somebody this time was a young doctor without patients. He soon resigned, and I was allowed the privilege, at $125 a month, of conquering a peace by subduing the young hoodlums, or of meeting the fate of my predecessor.

This was how I became a schoolmaster, and how I won my way into the noblest profession—I think that is what they call it sometimes in educational conventions.

For eight successive years I taught the same school, and—I am am ashamed to own it, and would not tell it were it not necessary to illustrate what I intend to present—I had the cowardice, like other teachers with me, to submit to eight annual examinations, in order to determine my fitness, at each annual revolution of the sun, to teach the same school each succeeding school year.

Nor was this the end of humiliation and insult. After getting a "bran new" certificate at the end of each year, before I could go on again, I had to be elected by the votes of twelve members of the Board of Education, because my term of office lasted only one year. This annual election system was handed down to us from the primitive New England "town meetings." I believe that here in Boston, and in all New England cities and villages, and, in fact, in most parts of the United States, it is still kept up. A teacher holds the office only one year, and then he is at the mercy of any school director, or local member of the board, who may have some spite to wreak, or some relative to put in. Much as I honor the occupation of teaching, I am not in love with a system that tends to take all the manliness out of a man, and all the independence from a woman.

Under such a barbarous system of office-holding, rather than have a son of mine become a common-school teacher, I would apprentice him to the trade of a tanner, a tailor, or a shoemaker. He might then stand some possible chance of rising in the political world. For myself, rather than teach under it, I would contest with Nasby the postmastership of the Confederate Cross-Roads.

At length, dragged out of my bed, after a typhoid fever that brought me to the verge of the grave—a sickness brought on by over-work, worry and anxiety—in order to be run through the examination-mill a *ninth* time, the hereditary blood of my grandfather, who "fit" in the Revolution, rose up in rebellion. I vowed to break up and root out the annual-examination farce, and the New-England-town-meeting-annual-election humbug, both of which had followed me across the continent, like the ghost of some grim old Puritan, sticking closer than the accent of Yankee-land in our mother tongue.

So I left the school-room, went into political conventions, secured a nomination for the only office ever open to a schoolmaster, that of State Superintendent of Public Instruction, stumped the State, won two successive elections, and the third time, with my whole party, won a defeat; framed a school-law; established free schools; lobbied legislatures; secured a legal recognition of professional teachers; abolished the New England annual-examination farce; and, in San Francisco, broke up the annual rotation-in-office election system; placed the examination of teachers throughout the State exclusively in the hands of experienced teachers, thereby ruining the occupation and the glory of many a learned committee-man; secured life diplomas for experienced and capable teachers; gained a legal recognition of the normal school diplomas of all State normal schools in the United States; and, by law, made valid in California the life diplomas and State certificates granted to teachers by other States.

All these reforms cost me years of hard work and determined effort, and you will understand why I entertain strong convictions on the subject of teachers' certificates.

For nearly twenty years, on the western verge of the continent, I have been engaged in a kind of border warfare in education. My educational notions have changed since I taught school near Boston. Living in a State whose people have been gleaned from every other State in the Union, from France, Germany, Italy, England, Ireland, Australia, and China, new conditions have made new questions to be decided, and new issues to be met.

While I fully recognize all that is good in New England schools, school laws, school customs and usages, I take satisfaction for past suffering, in hurling a few brick-bats into the windows of the old school-house where I was flogged.

Before touching on the subject of professional certificates, the two weak points of our public school system must be taken into account.

1. Of the three hundred thousand persons that "keep school" in our country, not more than one tenth can be regarded as professional teachers, that is, teachers trained to their business, and intend-

ing to pursue it for a term of years. From the various normal schools altogether, there are graduated, annually, not more than two thousand at a very liberal estimate, and of these at least one half drop out of the occupation in five years.

Most of our schools *outside* of our large cities, and many of the lower classes *within* our cities, are "kept," not taught, by unskilled and untrained labor, at the wages of unskilled labor. The pay of these unskilled "school-keepers" is less than that of any class of artisans or mechanics in any occupation that requires a trained apprenticeship.

These "school-keepers" are quite as good as the people deserve, and in most cases better than they ought to get for the wages paid. Until the people recognize the necessity of schools all the year round, until they recognize that teaching is an art, until they are willing to pay for skilled training, instead of mere "school-keeping," the broken summer and winter schools, kept by young girls waiting to get married, and by boys working their way through college, or into other occupations and professions, or by migratory Ichabod Cranes, must serve the purpose of keeping the children out of utter barbarism, by giving them a chance to learn to read and write, and reckon dollars and cents.

The abstract theory of our school system is fine enough, but the census statistics loom up in fearful significance as a dark background. We shall learn before long that mere reading and writing do not constitute education, and that schoolmasters and schoolma'ams are not necessarily teachers.

It is a quarter of a century since I went to school in my native village. I return and find the school there is no better than when I was a school-boy. That village school is a fair type of many schools all over our country. It will not do to pick out a few cities, and shut our eyes to the rural districts.

When I went to school, we boys had neither training nor culture. We learned to read and write and cipher, and memorized text-books, but we were not *educated;* and hundreds of thousands of boys and girls, all over our country, are doing the same thing at the present time.

It matters but little how the temporary keepers of schools of this type are examined. Still, there ought to be a plan devised by which the untutored, untrained and unskilled "school-keeper" shall not be placed on the same footing and paid the same wages as the accomplished graduate of a normal school, or the self-made teacher, trained in actual work in the school-room.

Schools of this class were well enough in the ruder years of the republic, when men and women were subduing the wilderness, driving out the savages, and laying the rough foundations of a great nation. But the time is now rapidly coming when, in consequence of a denser population, the struggle for existence will become fiercer, when there will no longer be millions of acres of fertile land to be taken up at nominal prices, and made productive by unskilled labor. The time is coming when our artisans and mechanics must be trained to compete with those from the technical and industrial schools of European countries.

Our schools in the small villages and farming districts must be reorganized to meet this new order of things, and the people must employ skilled teachers, and pay them the wages of skilled labor.

2. The other radical defect in the practical working of our school system is the short terms of school officers and superintendents, and their election by direct vote of the people in general elections.

Annual elections suited the genius of New England towns when the government was the purest type of a democracy, and when the machinery of great political parties was unknown; but, applied to great cities, to States, and to the broader expanse of the West, the short term of office and the annual election have been ruinous in their results, not only in educational offices, but in all others.

There can be no steady progress in public schools without long-continued, systematic efforts; and there can be no *system* when one set of school officials succeeds another as often as the seasons change. By the time one set of school officers has learned something about the condition and wants of the schools, by some change in the politics of the city or town, a new set succeeds, bent on reforming the work of their predecessors.

In many parts of our country, already, school boards elected by one political party feel under no obligation to retain in place the teachers appointed by the opposite party, and the outrageous annual-election farce, which cowardly teachers have so long submitted to without a struggle, affords a fine opportunity to drop out the old ones and run in the new.

Gradually, but surely, the schools are coming to be considered as legitimate party spoils of the victors, and the struggle for position on boards of education in all our great cities is mainly to control the patronage of appointments. There has been a great deal of talk about reform in civil-service appointments, but the country stands in greater need of reform in the manner of making educational appointments. There is more favoritism, more of politics and church, mixed up in the annual appointments of the 300,000 teachers in the country than in all the custom-houses; and there is more ignorance and unfitness for position than in all the post-offices and civil-service places taken together.

I make no random assertions. I speak from a thorough personal knowledge of our State; and teachers and educators from other States affirm the same condition of things with them. It is undoubtedly worse in the newer States than in the older, and worse in the States evenly balanced, and subject to frequent political changes, than in the one-sided States always controlled by the same political party. Right here in Boston, the centre of conservatism, there is little change, because for twenty-five years there has been no change in the political character of the Board of Education. But, each succeeding year, every one of the thousand teachers here feels that it is possible for one single enemy on the Board to secure, by persistent misrepresentation, and by trading votes, the removal of any teacher. Occasionally, even in Utopia, it happens that a teacher is "left out," and consequently no teacher can act or can think independently; and it is even whispered that it makes a material difference with a man's chances whether he be a believer in Cotton Mather or in Darwin.

If the Boston Brahmins like this condition of petty servitude to school directors, I am perfectly willing they shall fold their arms with all due meekness and gratitude, leaving the work of reformation to outside barbarians. They get better salaries than we do out West, and consequently are conservative.

Until there is a reform in these defective points of our school system, it seems to me there can be no marked and permanent improvement in our public schools as a whole. There will be individual schools that, under superior teachers, will attain a high degree of excellence; but the general average of the schools can not be raised much higher than it is, because the system neither encourages independent thought nor tolerates progress.

Puttering in conventions over the little details of teaching arithmetic, grammar, and geography, will avail nothing. Men are wanted to shape legislation, to dig out the *debris*, and with strong and rough hands to lay the superstructure of a better system of American school supervision and school teaching.

There are some men and women engaged in public school service who make teaching a life-work, who understand their business, and who are earnestly devoted to their work, and the rights and privileges of this class demand a careful consideration. There are only a few States that have any system of professional examinations by which a public school teacher can secure a professional life diploma, and thereafter be exempted from the humiliation of periodic examinations by petty school officials, just emerging from babyhood of official ignorance of the whole subject of education.

And even if a life certificate can be secured in a few States, such as Illinois, Ohio, Iowa, or California, it is of no legal value outside of the particular State in which it is granted. California is the only State that recognizes by law the State diplomas and certificates of other States, by placing them on an equal footing with her own. Were I, after twenty years of continous service as a teacher, as State Superintendent, and as Deputy City Superintendent of San Francisco, holding in my possession dozens of defunct certificates, and a life diploma of the State of California, were I to go back to my native town, and seek employment in my native State by teaching the little "Deestrict School" that I went to when a barefoot boy, I should have to "pass examination" to determine my fitness to teach a little squad of boys and girls to read and write. The school law of New Hampshire not only fails to recognize the educational diplomas of mushroom States like California; but, with true Puritan stubbornness, neglects to provide her own sons, who pick up education enough to become teachers, with any kind of a State document which they can carry with them to the State where they go to earn a living.

It would be the same were I to go "looking out for a school" in Maine, or Vermont, or Massachusetts, or Rhode Island, or Connecticut, or any State in the Union except my own adopted State.

Were my esteemed personal friend Mr. Philbrick, the Superintendent of the Public Schools of Boston, crowned with the well-earned honors of twenty-five years of educational labor, to lose his position at the next annual election, and in consequence, were to emigrate to California, to teach school to earn a living, he would have to pass a rigid written examination, before he could draw a dollar of the school fund for teaching the smallest school, in the roughest mining camp in the State. Massachusetts has provided no means of giving her educational veterans a certificate of public-school service.

No State in the Union, except California, recognizes by law the normal school diplomas of other States. In fact, many of the States fail to recognize by law the diplomas given to the graduates of their own normal schools.

There ought to be, in every State, a State Board of Examination, made up exclusively of professional teachers, including the State Superintendent of Public Instruction, having power to issue life diplomas to experienced teachers of the highest rank, and certificates of lower grades to younger teachers, of lower rank; these diplomas and certificates to be issued only upon actual examination in writing, and the record of examination to be indorsed upon the certificates. There ought, also, to be a system of broad and liberal legislation in all the States, by means of which a professional teacher holding a diploma or certificate in one State, should be guaranteed a legal recognition in all the other States.

It is true that this need is more felt in the newer Western and Pacific States than in the older ones. For instance, in California, our teachers are drawn from every other State in the Union. These teachers must pass a written examination in our State, before they can engage in teaching. This requisition often keeps them waiting for several months after their arrival. Occasionally a teacher comes bringing a State certificate or normal school diploma, which is at once recognized under our liberal school law.

But most of the States have failed to provide for any system of State certificates, by means of which their teachers can carry with them, when they emigrate, any written evidence of professional fitness.

If the older States do not feel the local need of some provision of this kind, they owe a duty to their educated sons and daughters, who seek a wider field of action in the newer States. They owe a duty to the cause of National American Education.

In addition to a State system of examination as a means of protecting the public schools against charlatans, ignoramuses, and humbugs generally, it is indispensable that every State have an efficient system of city, county, and township boards of examination.

These boards ought to be made up of each city, county, or town superintendent, together with from three to five professional teachers, themselves holders of high-grade certificates. They should have power to issue, on actual written examinations, certificates of different grades, valid for periods of time ranging from two to ten years, according to grade.

These boards ought to be paid a reasonable sum for their work, otherwise it will not be well done. They ought to be made up exclusively of practical teachers, for the same reason that only lawyers can legally examine law students applying for admission to the bar, that only physicians examine medical students, and that only clergymen pass on the fitness of theological students to enter the ministry. By combining a system of State, city, county, and town examinations, together with inter-state legislation, something might be done to raise the standard of public school teaching.

It is a matter of surprise that so little has already been done in this direction. It can only be accounted for by the fact that nine tenths of the men and women engaged in keeping school are intending and expecting to get out of the business as soon as they can. Otherwise, they would never submit to the humiliation of successive examinations by petty officials, who often know little or nothing about education, but who delight in a brief official importance.

It is urged against this plan of competitive, professional examinations in writing, that "percentages" represent mere scholarship, and fail to gauge the power to discipline, the tact to manage, and the skill to teach.

This may be true to some extent, but it is also certain that, while some good scholars may *fail* when submitted to the final test of the school-room, no ignorant teacher can possibly make a good teacher under any circumstances. There is a grade of scholarship below which no man or woman is fitted to make a trial of teaching. Above this standard, some will succeed and some will fail. So it is with graduates of the law schools, the divinity schools, and the medical schools.

It may be urged that boards of examination will show favoritism in issuing certificates to friends. So they will, unless the people elect incorruptible school officers, and appoint incorruptible teachers. The best laws ever framed, and the best systems ever devised, are never binding on corrupt or incapable executive officers.

It may be urged that the diploma of a college ought to be taken as a valid certificate of fitness to teach. Now a college-bred young man *may* or *may not* be qualified to teach. I have known many young men coming to California, with flying colors and fresh diplomas, who ignominiously failed to secure a certificate to teach even the lowest grade country school, on an examination in arithmetic, grammar, geography, history, reading, and spelling, so elementary in its character, that to a pupil of average attainment in the second grade of an ordinary grammar school, it would have been mere play. They not only showed no "fitness to teach," but they exhibited a most lamentable ignorance of the very elements required to be taught in every common school. They might have been brilliant in the dead languages, but they misspelled their mother tongue, they murdered English, and they couldn't cipher. There can be no safe and sure test, except actual examination.

I do not deny that the hobby of written examinations may be ridden to death. It has been wickedly said by somebody—doubtless some luckless examinee—that the leading object of many examinations is to give the examiners a chance to show off their own attainments. I have seen many sets of questions that seemed to be fossil curiosities, picked up during a life-long search after abnormal things —"tough sums" in arithmetic and algebra, the product of some mathematician run to seed; gleanings of the tag ends of the countless rules, and notes and exceptions, and annotations and explanations, and illustrations and idioms, of Lindley Murray, that great grammarian who wrote bad English, and made sad the hearts of unnumbered generations of school boys and school girls; twisted elliptical sentences to be parsed according to Smith, or Brown, or Greene, or Wells, or Weld, or Sanborn, or Kerl, or Hart, or Clark, or Quackenbos, or Bullion, or Pinneo, or Nokes, or Stokes, or Niles, or Stiles, or Thompson, or Pickwick; unheard-of words of crooked orthography, the gnarled growth of centuries of changes of the English tongue, strung together like onions, in a way that would have brought tears to the eyes of old Webster himself, that dear old philological bush-ranger, who fought orthography on his own hook, in defiance of all usage, and of all laws of linguistic warfare; questions in geography on zig-zag boundaries, on the length of all the rivers of all the world, from the Amazon down to the trout-brooks that we fished in when boys; on the distance of the classic towns of "You Bet" and "Red Dog," in California, from Nijni Novogorod and the sources of the Nile; on the direction of Brandy Gulch and Whisky Cañon from Ujiji and Petropaulovski; questions in history requiring the year and the day of the month of the settlement of every State in the Union, supplemented by senseless interrogatories on historical myths known only in our school text-books; impracticable questions on theory and practice of teaching, about what ought to be done under impossible conditions; questions about elements of penmanship that even such accomplished penmen as Greeley, or Choate, or Napoleon Bonaparte, couldn't answer; questions on Sanscrit roots no Brahmin ever heard of; questions on the constitution that would have floored the "Great Expounder;" questions on physiology that would puzzle Darwin; questions on natural philosophy at which Huxley or Tyndall would be dumb; questions which showed the examiner to be "stick, stark, staring mad," and which no sane man could answer. But a practical system of examinations presupposes a common-sense style of conducting them.

In conclusion, I submit the following propositions for the consideration of teachers, and educators, and legislators:

1. A comprehensive system of State, city, county, and town Boards of Examination.
2. Boards of Examination to be made up of State, city, county, or town superintendents, together with a limited number of professional teachers, appointed in the manner best suited to the school systems of the different States.
3. A graded series of teachers' certificates, from life diplomas down to temporary certificates, valid for one year, granted on actual examination only.
4. Examinations to be conducted in writing, and the percentages obtained in each study to be indorsed on the certificates.

5. A legal recognition by each State of the professional certificates issued in other States.

6. A provision for the legal recognition, by Boards of Examination in each State, of the normal school diplomas issued by the normal schools of other States and other countries.

7. A determined and combined effort to shape legislation so as to secure longer terms of office to State, city, county, and town superintendents, to members of Boards of Education, and to school trustees, thereby securing some degree of uniform progress in educational management.

8. A war of independence, to be waged against the outrageous system of the annual election of teachers, a plan which reduces them below the level of the holder of the smallest post-office in the gift of a victorious political party.

SPECIMEN SET OF QUESTIONS.

QUARTERLY EXAMINATION, JUNE, 1876.

ORDER OF EXAMINATION.

Subject	Credits	Subject	Credits
1. General Questions.		13. Penmanship	25
2. Orthography	100	14. Algebra	50
3. Grammar	100	15. Natural Philosophy	50
4. Written Arithmetic	100	16. Physiology	50
5. Geography	50	17. Natural History	50
6. *Reading (with oral exercises)	50	18. Constitution of United States and California	25
7. Theory and Practice	50	19. School Laws of California	25
8. Defining (word analysis)	50	20. Industrial Drawing	25
9. Mental Arithmetic	50	21. Vocal Music	25
10. *Oral Grammar	25		
11. History of the United States	50		
12. Composition	50	Total	1000

* The *Oral* Examination may be conducted at any time, by taking each applicant separately.

1. GENERAL QUESTIONS.

1. Name, age, birthplace.
2. Where educated.
3. Experience in teaching.
4. What certificate, if any.
5. Are you an applicant for a State certificate ?

2. SPELLING.

I. DICTATION PARAGRAPH.

[50 Credits. Three Credits off for each misspelled word, or misplaced capital.]

Had the Plantagenets, as at one time seemed likely, succeeded in uniting all France under their government, it is probable that England would never have had an independent existence. The noble language of Milton and Burke would have remained a rustic dialect, without a literature, a fixed grammar, or a fixed orthography, and would have been contemptuously abandoned to the use of boors. No man of English extraction would have risen to eminence, except by becoming, in speech and habits, a Frenchman.

II. WORDS.

[50 Credits. One Credit off for each misspelled word.]

harangue	vignette	diphtheria	corridor
fricasee	guarantee	professor	kindergarten
maintenance	rendezvous	Pestalozzi	convertible
blamable	curable	metempsychosis	vacillation
feasible	responsible	vaccination	indestructible
inexorable	noticeable	anonymous	musn't
independence	suppliance	wasn't	curriculum
contrivance	perseverance	immaculate	avoirdupois
farinaceous	sacrilegious	bissextile	technology
Isaiah	Matthew	sphericity	philologist
hieroglyphics	domicile	tyrannical	ammunition
defendant	pharmacy	inflammable	metaphysician
Buddhism			Mohammedanism

3. GRAMMAR.

[100 Credits. Time, 1½ hours.]

1. Write a synopsis of the verb *to speak*, in the indicative mood, third person, singular number, passive voice.

2. State three cases where the relative *that* must be used in preference to *who* or *which*, and illustrate each case by a sentence.

3. State all the *noun-suffixes* and *verb-suffixes* of inflection, in English.

4. Write the plurals of—1, focus; 2, index; 3, his; 4, memorandum; 5, animalcule.

5. Correct such of the following as are not, in your opinion, good English:

I. You had better go.
II. I had rather not do it.
III. The ship was soon lost sight of.
IV. It is the strongest case I ever heard of.
V. "The deadest piece of ironmongery in the trade."

6. "The squirrel eyes askance the chestnuts browning." Parse, with brief forms: 1, squirrel; 2, eyes; 3, askance; 4, browning; 5, chestnuts.

7. "Let not Ambition mock their useful toil,
Their homely joys and destiny obscure;
Nor Grandeur hear, with a disdainful smile,
The short and simple annals of the poor."

I. What kind of a sentence?
II. How many statements, or propositions?
III. Why a comma after *toil?*
IV. Why a semicolon after *obscure?*
V. Derivation of *simple?*

8. Parse, with brief models: 1, ambition; 2, grandeur; 3, hear; 4, obscure; 5, why are ambition and grandeur capitalized?

9. State five ways in which you can make use of a reading lesson in connection with grammar?

10. Correct the following sentences, and give a general rule or direction to pupils, covering each case:

I. The lecture was brief, short, and concise.
II. She is a teacher whom all are pleased with.
III. A pin was accidentally swallowed by a little girl without a head.
IV. We reached home, at length, after great difficulty, in a blinding snow-storm, through deep snow drifts.
V. It can be no worse for us, if we fail.

4. WRITTEN ARITHMETIC.

[100 Credits. Time, $2\frac{1}{2}$ hours.]

[NOTE.—Leave all your work on the paper; make no analysis or explanation unless called for, and then give in full.]

1. Perform the following operations: Multiply 3.05 by $2\frac{1}{5}$, subtract 0.21, divide the result by $\frac{1}{4}$, and add to it the quotient of 9 divided by 1-900th.

2. A man owned a square field, containing ten acres. He gave enough from it for a street 4 rods wide, all around it. How much land had he left?

3. How many feet of siding, six inches wide, will cover the sides of a house which is 24 feet by 30 feet, and 15 feet high, allowing $\frac{1}{6}$ for the lap. (No gable ends.)

4. A water tank is $3\frac{1}{2}$ wide and $5\frac{1}{2}$ feet long. How deep must it be to hold 8 hogsheads?

5. A man sold two horses for $240 each; on the one he gained 20 per cent., and on the other he lost 20 per cent. Did he gain or lose on the two transactions, taken together, and how much?

6. A vertical pole 99 feet high is standing in a public park, equally distant from the four corners of the park. The park is rectangular, and 16 rods by 36 rods. How far is it from the top of the pole to a corner of the park?

7. A merchant sold goods at 30 per cent. profit, and paid $\frac{1}{8}$ per cent. of his gross receipt for expenses, what is his net gain on sales amounting to $8,000?

8. Deduce the multiplier used in compound interest for finding the compound interest on any sum of money, at 5 per cent., for 5 years.

9. An eccentric old lady papered the walls of her room with 3 cent postage stamps. Her room was 16 by 10 feet, and 12 feet high; it had 2 windows, each $5\frac{1}{2}$ by 4 feet, and 2 doors, each 6 by 3 feet. A postage stamp is 1 inch long by 15-16 wide. What was the cost of papering her room?

10. On a promissory note from John Doe to Richard Roe, San Francisco, January 4, 1874, for $1,200, payable on demand, 10 per cent. a year, there were paid: March 19, 1874, $300; Aug. 15,

1874, $200; Dec. 21, 1874, $150. Write the note in due form, and compute the interest by the Business Rule up to the time of payment, Jan. 4, 1875.

5. GEOGRAPHY.

[50 Credits. Time, 1 hour.]

1. On a steamer trip from New Orleans to Pittsburgh, name the five largest cities you would pass, and the State in which each is situated.
2. State the following facts about Europe: 1, area; 2, population; 3, five chief cities; 4, height of Mt. Blanc; 5, five chief rivers.
3. What is the estimated population, 1876, of: 1, San Francisco; 2, California; 3, the United States; 4, Philadelphia; 5, St. Louis.
4. Name the five most populous islands in the world, in the order of population.
5. At what places on the earth is the sun vertical at noon, at least once a year?
6. How is it proved that the earth is an *oblate-spheroid?*
7. State the chief cause of ocean currents, and also two minor causes that influence them.
8. State the causes of the dense fogs that prevail off the coast of Chili and Peru, Oregon and California.
9. Name the three chief cities of: 1, New England; 2, the Middle States; 3, the Southern States; 4, the Western States; 5, the Pacific States.
10. Name the three leading countries in the production of each of the following: 1, cotton; 2, sugar; 3, gold; 4, iron; 5, wool.

6. READING.

[25 Credits. Time, 30 minutes.]

1. Illustrate the use of each of the following marks: 1, macron; 2, breve; 3; diaeresis; 4, cedilla; 5, caret.
2. Write ten words having the sound of ȧ in *half*.
3. By means of *accent*, and the notation of vowels used in Webster's Dictionary, indicate the correct pronunciation of the following words: 1, interesting; 2, museum; 3, irreparable; 4, tirade; 5, irrevocable.

4 and 5. Make the marks used in Webster's Dictionary to indicate the sound of each vowel in each of the following words: [Examiners will write the words upon the blackboards, omitting the notation. *One credit off for each error in notation.*]

āle	ĕnd	ōld	ŭp
ärm	vẽrge	ŏdd	ru̥de
a̤ll	pre̱y	möve	pụll
ădd	hêir	dọne	ûrge
ȧsk	pīne	wọlf	mōōn
whạt	pĭn	nôr	fo͝ot
âir	pïque	ūse	flȳ
ēve	thīrst		

7. METHODS OF TEACHING.

[50 Credits. Time, 1 hour.]

1. Explain the distinctive features of the methods of instruction introduced by Pestalozzi.
2. Name three important educational topics that are attracting the attention of educators, teachers, and school officers.
3. Name five books on *Teaching* that you would recommend to persons ignorant of both the science and the art of teaching.
4. What is the so-called *Grube System* of teaching arithmetic to beginners?
5. In addition to teaching the table, how would you teach square measure to a class?
6. Write ten questions on the local geography of the place where you are passing examination, such as you would put to a class of beginners.
7. Can you name two leading defects in the text-books on grammar now in use in this State?
8. What criticisms do you make on the arithmetics in use?
9. Explain the chemical changes that take place in the burning of a candle.
10. Explain to a class the cause of the strong sea breezes that prevail in Summer along the coast of California.

8. DEFINING AND WORD ANALYSIS.

[50 Credits.]

1. Derivation and root meaning of: 1, orthography; 2, syntax; 3, geography; 4, botany; 5, calculate.
2. Define *impediment*, and give two synonymous words.
3. Explain the difference between *diurnal* and *daily*, *rotation* and *revolution*.
4. Make a list of the Anglo-Saxon *prefixes* and *suffixes*.
5. What classes of words in our language are mainly of Teutonic or Anglo-Saxon origin; of Romanic origin?
6. Derivation and meaning of: 1, scrupulous; 2, supercilious.
7. Write a single sentence containing both *shall* and *will* correctly used.
8. Origin of: 1, volcano; 2, bonanza; 3, demijohn; 4, arcadian; 5, sybarite.
9. Define the expression, "resumption of specie payments."
10. Derivation of: 1, centennial; 2, exposition; 3, Philadelphia; 4, the title "Dom;" 5, international.

9. MENTAL ARITHMETIC.

[50 Credits. Time, ½ hour.]

[NOTE.—Questions to be read by the Examiner; only the answers required.]

1. What is 500 per cent. of 2/5?
2. What is the interest on $60 for 2½ months, at 6 per cent. a year?

3. One-half and one-fifth of a number, plus 6, equals the number; find the number.
4. Add 2/5 and 3/8.
5. How many feet in 40 rods?
6. At $12\frac{1}{2}$ cents each, how many oranges can be bought for $40?
7. Divide the decimal .4 by the decimal .05.
8. How many ounces in $4\frac{3}{4}$ pounds of gold?
9. In 9 rods, how many feet?
10. How many inches in 5/9 of a square foot?
11. Find the product of $5 \times 4 \times 6 \times 0 \times \frac{1}{2}$.
12. $150 - 20 - 8 - 5 - 9 - 10 - 9 - 6 - 8 - 6 - 7 - 6 - 8 - 7 - 9 - 8 - 7 = ?$
13. $1000 - 300 - 200 - 100 - 200 - 70 - 20 - 2 \div 9 \times 6 - 9 \div 7 = ?$
14. How many inches in 5/12 of a cubic foot?
15. How many times is $\frac{1}{2}$ a dollar contained in $\frac{1}{4}$ of a dollar?
16. Cost of $6\frac{1}{2}$ yards of calico, at 15 cents.
17. One thousand is five-sixths of what?
18. Four-fifths is what part of twenty?
19. Prime factors of 1728.
20. Interest of $1, at 6 per cent., for 2 years, 9 months, 21 days.
21. Interest of $300, for 2 years, 11 months, at 4 per cent.
22. $20 is what per cent. of $30?
23. Find $66\frac{2}{3}$ per cent. of $1200.
24. 24 is 120 per cent. of what?
25. What number, increased by 80 per cent.= 36?

11. HISTORY OF THE UNITED STATES.

[50 Credits ; 5 Questions, 8 Credits each.]

1. For what events in the history of the Revolution is Philadelphia distinguished? Boston?
2. Name four leading colonial wars, and one leading event in each.
3. Of the distinguished Americans during the Revolutionary war, name two leading statesmen, four leading generals, two leading orators, one foreign minister, and one leading financier.
4. During the war of secession, name four Union victories, and four Confederate victories, giving the year and the name of the victorious commander.
5. Name ten signers of the Declaration of Independence.

[One Question, Ten Credits.]

6. State in what way in our history the following persons distinguished themselves: 1, Alexander Hamilton; 2, Robert Morris; 3, Benjamin Franklin; 4, Charles Sumner; 5, John C. Calhoun.

12. COMPOSITION.

[50 Credits. Time, 1 hour.]

1. Write five brief directions about composition-writing, such as you would give to the highest grade in a Grammar School.
2. Write two directions about *paragraphing*.

3. What kind of composition-exercises would you give to children in a Primary School, during their third school year?

4. Give the "heads" of a composition about *Government.*

5. Write the most important rules of punctuation that you would give a class in composition, as follows: 1, two rules for the comma; 2, two rules for the semicolon; 3, one rule for the dash; 4, two rules for the exclamation mark; 5, two rules for quotation marks.

14. ALGEBRA.

[50 Credits; 5 Questions, 8 Credits each.]

1. Find the square root of $4a^4 - 12a^3 + 25a^2 - 24a + 16$.

2. Divide the number 5 into two such parts that twice their product increased by the sum of their squares may be equal to 25.

3. Find the value of x and y:

$$x^2 + xy = 28$$
$$y^2 + 3xy = 45$$

4. Difference between a pure and an affected quadratic equation?

5. Extract the cube root of $a^6 - 6a^5 + 15a^4 - 20a^3 + 15a^2 - 6a + 1$.

[One Question, Ten Credits.]

6. What are logarithms, who invented them, and what are their uses?

15. PHYSICS.

[50 Credits; 5 Questions, 8 Credits each.]

1. How far will a cannon ball, dropped from a height, fall in 4 seconds?

2. Give four illustrations of the correlation of *heat* and *motion.*

3. How is light supposed to be diffused.

4. A body would weigh 4 tons, 8,000 miles above the earth's surface, find its weight at the surface.

5. On what law of light does the action of the microscope depend?

[One Question Ten Credits.]

6. What are the laws discovered by Kepler that govern the motions and distances of the planets?

16. PHYSIOLOGY AND HYGIENE.

[50 Credits; 5 Questions, 8 Credits each.]

1. State two differences between the veins and the arteries.

2. State the difference between the functions of the cerebrum and the cerebellum.

3. Direct a class how to treat *headaches;* common *colds.*

4. In case the artery of the wrist or the ankle were cut, direct a pupil how to stop the bleeding until the arrival of a physician.

5. Give a class five rules for taking care of their eyes.

[One Question, Ten Credits.]

6. State the locality of: 1, the *patella*; 2, the *ulna*; 3, *scapula*; 4, *tibia*; 5, *hyoid bone*.

17. NATURAL HISTORY.

[50 Credits.]

1. What changes take place in the organs of a flower when it is made "double" by culture?
2. Name and classify five of the most beautiful flowers, indigenous to California.
3. Give the transformations of the frog.
4. How does the natural system of classification differ from the artificial system?
5. Mention the principal forest trees of this State.
6. What are the chief wild animals of this State, and where found?

18. CONSTITUTIONS OF THE UNITED STATES AND CALIFORNIA.

[25 Credits; 5 Questions, 4 Credits each.]

1. When was the Constitution of the United States framed; who was President of the Convention, and when was it adopted by a majority of the States.
2. Name five rights of the people guaranteed by the Constitution of the United States.
3. State the substance of two important amendments to the Constitution of the United States.
4. How is the United States Constitution amended?
5. What educational provisions does the Constitution of California contain?

[One Question, Five Credits.]

6. In framing the Constitution, why was each State, large or small, allowed two Senators?

19. SCHOOL LAW.

[25 Credits.]

1. What are the conditions for obtaining a life diploma?
2. In what three different ways are school moneys raised by taxation?
3. Name five provisions of the school law that are, in your opinion, good ones.
4. What are the provisions of the State law about educating negro children?
5. How is the State University supported?

20. DRAWING.

[25 Credits.]

1. Name any benefits derived from the study of drawing in the public schools.
2. What system of drawing has been adopted in this State?
3. What are the distinctive features of this system?
4. In a graded school, how much time would you give for drawing? In an ungraded school?
5. Define: 1, a right-angled triangle; 2, a circle; 3, a surface; 4, a vertical line; 5, a perpendicular line.

21. MUSIC.

[25 Credits.]

1. How can a teacher that cannot sing have singing in school?
2. Name two benefits arising from school singing.
3. How much time ought to be given to singing, and when should the time be taken?
4. What text-books on music have been adopted by the State Board of Education?
5. Write the scale.

VII. THE PROFESSIONAL TEACHERS OF CALIFORNIA.

LIST OF THE HOLDERS OF LIFE DIPLOMAS

WHICH HAVE BEEN ISSUED ONLY TO HOLDERS OF EDUCATIONAL DIPLOMAS THAT HAVE HAD TEN YEARS' EXPERIENCE IN TEACHING.

[The names of holders of diplomas who have permanently engaged in other pursuits are marked †; the names of holders deceased are marked *.]

Abbott, Warren .... '71
Aldrich, Abbie F............ '76
Allen, L. D................. '71
Allsopp, J. P. C............ '69
†Ames, Charles C........... '69
Ames, Martha............... '75
Anderson, J. W............. '68
Anderson, Mrs. C. A........ '73
Ashton, Mrs. N. J.......... '76
Atwood, Mrs. C. L.......... '67
Austin, Miss Minnie F...... '66
Babcock, W. S.............. '76
Bagnall, John .... '67
†Bailey, C. P.............. '68
†Baker, George F........... '73
Baldwin, Miss Nellie .... '75
Barnard, Miss A. S.......... '75
Barr, Miss Sara A........... '73
Batchelder, H. T........... '73
Baumgardner, Mrs. E. M.... '76
Beals, Mrs. C. R............ '72
Benjamin, C. V............. '72

Bennette, Fanny E. .... '69
Bennett, Miss Mary H. ...... '74
Black, Samuel T. .... '72
Black, Charles M. .... '74
Bloomer, A. C. .... '76
*Bodwell, Miss Mary L. ..... '66
Bolander, H. N. .... '68
Bradley, Theodore .... '66
Bragg, Mary J. .... '75
Braly, John H. 69
Brodt, A. W. .... '71
Brown, George .... '66
†Brown, F. R. .... '67
Brown, Miss S. L. .... '74
Bryerly, John R. .... '76
Buckman, F. S. S. .... '75
Bugbey, Mrs. B. N. .... '76
Bunnell, George W. .... '66
Burke, Lizzie K. .... '73
Campbell, Miss C. C. .... '72
Campbell, F. M. .... '73
Carlton, H. P. .... '66
†Casebolt, Miss M. A. .... '72
Castelhun, Miss Maria A. .... '74
Chapman, M. V. .... '72
Chalmers, Miss Annie B. ..... '75
Chestnutwood, Mrs. J. A. .... '75
Chestnutwood, Jno. A. .... '73
Childs, C. W. .... '68
Clappe, Mrs. L. A. K. .... '68
Clark, Dorcas .... '67
Clark, Mary E. .... '67
†Clark, Miss H. M. .... '66
*Clark, L. R. .... '70
Clark, M. C. .... '75
Cleveland, Miss E. A. .... '73
Coe, Eli G. .... '71
Conklin, E. B. .... '71
†Cook, Mrs. P. .... '70
Cook, Miss Hannah .... '73
†Cottle, Melville .... '69
Crane, Amanda .... '76
Craven, Andrew F. .... '74
Crawford, Mrs. J. F. .... '74
Crawford T. O. .... '75
Crosette, F. M. .... '76
Cross, C. W. .... '75
Crowhurst, Wm. .... '75
Crowell, C. H. .... '73
Cummings, C. C. .... '66
D'Arcy, Miss M. E. .... '72
Davies, J. S. .... '76
Davis, Mrs. Imogene W. ..... '75
Deane, Mrs. Margaret .... '71
Deetkin, Mrs. Lizzie G. ...... '74
Denman, James .... '66
Dodge, W. C. .... '74
Dooner, John .... '75
Drake, A. J. .... '71
Drake Chas. M. .... '76
Duane, Mrs. A. S. .... '72
DuBois, Mrs. A. E. .... '68
Dubois, J. B. .... '76
Duenkel, Wm. .... '75
Dwyer, James .... '75
†Eickhoff, J. Henry .... '73
Farley, A. J. .... '72
Field, Miss Carrie P. .... '75
Finch, J. B. .... '71
Fink, Augusta P. .... '75
Fisk, Julia A. .... '76
Fitzgerald, A. L. .... '71
Foster, Mrs. J. A. .... '73
Foster, Mrs. Emily .... '74
Fowler, Miss Laura T. .... '68
Freeman, G. N. .... '75
Fry, W. H. .... '72
†Fuller A. L. .... '69
Furlong, George .... '76
Gabriel, Mrs. C. E. .... '74
Garrison, Gazena A. .... '76
* Gates, Freeman .... '72
Gorman, W. J. .... '73
Goodrich, A. H. .... '68
†Graf, Miss Minnie .... '72
Grant, Miss Ella G. .... '75
Grant, Miss Helen A. .... '75
Gray, John C. .... '69
Greer, Miss Jane E. .... '75
Griffith, Mrs. Aurelia .... '71
Gunn, Miss S. M. .... '75
Gwinn, James M. .... '71
† Hamilton, Miss Addie ...... '73
† Hammond, Josiah Shaw .... '73
Harlow, James .... '67
† Hart, W. C. .... '73
Hall, Frances M. .... '76
Hatch, J. L. .... '75
Hayes, John .... '76
Henning, Irving P. .... '75
Herbst A. .... '73
Higby, H. C. .... '75
Hill, Miss A. H. .... '73
Hill, Whitman H. .... '71

Hodgdon, Miss S. J. . . . . '72
Hoffman, Mrs. Mary L. . . . . . . '73
† Hoitt, Ira G. . . . . '66
† Holbrook, T. W. J. . . . . '66
Holder, W. W. . . . . '71
† Holmes, Ahira . . . . '66
† Holmes, Ellis H. . . . . '66
Houghton, Miss E. W. . . . . . . '66
Howe, H. H. . . . . '68
† Howe, J. M. . . . . '67
Howe, Converse. . . . . '75
Hucks, Annie E. . . . . '75
Hudson, J. A. . . . . '73
Humphrey, E. D. . . . . '68
Humphreys, Miss L. A. . . . . . '74
Humphreys, Miss M. A. . . . . . '74
Hunt, Miss Carrie L. . . . . '70
Hurley, Miss J. M. A. . . . . '73
Hutton, Chas. E. . . . . '73
Houghton, George E. . . . . '76
Itsell, A. J. . . . . '74
Jackman, Samuel H. . . . . '70
Jessup, Miss S. A. . . . . '72
Jewett, Annie S. . . . . '76
Jewett, Miss Susan N. . . . . '72
Johnson, J. W. . . . . '76
Johns, Charles T. . . . . '71
Johnson, J. G. . . . . '70
Jones, George W. . . . . '71
Jones, Thornton J. . . . . '75
Keegon, Mary A. . . . . '75
Kelso, John R. . . . . '76
Kennedy, Kate . . . . '67
Kennedy, J. G. . . . . '71
Kennedy, W. W. . . . . '71
Kercheval, Miss Jennie G. . . . '69
Kincaid, Mrs. Mary W. . . . . . . '76
Kingman, Mrs. M. F. . . . . '75
Kinne, H. C. . . . . '72
Kirkpatrick, J. M. . . . . '69
Knowlton, Ebenezer. . . . . '66
Lamb, Miss Irene. . . . . '73
† Leadbetter, W. R. . . . . '70
† Leggett, Joseph . . . . '72
† Leonard, T. C. . . . . '66
Levinson, Miss Rosa. . . . . '72
Levy, Daniel . . . . '73
Lighthall, G. E. . . . . '71
Lillie, John B. . . . . '75
Lipowitz, Max. . . . . '75
† Littlefield, J. D. . . . . '66
Loomis, Miss Amanda. . . . . . . '68
Loudon, Jacques. . . . . '76
Lovett, C. M. . . . . '75
Lubeck, Mrs. Julia M. . . . . . . '75
Luckey, W. T. . . . . '67
Lynch, Miss Frances. . . . . '66
Mack, George C. . . . . '66
Mackall, J. N. . . . . '72
† Makinney, H. E. . . . . '68
Mann, Azro L. . . . . '67
Manning, Miss Agnes M. . . . . '73
† Marks, Bernhard . . . . '66
* Marriner, R. K. . . . . '66
Marsh, Mrs. S. W. . . . . '71
† McBride, H. E. . . . . '75
McCarty, A. F. . . . . '75
McChesney, J. B. . . . . '67
McDonald, A. H. . . . . '68
McDonald, Mrs. A. H. . . . . '75
McDonald, W. P. . . . . '75
McFadden, Miss Agnes. . . . . . '75
McFadden, W. M. . . . . '71
Menefee, C. A. . . . . '71
Metzger, C. L. . . . . '75
Middleton, Mrs. Eliza F. . . . . '75
Miller, Miss Ora E. . . . . '73
Millette, Percival C. . . . . '71
Milliken, Mrs. Ellen A. . . . . . '73
McGlashan, C. F. . . . . '76
Mumford, Mrs. M. E. . . . . '76
Minns, George W. . . . . '66
Moore, John A. . . . . '71
Morgan, Mrs. L. A. . . . . '72
† Morrill, Joseph C. . . . . '67
Morris, George F. . . . . '67
Morris, N. Z. . . . . '73
*Morse, Augustus, Jr. . . . . '67
Murphy, Miss Mary M. . . . . . '75
Myrick, Thomas S. . . . . '66
Moore, Mrs. Mary B. . . . . '75
Mayborn, Mrs. M. J. . . . . '76
McKenzie, Margaret. . . . . '76
McCormick, Harriet. . . . . '76
Nelson, Henry A. . . . . '71
Nicholson, Thomas. . . . . '74
† Nutting, H. N. . . . . '66
O'Connor, Joseph . . . . '71
Olinger A. F. . . . . '72
Otis, James . . . . '73
† Overend, Miss Lizzie. . . . . . . '73
Oliner, A. W. . . . . '76
O'Conner, Maria E. . . . . '76

†Parker, Miss Jean .... '71
Pascoe, Miss Mary I......... '72
†Pearson, Dana C............ '75
Peck, George H............. '75
†Pelton, John C............. '66
†Penwell, S. A.............. '68
Phelps, Mrs. M. W.......... '74
Potter, M. B................ '71
Powell, Miss Elizabeth...... '75
Power, Frank .... '71
Prescott, Miss D. S.......... '71
Preston, E. M.............. '69
†Price, Caroline .... '67
Prior, Philip................ '71
Putman, J. E............... '75
Randall, A. H.............. '68
Rattan, Volney.............. '74
Redway, J. W.............. '76
Reed, L. W................ '70
Reynolds, Mrs. F. E......... '72
Rogers, James.............. '76
Rose, T. H................. '68
Rousseau, E............... '69
Rowe, Miss A. A............ '73
†Rowell, W. K.............. '66
Ryder, Miss L. E............ '76
Salisbury, Mary A.......... '76
Sanders, W. A.............. '69
Sankey, M. J............... '75
Schellhous, E. J............ '69
Seawell, J. H............... '76
Shaw, Miss E. A............ '72
Shearer, S. M.............. '72
Shearer, Mrs. C. O.......... '73
Sherman, E. B.............. '76
Sherman, Fannie M.......... '75
Shipley, J. C................ '73
Short, Miss Julia B.......... '75
Sibley, J. M................ '66
†Simon, Miss Frances........ '72
Simonton, George W......... '66
Slavan, Miss A. E........... '72
Sollinger, J. A.............. '76
Smith, Miss Annie .... '68
Smith, Miss Carrie L......... '72
Smith, Chas. S.............. '76
Smith, Miss Jessie .... '72
Smith, W. A. C............. '68
Smith, Miss Jennie.......... '74
Southworth, Mrs. E. A....... '68
Standeford, Mrs. N. D....... '75
Steel, Thomas H............ '75
Stincen, Miss Alice M........ '73
†Stone, H. P................ '71
Stone, D. C................ '66
†Stone, Mrs. B. H.......... '73
Stowell, Fannie A........... '74
Stowell, Miss M. E.......... '72
Stowell, Miss P. M.......... '72
Stratton, James............. '66
Sullivan, Miss Kate.......... '72
Sumner, J. H............... '73
Swett, John .... '67
†Swett, Mrs. Mary L......... '66
†Swezey, S. I. C............ '67
† Tait, George .... '66
† Taylor, Robert .... '66
Temple, Miss Emma .... —
Templeton, Miss L. S........ '72
Templeton, M. L............ '67
Thompson, Helen............ '72
Thurber, A................. '71
Thurston, E. T............. '69
† Trafton, Dr. A............ '71
Thurton, Sarah L............ '75
Todd, H. J................. '76
Towle, C. B................ '76
† Upham, Isaac............. '69
Walsh, Miss Nellie E......... '75
Warren, C. G............... '69
Warren, R. B............... '70
Waterman, S. D............ '71
Watson, Mrs. C. R........... '72
Watson, Miss Mary J......... '72
Watkins, Emory .... '75
Watson, B. J............... '75
Watson, Miss Lizzie J....... '74
Weir, Miss Sarah J.......... '68
Wells, Mrs. Laura H......... '71
Wermuth, Hamilton.......... '71
Wheelock, Mrs. D. B........ '73
White, Silas A.............. '71
White, T. B................ '72
White, William............. '68
White, Miss Louisa E....... '75
Williams, W. J. G.......... '69
Wilson, H. R............... '71
Wilson, Jas. K.............. '75
Wood, Mrs. E. A........... '72
Woodruff, Miss Frances A... '70
Woodworth, Miss Janette E.. '75
Woodworth, Mrs. A. W..... '75
Wright, Mrs. A. E.......... '76
Westby, Miss S. M.......... '76
Wade, Margaret .... '76
Yates, W. A................ '74

VIII. HOLDERS OF STATE EDUCATIONAL DIPLOMAS

NOTE.—State diplomas are issued only to persons that have been holders of First Grade Certificates for at least one year, and that have taught at least five years.

*Deceased. †Not teaching.

Ables, Thomas J.
Adams, Clara A.
Adams, W. J.
Aldrich, Abbie F.
Alderson, M. J.
Alexander, Mary J.
Ames, Martha.
Anderson, C. A.
Ashbrook, M. V.
Ashbrook, T. P.
Ashley, Ella E.
Ashley, Julia V.
Ashton, Mrs. N. Jennie.
Augustine, S. M.
Ayers, Mary J.
Babcock, William S.
Baker, Samuel D.
Baldwin, F. D.
Banks, Jerome.
Barbour, Aaron C.
Barthelow, Mrs. A. W.
Beck, Mrs. N. B.
Betancue, Lizzie.
Biggs, Thomas.
Bightmire, S. A.
Bissell, Joseph.
Bloomer, A. C.
Boardman, C. F.
Bolton, H.
Bonnard, Eureka A.
Boyle, Sarah J.
Boynton, Kate.
Boynton, S. S.
Bradshaw, W. R.
Bragg, Mary J.
Breschen, Seraphine.
Brier, K. W.
Brigham, Fannie E.
Brigham, Julia P.
Broadbent, E.
Brooks, E. R.
Brophy M.
Brown, A. G.
Brown, Chas. W.
Brown, George J.
Brown, J. B.
Brown, Sarah E.
Brumsley, M. I.
Bryant, Annie.
Buckman, F. S. S.
Bunnell, Mrs. Alice.
Bush, Mrs. E. A.
Butterfield, S. H.
Carr, Ezra S.
Campbell, Amy T.
Case, E. L.
Castelhun, Mary A.
*Chase, Carrie M.
Chesnutwood, Mrs. J. A.
Ciprico, Anita C.
Clark, W. J.
Clay, William T.
Colby, Julia E.
Congdon, Jas. S.
Connolly, J. J.
Conrad, C. C.
Cooper, Mrs. F. A.
Cory, A. A.
Coulter, Leonard.
Crane, Amanda.
Crane, George.
Crawford, T. O.
Crichton, Mrs. A. M.
Crocker, L. H.
Cross, C. W.
Crothers, Margaret I.
Culbertson, Mary K.
Curragh, J. M.
Daniels, Mrs. S. B.
Davidson, Mrs. Nannie S.
Davis, Mrs. Imogene.
Davis, J. T.
†Davis, Sadie.
DeNure, D. D.
Dixon, Bessie.
Dolliver, Clara G.
Dooner, John.
Doyle, Irene.
Doyle, Mrs. James A.
Dozier, A. W.
Dozier, Melville.
Drake, Charles M.
Drake, Elmer.
DuBois, John B.
Dunbar, Annie S.
Dunbar, S. G. S.
Dwyer, James W.
Edwards, W. H.
Elliott, Ella J.
Elliott, Mary E.
Ellis, Mary C.
Estabrook, Mary A. H.
Evans, Ellen A.
Evans, Ellen G.
Fairchild, Hattie M.
Fallon, Joseph K.
Feller, Lorenzo.
Fenton, H. W.
Fisk, Juliet A.
Flint, Almira T.
Floyd, Enos F.
Folger, H. C.
Fonda, Charles E.
Foss, B. R.
Foss, Wm. F. F.
Foster, Mrs. Julia.
Fowler, B. F.
Fox, John.
Frissell, Sarah E.
Furlong, Robert.
Gabriel, Mrs. C. E.
Garlick, J. P.
Garrison, Gazena A.
Geer, Emily F.
Geis, S. W.
Germain, Clara.
Goepp, G.
Godfrey, G. K.
Gordon, Wellington.
Gould, M. J.
Granger, F. C.
Grant, E.
Gray, Annie L.
Greer, C. E.
Gunn, E. L.
Gunn, Sarah W.
Guthrie, N. L.
Goodcell, Henry, Jr.
Garin, Paul A.
Greer, Mary D.
Haislip, Benjamin F.
Hall, Annie J.
Hall, F. M.
Hall, Maggie J.
Ham, Charles H.
Hayburn, Annie T.
Hamilton, Hiram M.
Hamilton, Rev. Hiram.
Hamilton, Mrs. W. H. H.
Hamilton, James T.
Hamill, Amelia.
Harkness, Margaret.
Hartmeyer, Mrs. S. L.
Harvey, Oliver T.
Havens, Carrie.
Hawks, Carrie M.
Hawkins, J. O.
Hazen, J. P.
Heckman, H. H.
Henning, Irving P.
Hewett, Roscoe.
Hiatt, Pleasant.
Higby, H. C.
Hinton, J. M.
Hoffman, Mrs. Mary L.

Horton, Geo. Wallace.
Holbrook, Edw.
Holmes, M. D,
Howard, Emma.
Howe, Converse.
Howe, E. P.
Howell, S. S.
Hubbell, S. C.
Hughes, A. B.
Humphreys, L. A.
Humphreys, M. A.
Hunt, B. E.
Huntsinger, Mrs. Jennie.
*Ingraham, Mrs. R. F.
Jacks, Fannie.
Jamison, J. H. S.
Janes, Emma.
Jaycoax, Mrs. A. S.
Jenks, David W.
Jewett, Annie S.
Jewett, Fidelia.
Johnson, G. N.
Johnson, G. W.
Johnson, Joseph W.
Jones, Addison.
Jordon, John F.
Jordan, Maggie L.
Kane, Richard.
Keegan, Mary A.
Kellogg, M. D.
Kelso, John R.
Kelton, Mrs. Mary A.
Kendall, Sylvia A.
Kennedy, J. F.
Kenniston, Chas. M.
Kerr, Theodore T.
Kimball, C. A.
King, Charles E.
King, R. M.
Kingman, Mrs. M. V.
Kinkade, Letitia.
Klink, John F.
Knighton, William A.
Knowlton, E. L.
Kottinger, H. M.
Kratzer, Lella.
Lafferty, I. N.
Lambert, Daniel.
Lander, F. L.
Langan, George.
Laurie, B. M.
Law, John K.
Leach, Miss Mira.
Libby, Mrs. Joseph S.
Lighte, Pauline S.
Lillie, Sarah P.
Lippowitz, Max.
Little, Mary.
Loag, Emily T.
Lloyd, Mary A.
Loofbourrow, Elias.
Lovett, Charles E.
Lynch, Miss Tillie S.
Lynch, W. F. B.
Lyser, Albert.
Magoon, Wm. H.
Martin, A.
Martin, E. J.
Martin, James M.
Marvin, A.
Mathews, Mrs. M. E.
McArthur, Annie.
McCarty, Thomas.
McColgan, Kate F.
McCormack, Harriet T.
McDonald, Mrs. N. R.
McDonald, W. P.
McDonald, Kate.
McDonald, J. J.
McDonall, Mrs. J.
McEwen, John.
McFadden, John.
McGowan, Patrick H.
McHugh, Peter.
McKean, Lottie.
McKusick, H. P.
McManus, A. C.
McPhee, V. J.
McReynolds, Jos.
Mea, John F.
†Meagher, John F.
Merrill, Ida M.
Merritt, Julia E.
Metzger, C. L.
Michener, Mrs. M. E.
Middleton, A. W.
Middleton, Mrs. Eliza F.
Miles, Mrs. R. S.
Miller, John.
Miller, Lafayette.
Miller, N. J.
Miller, John H.
Milliken, Mrs. E. A.
Minta, Wesley.
Mitchell, Fannie.
Mondram, F. V. C.
Montgomery, A. S.
Moore, Mrs. B. F.
Morford, N. A.
Morgan, Richard.
Morgan, Rose E.
Mullens, H.
Mumford, Mrs. M. E.
Murnan, John T.
Murphy, Mary.
Norman, L. F.
Norvell, Jos. A.
Neill, M. A. O.
O'Connor, Maria.
O'Laughlen, Mrs. Nellie.
Oliver, A. W.
Oliver, Mrs. C. F.
Oliver, J. C.
Ormstrong, Flora S.
Otis, C. W.
Overend, E.
Owen, Georgie.
Owens, Nellie M.
Page, Lizzie.
Palmer, R. M.
Parker, Flora A.
Parker, James L.
Peachy, Thomas G.
Peadry, Frank A.
Pearce, Carrie.
Peck, A. W.
Pedler, F. A.
Pendegast, H. B.
*Penwell, Mrs. L. M.
Pitcher, Charlotte M.
Powell, David.
Powell, Elizabeth.
Powers, Talbot P.
Prag, Mary
Pratt, Mary E.
Price, Harrison.
Putnam, J. E.
Ray, J. H.
Rayl, Mrs. Martha.
Reavis, Walter Scott.
Redway, Jacques W.
Renfro, Lewis C.
Rice, L.
Righter, F. M.
Roberts, Lizzie.
Robertson, William A.
Robertson, George B.
Robinson, Mrs. M. S. P.
Rogers, Arthur.
Rogers, James.
Roper, J. W.
Royall, J. P.
Royce, Ella J.
Ryan, Amanda.
Ryder, L. E.
Sankey, Mrs. Mary J.
Saunders, Samuel.
Saxon, T. A.
Sears, Marion.
Seawell, J. H.
Shaw, Annie J.
Shearer, Mrs. C. C.
Sherman, E. B.
Sherman, Ella Imogene.
Sherman, M. F.
Sexton, Mrs. Ella M.
Sickal, M. T.
Sill, Prof. E. R.
Sinex, Rev. J. H.
Slack, Clay H.
Smith, James D.
Smith, Ansell.
Smith, Grace.
Smith, James D.
Sollinger, J. A.
Soule, Maria L.
Southeimer, Jno. J.
Spring, Mrs. Fannie.
Squires, W. E.
Standish, H. M.
Standeford, N. D.
Stegman, Mattie A.
Stevenson, Helen R.
Stincen, Emma E. C.
Stoddard, C. W.

Stone, W. W.
Stowell, F. A.
Sturges S.
Swain, Orlando E.
Swan, Amanda.
Taylor, Mrs. H. P
Thomas, J. R.
Thompson, Louisa
Thompson, J. N.
Tillotson, Henry Ira
Todd, H. J.
Towle, Mrs. Lizzie B.
Towle, S. G.
Trout, Daniel H.
True, Charles F.
Turner, H. F.
Underwood, J. G.
Van Dorn, V. J.
Van Schaick, Mrs. Mary A.
Vestal, F. A.
Walbridge, Jennie M.
Waldron, S. A.
Walker, Alice
Walker, Charles H.
Wallace, Alma
Wallace, W. B.
Walter, Emelyn.
†Wanzer, Mrs. L. M. F.
Ward, Mary A.
Webb, Sallie B.
Weeks, M. D.
Wells, Addie H.
Wells, Jos. H.
Wenk, Robert E.
Westbay, L. M.
Weston, Ada.
Wheelock, Mrs. D. R.
White, Emmons.
White, Mrs. Sara.
White, A. F.
Whitmore, Ella L.
Wicks, John T.
Wideman, James
Wilson, H. C.
Wood, Jessie.
Wood, Mrs. N. A.
Woodward, Mrs. N. Zoraida.
Wooll, Hattie.
Wozencraft, W. R.
Wright, Mrs. E.
Wright, J. M.
Wythe, Sarah J.
Yates, Lizzie.
Young, Nestor A.
Yule, John.
Zimmerman, William.
Tyrus, Mary A.

IX. NOTES OF PROMINENT TEACHERS.

D. C. Stone taught in Marysville, from 1854 to '68, and organized there one of the best schools in the State. In 1868, he removed to Oakland, and established a "Family School." In 1873, he was appointed teacher of natural sciences in the San Francisco Girls' High School, and, in 1876, was made Deputy City Superintendent.

J. B. McChesney began teaching at Forbestown, 1857, but soon removed to Nevada City, where he organized first a Grammar School and then a High School. In 1865, he was made Principal of the Oakland High School, where he is still teaching.

*Freeman Gates was a pioneer in the schools of San Jose, and afterwards County Superintendent. He subsequently founded the San Jose Institute.

Joseph Leggett founded the Grass Valley High School, with brilliant success; studied law; removed to San Francisco; was made Examining Teacher, in 1872; Deputy City Superintendent, 1874 and 1875; and a lawyer in 1876.

Melville Cottle was a pioneer teacher in Stockton, and was four years County Superintendent of San Joaquin County.

Isaac Upham taught in Butte County for several years; organized a fine school at Oroville, and was subsequently an able County Superintendent of Butte County and of Yuba County.

George H. Peck taught the first Public School in Sacramento, 1854; taught in San Francisco, from 1860 to 1865; and was County Superintendent of Los Angeles, in 1874–'75.

*Augustus Morse, Jr., was a teacher at Martinez; afterwards Principal of the Grass Valley High School, and then County Superintendent of Nevada County.

A. H. Randall organized the Stockton High School, which he has made one of the most thorough in the State.

A. H. Goodrich was a pioneer teacher in Placer County, where he held the office of County Superintendent for four years, and where he is still teaching.

George W. Simonton taught for many years at Vallejo, and was for four years County Superintendent of Solano County.

Dr. E. J. Schellhouse has taught for twenty years in various counties in the State, and is well known as an enthusiastic lecturer.

Dr. T. H. Rose taught several years at Benicia, made a fine Grammar School at Los Angeles, and organized a High School.

J. M. Sibley, in 1854, founded the Folsom Grammar School, in which he taught for ten years. He subsequently taught at Oakland and Sonoma, and for the last ten years has been teaching in the San Francisco Boys' High School.

A. H. McDonald, Principal of the Sacramento Grammar School, has taught for many years in various parts of the State.

F. M. Campbell began teaching near Vallejo; was for several years a popular teacher in the Brayton College School, and for six years has been the efficient City Superintendent of the Oakland Schools.

George W. Bonnell was Principal of the Spring Valley School, San Francisco; was afterwards Principal of San Francisco Latin School; and is now Professor of Latin and Greek in the State University.

Professor Martin Kellogg was for several years Professor of Ancient Languages in the College of California, and has been from the beginning a Professor in the State University; he contributed some valuable articles to the *California Teacher*, and has frequently lectured at State institutes.

W. C. Dodge, who began teaching in the State in 1854, has taught for many years in Alameda County.

M. L. Templeton was Principal of the Sacramento High School, and afterwards of the Woodland Grammar School, in both of which he was eminently successful.

B. J. Watson was for many years a prominent teacher in Nevada County, where he became County Superintendent.

Alfred Thurber founded the Pacheco School, and has been for six years County Superintendent of Contra Costa.

Sparrow Smith was for many years a teacher in Sacramento County, and also County Superintendent.

George K. Godfrey was a pioneer in the northern counties of the State. He has served twelve years as County Superintendent in Shasta and Siskiyou Counties.

C. W. Childs was for several years a teacher in El Dorado County; he is now Principal of the Suisun School, and County Superintendent of Solano County.

H. T. Batchelder has been a leading teacher in Butte County for many years, and also a County Superintendent.

John Bagnall was for many years a teacher in various of the central counties, and was one term County Superintendent of Alpine County. He has been for several years in San Francisco, noted for his success as a teacher in the evening school. Under disabilities, which would have discouraged most men, he has done vastly more in education than hundreds of other teachers who walk without crutches.

Azro L. Mann taught for several years at Marysville, but has gained his reputation chiefly by his success as head of the classical department of the San Francisco Boys' High School.

Mrs. Maria McGilvray, twenty-two years a teacher in various parts of the State, is still a vigorous and capable worker.

Mrs. J. H. Nevins has been twenty-three years a teacher in the State, thirteen of which have been in San Francisco.

James Stratton began teaching in the State in 1853; was several years Principal of the Washington School, San Francisco, and is now Principal of a Grammar School, in Oakland.

Miss Mary A. Hoyt taught the first Grammar School in

Los Angeles, where she was for many years a successful educator.

Percival C. Millette, a pioneer, was County Superintendent of Placer County in 1857, and has taught ever since in numberless county schools.

X. STATE EDUCATIONAL SOCIETY.

In his circular calling the State Teachers' Institute of 1863, Superintendent Swett thus alluded to the importance of a State Society:

Educational conventions, in every part of our country, express a general desire for a distinct and definite recognition of the occupation of teaching by forms equivalent to those now existing in law, medicine, and theology. It is true, there are many who make teaching a temporary occupation, a stepping-stone to other pursuits, and there is no objection to this when they are duly qualified for the noblest of human duties; but there is a large class, becoming larger every year, who desire to make it the occupation of a life—an occupation which calls for a range of acquirements and a height of qualifications fully equal to that of the liberal professions.

Why should not the pioneer teachers of this State, in the next Institute, take similar measures of self-organization, self-recognition, and self-examination, and raise themselves above the humiliating necessity of submitting to an examination by members of other professions, or of no professions at all? A State Educational Society could be organized by those who shall pass the next examination by the State Board, those who hold diplomas of graduation from normal schools, and the Professors in the various colleges and collegiate schools of the State. This society could become legally incorporated at the next session of the Legislature, and other members could be admitted from time to time, by passing a regular examination, and receiving diplomas. Such certificates would soon be gladly recognized by unprofessional examiners—many of whom, though men of education, feel that they are not duly qualified to sit in judgment on the competency of teachers for their peculiar work—as the best possible assurance of fitness to teach. And teachers may rest assured that legislative enactments would soon follow, making such diplomas *prima facie* evidence of ability to teach in any part of the State, without further examination.

Some such steps we are called upon to take by the large number of accomplished men and women who are entering on our vocation. We are called upon to act, not only in justice to scholarship and talent, but in self-defense against impostors and pretenders; and we may honestly avow a desire to exclude all who unworthily or unfitly intrude themselves into the noble office of teaching.

A State Society would unite the teachers of our State in the bonds of fraternal sympathy; a certificate of membership would entitle the holder to the aid of members in all parts of the State; it would be a passport of employment when he should change his residence; it would entitle him to the substantial benefits of an honorable reception among all teachers; and a small annual membership fee would soon constitute a fund for the establishment of a teacher's journal, as the organ of the society.

The subject of a State professional society being brought before the Institute, the plan was advocated by John E. Benton, Theodore Bradley, and others.

A committee was appointed with Mr. Bradley, Chairman, who made a report, and requested all interested in forming such a society to meet after the final adjournment of the Institute.

A State Educational Society was soon afterwards formed on the plan recommended, with the following constitution:

PREAMBLE.

We, as teachers of California, in order to further the educational interests of the State, to give efficiency to our school system, to furnish a practical basis for united action among those devoted to the cause in which we are engaged, and for those purposes to elevate the office of teacher to its true rank among the professions, do hereby adopt the following

CONSTITUTION.

NAME.

SECTION 1. This organization shall be known as the "California Educational Society."

SEC. 2. All holders of State Life Diplomas, or State Educational Diplomas, shall be eligible to membership on the recommendation of the Executive Committee, and the payment, in advance, of an admission fee of five dollars.

SEC. 3. Any member may be expelled for unprofessional conduct by a two-thirds vote of members present at any regular meeting; *provided*, that a copy of the charges be deposited with the Recording Secretary at least four weeks before the meeting at which the charges are acted upon, and immediate notice thereof be given to the accused.

The society assumed the publication of the *California Teacher*, and elected annually a Board of Editors, until 1873, when the control of the journal passed into the hands of the State Superintendent.

LIST OF MEMBERS OF THE STATE EDUCATIONAL SOCIETY.

[NOTE.—The names of deceased members are marked *; of those retired from the profession †.]

Anderson, J. W.
Anderson, Mrs. A. B.
Atwood, Mrs. C. L.
Austin, Miss M. F.
Allen, L. D.
Adams, J. G.
Bradley, Theodore.
Bagnall, John.
Bolander, Henry N.
Brown, George.
†Brown, F. R.
Braly, J. H.
Brodt, A. W.
†Baker, G. F.
Beanston, George.
Bennette, Fannie E.
Barre, Miss S. A.
Bragg, Mary J.
Baldwin, Nellie.
†Brown, Louisa.
†Cottle, Melville.
Cleveland, Miss E. A.
Cook, Hannah.
Denman, James.
*Deal, M. S.
Dubois, Mrs. A. E.
Deane, Mrs. Margaret.
Dolliver, Clara J.
Doud, Nettie.
Deetken, Mrs. L. G.
†Fitzgerald, O. P.
†Flood, Noah F.
Fuller, A. L.
Finch, J. B.
Farley, A. J.
Fenton, H. W.
Fitzgerald, A. L.
Fink, Miss A. P.
Field, Miss C. P.
Fowler, Laura S.
Goodrich, S. H.
†Holmes, Ahira.
†Holmes, Ellis H.
Humphrey, E. D.
Higbie, Alfred.
†Huntley, O. H.
†Hoitt, Ira G.
Howe, Converse.
Hunt, Carrie L.
Hucks, Annie.
Johns, Chas. T.
Kellogg, Martin.
Knowlton, Ebenezer.
Kennedy, W. W.
Kennedy, J. G.
Kennedy, Kate.
Kincaid, Mary W.
†Leonard, T. C.
†Louttit, J. A.
Lyser, Albert.
Levison, Rosa.
Myrick, Thos. S.
†Marks, Bernhard.
McGlynn, A. E.
Makinney, H. E.
*Morris, Geo. F.
McChesney, J. B.
†McBride, H. E.
Moore, John A.
Nutting, H. N.
Nicholson, Thomas.
O'Connor, Joseph.
Peck, Geo. H.
†Pelton, John C.
Preston, E. M.
†Penwell, S. A.
Prior, Philip.
Pascoe, Mary.
†Parker, Jean.
Prescott, Miss D. S.
†Rowell, W. K.
Randall, Ambrose H.
Rousseau, E.
Rattan, Volney.
†Swezey, S. I. C.
Stratton, James.
Swett, John.
Smith, Sparrow A.
Stone, D. C.
Sibley, J. M.
Schellhouse, E. J.
Scott, M. M.
Smith, Jessie.
Smith, Jennie.
Stowell, Miss M. E.
Stowell, Miss P. M.
Slaven, Miss A. E.
Sullivan, Kate.
Sumner, J. H.
Stone, W. W.
Smith, J. D.
Shaw, Miss E. A.
†Tait, George.
*Townsend, Dennis.
Templeton, M. L.
Thurston, E. T.
Thompson, Helen.
True, Chas. F.
Upham, Isaac.
White, Silas A.
White, William.
Winn, A. T.
Williams, W. J. G.
Warren, R. B.
Wermouth, Hamilton.
Wade, Margaret.
Zimmerman, Wm.

PRESIDENTS OF THE STATE EDUCATIONAL SOCIETY.

1. John Swett.
2. George W. Minns.
3. Theodore Bradley.
4. James Denman.
5. D. C. Stone.
6. Bernhard Marks.
7. John Swett.
8. E. H. Holmes.
9. J. W. Anderson.

SECRETARIES.

1. Bernhard Marks.
2. Silas A. White.
3. Mrs. C. L. Atwood.
4. Mrs. Aurelia Griffith.

XI. STATE SERIES OF TEXT-BOOKS.

In 1864, the State Board of Education, consisting of Governor Stanford, Surveyor-General Houghton, and State Superintendent Swett, met and adopted a State series of text-books, taking the series recommended by vote of the State Teachers' Institute that met in San Francisco, May 7–10, 1863.

BOOKS ADOPTED.

Eaton's Series of Arithmetics;	Quackenbos's English Grammar;
Cornell's Primary Geography;	Willson's Series of Readers;
Warren's Intermediate Geography;	Willson's Speller;
Greene's Introductory Grammar;	Quackenbos's History of the U. S.

In 1866, the Board, reorganized under the Revised School Law, Governor Low, Chairman, met and readopted, for a term of four years, the list of 1864, with the exception of the geographies and Quackenbos's Grammars, which were indefinitely continued, but not readopted for four years. Clarke's Geography was also added to the list of geographies, and the Spencerian and Payson, Dunton & Scribner's Penmanship were continued in use.

In 1869, the Board, Governor Haight, Chairman, Superintendent Fitzgerald, Secretary, adopted Monteith's Series of Geographies, in place of Cornell's, Warren's and Clarke's, and Brown's Grammars, in place of Greene's and Quackenbos's—the change to take effect July, 1870.

In 1870, July 12–13, the State Board met, and, under the re-enacted California School Law, adopted the following

STATE SERIES.

McGuffey's Series of Readers;	Willson's Spellers;
Robinson's Series of Arithmetics;	Cutter's Physiologies;
Monteith's Series of Geographies;	Payson and Dunton's Penmanship.
Brown's Series of Grammars;	

A year later, the Board added to this list Swinton's Condensed History of the United States, and Swinton's Word Analysis.

In 1874, June 22d, in compliance with a new section of the School Law, the Board passed a resolution inviting publishers to lay before them, on or before January 5th, 1875, proposals for supplying text-books for use in the public schools of the State.

January 5th, 1875, the Board met—Governor Booth in the chair, and Superintendent Bolander, Secretary—considered the proposals received, and adopted the Pacific Coast Readers, in place of McGuffey's; Cornell's Geographies, in place of Monteith's; Spencerian Penmanship, in place of Payson, Dunton & Scribner's; and readopted Robinson's Arithmetics and Cutter's First Book in Anatomy, Physiology, and Hygiene. The Board also recommended Swinton's Language Series for teachers and school libraries.

On February 3d, 1876, a writ of *certiorari* was issued by the Sixth District Court, Sacramento, Judge Ramage, against the introduction of the new Readers. The case was carried to the Supreme Court, which, on April 19th, 1875, declared the action of the Board, in adopting the Pacific Coast Readers, null and void, on the ground that the record did not show that six months' notice of a proposed change in Readers had been given, as required by law.

On June 1st, the Board again met, and advertised for proposals for all the books, it being considered that the ruling of the Supreme Court, on Readers, applied to all the books adopted at their former meeting.

Dec. 5th, 1875, the Board again met, pursuant to advertisement, to adopt text-books, but were enjoined by Judge Braynard, County Judge of Tehama County, and Judge Reardon, District Judge of the Fourteenth District, "from receiving, opening, or acting in any manner upon proposals for supplying Readers and Geographies, or taking any action whereby any Readers other than McGuffey's, or any Geographies other than Monteith's, may be used in the public schools of this State." The Board being still free to act upon all other books, adopted Robinson's Arithmetic, Swinton's Word Analysis, Spencerian Penmanship, Smith's Drawing, Mason's Music Reader's, and Cutter's First Book in Anatomy, Physiology, and Hygiene.

In the case of Readers and Geographies, the Board postponed action to Dec. 28th, the hearing of the injunctions being set respectively for Dec. 15th and Dec. 22d. Meanwhile, a bill was introduced into the Legislature, Dec. 9th, that the text-books in use in 1873–4–5, be continued in use in all the public schools of the State, until otherwise provided by statute. This bill became a law on Dec. 13th, when the injunction suits were at once dismissed.

As the case now stands, the old list of books throughout remains in the schools, and all power of changing is vested in the State Legislature.

XII. EDUCATION OF COLORED CHILDREN.

The Legislature of 1860 passed a law prohibiting colored (Negro and Mongolian) children from being admitted to schools for white children, under penalty of forfeiting all public moneys.

Previous to this, colored children were prohibited from attending schools for white children, but there was no penalty. The law had *allowed* trustees to establish separate schools for colored children, but had not *required* it.

The first legal recognition of the rights of colored children is found in the Revised School Law, 1866:

SEC. 57. Children of African or Mongolian descent, and Indian children, not living under the care of white persons, shall not be admitted into the public schools, except as provided in this act; *provided*, that, upon the written application of the parents or guardians of at least ten such children, to any Board of Trustees, or Board of Education, a separate school shall be established for their education, and the education of a less number may be provided for by the trustees in any other manner.

SEC. 58. When there shall be in any district any number of children, other than white children, whose education can be provided for in no other way, the trustees, by a majority vote, may permit such children to attend schools for white children; *provided*, that a majority of the parents of the children attending such school make no objection in writing, to be filed with the Board of Trustees.

SEC. 59. The same laws, rules, and regulations which apply to schools for white children shall apply to schools for colored children.

Under this qualified provision, most of the colored children in the State were admitted to school privileges, though in a few outlying districts—notably the city of Oakland—they were excluded from white schools, and were not allowed a separate school.

The Legislature of 1870 repealed Section 58, and left the colored question as follows:

SEC. 56. The education of children of African descent, and Indian children, shall be provided for in separate schools. Upon the written application of the parents or guardians of at least ten such children, to any Board of Trustees or Board of Education, a separate school shall be established for the education of such children; and the education of a less number may be provided for by the trustees, in separate schools, in any other manner.

In 1872, the Code Commissioners modified the law, under a decision of the Supreme Court, and the Legislature adopted it as follows:

SEC. 1669. The education of children of African descent, and Indian children, must be provided for in separate schools; *provided*, that if the directors or trustees fail to provide such separate schools, then such children must be admitted into the schools for white children.

In 1872, the Board of Education of Oakland admitted their eight colored children into the schools; and, in 1875, the San Francisco Board abolished the separate school of seventy-five colored children, and admitted the pupils to the white schools.

XIII. COURSE OF STUDY IN DISTRICT SCHOOLS.

The School Law of 1863-4 specified the studies to be pursued in the schools as follows: Arithmetic, Geography, Grammar, Reading, Writing, Spelling, History of the United States, Physiology, and such other studies as trustees might deem advisable.

The first "Course of Study for District Schools" was prepared by Superintendent Swett, and adopted by the State Board, June 8, 1866. At the same meeting, rules and regulations were also adopted.

This "Course of Study" was revised by the State Board in 1870, and again revised by Superintendent Bolander, and adopted by the Board in 1872.

In 1872, *Drawing* and *Music* were added to the list of regular school studies.

RULES AND REGULATIONS, 1866.

SECTION 1. Teachers are required to be present at their respective schoolrooms, and to open them for the admission of pupils at fifteen minutes before the time prescribed for commencing school, and to punctually observe the hours for opening and closing school.

SEC. 2. Unless otherwise provided by special action of trustees, or Boards of Education, the daily school sessions shall commence at nine o'clock A. M., and close at four o'clock P. M., with an intermission at noon of one hour, from twelve M. to one P. M. There shall be allowed a recess of twenty minutes in the forenoon session, from ten-forty to eleven o'clock, and a recess of twenty minutes in the afternoon session, from two-forty to three o'clock. When boys and girls are allowed separate recesses, fifteen minutes shall be allowed for each recess.

SEC. 3. In graded primary schools in which the average age of the pupils is under eight years, the daily sessions shall not exceed four hours a day, inclusive of the intermission at noon, and inclusive of the recesses. If such schools are opened at nine o'clock A. M., they shall be closed at two o'clock, P.M. In ungraded schools, all children under eight years of age shall either be dismissed after a four hours' session, or allowed recesses for play of such length that the actual confinement in the schoolroom shall not exceed three hours and a half.

SEC. 4. No pupil shall be detained in school during the intermission at noon, and a pupil detained at any recess shall be permitted to go out immediately thereafter. All pupils, except those detained for punishment, shall be required to pass out of the schoolrooms at recess, unless it would occasion an exposure of health.

SEC. 5. Principals shall be held responsible for the general management and discipline of schools; and the other teachers shall follow their directions and co-operate with them, not only during the school hours, but during the time when the pupils are on the school premises, before and after school, and during recesses. Assistants shall be held responsible for the order and discipline of their own rooms, under the general direction of the Principals.

SEC. 6. Teachers are particularly enjoined to devote their time faithfully to a vigilant and watchful care over the conduct and habits of the pupils during the time for relaxation and play, before and after school, and during the recesses, both in the school buildings and on the playgrounds.

SEC. 7. It is expected that teachers will exercise a general inspection over the conduct of scholars going to and returning from school. They shall exert their influence to prevent all quarreling and disagreement, all rude and noisy behavior in the street, all vulgar and profane language, all improper games, and all disrespect to citizens and strangers.

SEC. 8. Teachers shall prescribe such rules for the use of the yards, basements, and outbuildings connected with the schoolhouse, as shall insure their being kept in a neat and proper condition, and shall examine them as often as may be necessary for such purpose. Teachers shall be held responsible for any want of neatness or cleanliness about their school premises.

SEC. 9. Teachers shall give vigilant attention to the ventilation and temperature of their schoolrooms. At each recess the windows and doors shall be opened for the purpose of changing the atmosphere of the room. Teachers are cautioned against hot fires and a high temperature.

SEC. 10. Teachers shall enter in the school registers, in the order of their application, the names of all those applying for admission to the school, after the prescribed number of pupils have been received. Such applicants shall be admitted to seats whenever a vacancy occurs in any class for which they have been found duly qualified, in the order of their registration.

SEC. 11. Teachers are authorized to require excuses from the parents or guardians of pupils, either in person or by written note, in all cases of absence or tardiness, or of dismissal before the close of school.

SEC. 12. No pupil shall be allowed to retain connection with any public school unless furnished with books, slate, and other utensils required to be used in the class to which he belongs; *provided*, that no pupil shall be excluded for such cause, unless the parent or guardian shall have been furnished by the teacher with a list of books, or articles needed, and one week shall have elapsed after such notice without the pupil's obtaining said books. Books may be furnished to indigent children by the trustees, at the expense of the district, whenever the teacher shall have certified in writing that the pupil applying is unable to purchase such books.

SEC. 13. Any pupil who shall in any way cut or otherwise injure any schoolhouse, or injure any fences, trees, or outbuildings, belonging to any of the school estates, or shall write any profane or obscene language, or make any obscene characters or pictures on any school premises, shall be liable to suspension, expulsion, or other punishment, according to the nature of the offense. The teacher may suspend a pupil temporarily for such offense, and shall notify the trustees of such action. Pupils shall not be allowed to remain in any of the rooms that are provided with improved styles of furniture, except in the presence of a teacher or a monitor, who is made specially responsible for the care of the seats and desks. All damages done to school property by any of the pupils shall be repaired at the expense of the party committing the trespass.

SEC. 14. All pupils who go to school without proper attention having been given to personal cleanliness, or neatness of dress, shall be sent home to be properly prepared for school, or shall be required to prepare themselves for the schoolroom before entering. Every schoolroom shall be provided with a wash-basin, soap, and towels.

SEC. 15. No pupils affected with any contagious disease shall be allowed to remain in any of the public schools.

SEC. 16. The books used, and the studies pursued, shall be such, and such only, as may be authorized by the State Board of Education; and no teacher shall require or advise any of the pupils to purchase, for use in the schools, any book not contained in the list of books directed and authorized to be used in the schools.

SEC. 17. It shall be the duty of the teachers of the schools to read to the pupils, from time to time, so much of the school regulations as apply to them, that they may have a clear understanding of the rules by which they are governed.

SEC. 18. In all primary schools, exercises in free gymnastics, and vocal and breathing exercises, shall be given at least twice a day, and for a time not less than five minutes for each exercise.

SEC. 19. The following supplies shall be provided by the District Clerk, under the provisions of section forty-six of the Revised School Law, on the written requisition of the teacher, viz: clocks, brooms, dusting-brushes, wash-basins, water-buckets, tin cups, dust-pans, matches, ink, ink-bottles, pens, penholders, slate pencils, crayon chalk, hand-bells, coal-buckets or wood-boxes, shovels, pokers, soap, towels, thermometers, door-mats, scrapers, and stationery.

SEC. 20. Trustees are authorized and recommended to employ a suitable person to sweep and take care of the schoolhouse, and to make suitable provision for supplying the school with water.

RULES FOR PUPILS.

1. Every pupil is expected to attend school punctually and regularly; to conform to the regulations of the school, and to obey promptly all the directions of the teacher; to observe good order, and propriety of deportment; to be diligent in study, respectful to teachers, and kind and obliging to schoolmates; to refrain entirely from the use of profane and vulgar language, and to be clean and neat in person and clothing.

2. Pupils are required, in all cases of absence, to bring, on their return to school, an excuse in writing, from their parents or guardians, assigning good and sufficient reasons for such absence.

3. All pupils who have fallen behind their grade, by absence or irregularity of attendance, by indolence or inattention, shall be placed in the grade below, at the discretion of the teacher.

4. No pupil shall be permitted to leave school at recess, or at any other time before the regular hour for closing school, except in case of sickness; or on written request of parent or guardian.

5. Any scholar who shall be absent one week, without giving notice to the teacher, shall lose all claim to his particular desk for the remainder of the term, and shall not be considered a member of the school.

6. Each scholar shall have a particular desk, and shall keep the same, and the floor beneath, in a neat and orderly condition.

INSTRUCTIONS TO TEACHERS.

1. Teachers will endeavor to make themselves acquainted with parents and guardians, in order to secure their aid and co-operation, and to better understand the temperaments, characteristics, and wants of the children.

2. Teachers shall daily examine the lessons of their various classes, and make such special preparation upon them, if necessary, as not to be constantly confined to the text-book, and instruct all their

pupils, without partiality, in those branches of school studies which their various classes may be pursuing. In all their intercourse with their scholars, they are required to strive to impress on their minds, both by precept and example, the great importance of continued efforts for improvement in morals, and manners, and deportment, as well as in useful learning.

3. Teachers should explain each new lesson assigned, if necessary, by familiar remarks and illustrations, that every pupil may know, before he is sent to his seat, what he is expected to do at the next recitation, and how it is to be done.

4. Teachers should only use the text-book for occasional reference, and should not permit it to be taken to the recitation, to be referred to by the pupils, except in case of such exercises as absolutely require it. They should assign many questions of their own preparing, involving an application of what the pupils have learned, to the business of life.

5. Teachers should endeavor to arouse and fix the attention of the whole class, and to occupy and bring into action as many of the faculties of their pupils as possible. They should never proceed with the recitation without the attention of the whole class, nor go round the class with recitation always in the same order, or in regular rotation.

6. Teachers should at all times exhibit proper animation themselves, manifesting a lively interest in the subject taught, avoid all heavy, plodding movements, all formal routine in teaching, lest the pupil be dull and drowsy, and imbibe the notion he studies only to recite.

XIV. THE CALIFORNIA TEACHER.

At the State Teachers' Institute, May, 1863, it was voted to begin the publication of a monthly educational journal.

John Swett and Samuel I. C. Swezey were elected managing editors, and the first number of the *California Teacher* was issued July, 1863.

At the succeeding session of the Legislature, 1863–4, a law was passed, authorizing county superintendents to subscribe for a number of copies, at $1 a copy, to supply each Board of School Trustees with one copy.

In 1864–5, a provision was made in the Revised School Law, authorizing the State Board of Education to subscribe for a number of copies, sufficient to supply the clerk of each board of trustees, and each school library, with a copy of some educational journal, the subscription payable out of the State School Fund.

This provision placed the journal on a paying basis.

After the first year, the State Educational Society assumed the control of the *Teacher*, electing its editors annually. By the Revised School Law of 1865, the State Superintendent was made, *ex-officio*, one of the editors. Messrs. Swezey and Swett continued to edit the journal until July, 1868.

At the end of this time, Mr. Swezey made the following report:

OFFICE OF "THE CALIFORNIA TEACHER,"
302 MONTGOMERY STREET,
SAN FRANCISCO, June 17, 1868.

TO THE CALIFORNIA EDUCATIONAL SOCIETY.

GENTLEMEN: The undersigned, as acting publisher of the *California Teacher*, desires to present the following facts for your information:

1. The *California Teacher* was established at the State Institute, held in May, 1863, at the same time that your society was formally organized; since which time you have been recognized as the proper representative of the teachers' profession in this State. The Institute elected John Swett, Geo. Tait, Geo. W. Minns, and the undersigned, as resident editors; and, owing to the pressure of engagements upon the gentlemen named, the publishing duties were devolved upon the undersigned, who has continued to perform those duties through the entire five years, closing with the number for June, 1868.

At the close of the first volume, the authority of your society was editorially recognized in the following terms: "The *Teacher* will be guided by the wise hand of the California Educational Society, to which, indeed, we have hitherto looked, as the representative of the teachers in the State. What that society says in regard to editors, will be regarded as law; and whenever it desires a change, the resident editors of the first volume will rejoice in their relief from responsibility of no small magnitude, while they give a cheerful hand to their successors in office." (*California Teacher*, vol. 1, p. 310.)

On the 18th of June, 1864, your Society unanimously and formally consented to assume the responsibility of the publication, and thereupon unanimously elected as resident editors, John Swett, George Tait, and the undersigned. (*California Teacher*, vol. 2, p. 23.)

On the 5th of June, 1865, your Society elected John Swett, John C. Pelton, and the undersigned, as resident editors for the ensuing year. (*California Teacher*, vol. 3, p. 54.) Since that time there seems to have been no formal action taken upon this subject, though the principle has been regarded as settled that the State Superintendent and the City Superintendent of San Francisco should always be among the resident editors.

2. Under Section 84 of the Revised School Law, the State Board of Education, on the 13th of April, 1866, unanimously designated this journal as the official organ of education in this State. (*California Teacher*, vol. 3, p. 293.) And since that time the expenses of publishing the *Teacher* have been mainly met by the proceeds of the State subscription. This was to be expected. The proportion of teachers in any State who pay for an educational journal which they can read without paying for, is very small; and since the *Teacher* has been sent to every district, comparatively few private subscriptions have been received. The amount received at this date for subscriptions to vol. 6, commencing with the number for July, is $48.60.

3. As a matter of fact, the entire labor of conducting the *Teacher* has been performed by Mr. Swett and the undersigned [Mr. Swezey]. The two have acted in harmony, and have exercised a mutual supervision over each other. Any article or paragraph to which either has objected has been suppressed. The Department of Public Instruction in the *Teacher*, however, was under the exclusive control of Mr. Swett during his administration; while, as a general rule, the book notices were the special department of the undersigned, who has also attended to the proof reading, mailing, accounts, and business correspondence. The receipts of the first two years did not equal the cost of printing. The third year, the receipts and expenses were about equal. During the fourth and fifth years, the receipts have so far exceeded the expenses as to enable the undersigned to depute to other hands the actual drudgery of mailing; and at the end of the whole term, the two working resident editors are able to rejoice in the fact that they are neither material losers nor gainers pecuniarily in the conduct of their editorial experiments. Last year, the balance sufficed to meet a portion of the office rent of the undersigned, and to leave perhaps $25 per month to the editors, as compensation for the labor bestowed. During the year now ending, the same result is probable, though, as the bills are not all settled, it is impracticable to speak positively on the subject. At the close of each volume, Mr. Swett and the undersigned have divided equally the profits or the losses of the year, and commenced the succeeding one with clear books, to stand or fall on its own merits.

4. A grave practical question comes before your society to-day, arising from the following state of facts:

Upon the accession to office of the present State Superintendent, he assumed that, as a matter of course, the *Teacher* came under his personal and supreme control.

In the view of the undersigned, however, the *Teacher* is to be conducted by persons designated by your society; and they are to act until their successors are appointed—the statute giving the State Superintendent, as such, absolute control over simply his own department in the journal.

The Superintendent was informed, therefore, of the time by which the printers were expected to receive the matter for each monthly issue; that whatever space he required for his department was always to be at his service; and that, to avoid any apparent supervision of what he should choose to insert, the printers would be instructed to return the proof-slips of his department direct to his office, so that the appointed editors would not know what he should print, until they saw it in the completed journal.

This seems to have been unsatisfactory to the Superintendent, and he declines to accept the proposition, or to use the *Teacher* as provided by law.

At the last meeting of the State Board of Education, the Superintendent announced his intention, if the exclusive control of the *Teacher* should not be placed in his own hands, to commence the publication of an educational journal on his own account, which he should desire to have designated by the Board as the organ of the department. The Board so far deferred to his wishes as to formally rescind the designation of the *California Teacher*, and the matter was then left until after your present meeting should be held.

Should you abandon the plan hitherto acted upon, and elect the State Superintendent as controlling editor, there is no doubt that his objections to the designation of the *California Teacher* will be at once withdrawn; and it seems to be equally certain that, should you continue the plan hitherto acted upon, it will rest with the State Board of Education, to make choice between the journal responsible to the profession, as teachers of the State, and a journal under the supreme control of the present State Superintendent, as editor and publisher.

With the undersigned, as to the principle involved, there is no shadow of doubt. The example of all educational journals at the East, favors the plan heretofore acted upon, that the teachers, in their highest associated capacity, should name the editors, and the State Superintendent should have entire control, simply, of one department in the teachers' organ.

As to the few hundred dollars that may be saved in the publication of the *California Teacher*, each year, the undersigned, for himself (and, as he thinks, for Mr. Swett), is decided in the wish, that any other persons who think the amount received will properly pay for the responsibility attached, should be elected by your society to the editorial office.

All which is respectfully submitted.

SAMUEL I. C. SWEZEY.

In July, 1868, State Superintendent Fitzgerald and A. L. Fitzgerald were elected editors.

In 1872, the State Society elected John Swett, associate editor, with State Supt. Bolander; and, in the year following, the journal was taken out of the hands of the State Society, and its entire control was assumed by Supt. Bolander.

At this time, the State subscription amounted to $4,000 a year.

In 1876, the Legislature cut off the State subscription, which ended the publication of the *California Teacher*.

THE PIONEER JOURNAL.

The first educational journal published in this State was *The Bookseller*, published in 1860, by H. H. Bancroft & Co., and edited by John Swett. It maintained a lingering existence of a year, and then died of starvation.

It contained two fine articles by Starr King, one by Dr. Tuthill, and other able papers.

CONTRIBUTORS TO THE TEACHER.

The following list includes most of the teachers who were contributors to the State educational journal:

George W. Minns,
Mrs. Jennie C. Carr,
E. R. Sill,
Bernhard Marks,
Clara J. Dolliver,
John S. Hittell,
Daniel J. Thomas,
Laura T. Fowler,
Sparrow Smith,
Martin Kellogg,
D. C. Stone,
Ebenezer Knowlton,
Ralph Keeler,
Volney Rattan,
Dr. E. J. Schellhouse,
John Bagnall,
Charles Russell Clarke,
Dr. F. W. Hatch,
A. F. Hill,
Dr. T. H. Rose,
W. W. Holder,
William Swinton,
H. C. Kinne,
Joseph LeConte.

LEADING TOPICS.

Grammar—Hittell.
Heat as a Mode of Motion—Minns.
The Classics in School—Kellogg.
A Letter from 'Zekiel Stebbins—Minns.
Physical Culture—Swett.
Waste in School—Marks.
Africa and the Nile—Minns.
Constitution and Government—Thomas.
Juvenile Depravity in Schools—Swett.
School Libraries—Stone.
Geography of California—Marks.
Reverence for Children—Kellogg.
Teaching as a Profession—Marks.
Examination of Teachers—Swett.
Modern Languages—Keeler.
Practical Education—Kellogg.
Botany—Prof. Wood.
Co-education of the Sexes—Swett.
Against Medals in Schools—Marks.
Education in Great Britain—Rattan.
The Eldest Scholar—Keeler.
The True Teacher—Swett.
Arithmetic—Marks.
Etymology—Hill.
Pestalozzi—Carlton.
Marks's "Arithmetic"—Holder.
Composition—Bagnall.
Word-Analysis—Swinton.
Reading—Kinne.
Female Education—Mrs. Carr.
Botany for Schools—Bolander.

XV. HISTORICAL STATISTICAL TABLES.

1851-'76.

I. EXPENDITURES.

YEARS.	Assessed value of property.	YEARS.	Total expenditures.	Rate per $100.
1850-51	$57,670,689	1851-52	$33,449	.0679
1851-2	49,231,052	1852-3	65,645	.1016
1852-3	64,579,375	1853-4	275,606	.2890
1853-4	95,335,646	1854-5	334,638	.3009
1854-5	111,191,630	1855-6	305.221	.2938
1855-6	103,887,193	1856-7	307,832	.3240
1856-7	95,007,440	1857-8	339,914	.2696
1857-8	126,059,461	1859	427,003	.3444
1858-9	123,955,877	1860	474,263	.3618
1859-60	131,060,279	1861	470,113	.3172
1860-61	148,193,540	1862	441,228	.2985
1861-2	147,811,617	1863	483,407	.3014
1862-3	160,369,071	1864	655,198	.3763
1863-4	174,104,955	1865	883,116	.4893
1864-5	180,484,949	1866	859,229	.4680
1865-6	183,509,161	1867	1,163,348	.5816
1866-7	200,764,135	1868	1,151,407	.5255
1867-8	212,205,339	1869	1,290,585	.5418
1868-9	237,483,175	1870	1,529,047	.5868
1869-70	260,563,886	1871	1,713,431	.6572
1870-71	277,538,134	1872	1,881,333	.7001
1871-2	267,868,126	1873	2,113,356	.3321
1872-3	637,232,823	1874	2,111,155	.3992
1873-4	528,747,043	1875	2,658,241	.4347
1874-5	611,495,197			

FROM OFFICIAL REPORTS.

I. Total amount paid for teachers' salaries........ $14,463,846
II. Total amount paid for school-houses and sites.. 3,950,828
III. Total amount paid for incidentals 3,553,101
IV. Total amount paid for all purposes 21,967,775

ADDITIONAL EXPENSES—(ESTIMATED).

1. State University	*$850,000
2. State Normal School	500,000
3. Salaries of State Superintendents	75,000
4. Incidentals, printing, &c., of the State Superintendent's office	250,000
5. Salaries of County and City Superintendents, and incidentals paid from the general funds	800,000
Total	$2,225,000
Grand total of expenditures for Public School purposes	24,542,775

2. SCHOOL TAXATION, 1852-'75.

YEARS.	State School Fund apportioned.	Raised by county and city taxes.	†Raised from other sources.
1852	....	....	$2,417 00
1853	....	....	10,626 00
1854	$52,061 00	$157,702 00	42,557 00
1855	63,662 00	119,128 00	39,395 00
1856	69,961 00	121,639 00	28,619 00
1857	78,057 00	148,989 00	55,035 00
1858	53,405 00	162,870 00	85,107 00
1859	72,319 00	205,196 00	97,534 00
1860	81,118 00	230,514 00	122 858 00
1861	81,461 00	241,861 00	114,397 00
1862	75,412 00	294,828 00	141,806 00
1863	145,537 00	328,554 00	68,209 00
1864	132,217 00	260,842 00	84,084 00
1865	168,828 00	390,306 00	91,181 00
1866	132,410 00	470,668 00	79,600 00
1867	268,910 00	595,718 00	81,966 00
1868	252,603 00	654,738 00	73,986 00
1869	290,796 00	847,229 00	66,531 00
1870	360,447 00	839,756 00	63,441 00
1871	423,853 00	923,809 00	46,660 00
1872	424,022 00	1,249,943 00	232,075 00
1873	430,220 00	1,541,597 00	310,502 00
1874	428,418 12	1,332,208 82	345,316 95
1875	1,212,252 03	1,115,530 06	676,259 64
Totals	$5,298,869 35	$12,243,625 88	$2,960,162 59

*Exclusive of an endowment fund of $1,500,000.
†District Taxes, Rate Bills, etc.

3. SCHOOL STATISTICS, 1851-'76.

YEARS.	Children Listed by Census Marshals	Enrolled on School Registers	Average daily attendance.	Number of Schools.
1851	*5,906	1,846	......	......
1852	*17,821	3,314	......	35
1853	*19,442	4,193	2,020	111
1854	*20,075	9,746	4,635	168
1855	*26,077	......	6,442	227
1856	*30,039	......	8,495	321
1857	*35,722	17,232	9,717	368
1858	*40,530	19,822	11,183	432
1859	*48,676	23,519	13,364	523
1860	*57,917	26,993	14,754	593
1861	*68,395	31,786	17,804	684
1862	*71,821	36,566	19,262	715
1863	*78,055	36,540	19,992	754
1864	*86,031	47,588	24,794	832
1865	*95,067	50,089	29,592	947
1866	†84,179	50,273	33,989	913
1867	†94,213	62,227	43,271	1,083
1868	†104,118	65,828	43,681	1,228
1869	†112,743	73,754	49,802	1,354
1870	†121,751	85,808	54,271	1,492
1871	†130,116	91,332	64,286	1,550
1872	†137,351	94,720	65,700	1,654
1873	†141,610	107,593	69,461	1,868
1874	‖159,717	120,240	72,283	2,005
1875	§171,563	130,930	78,027	2,190

* Between four and fifteen years of age.
† Between five and fifteen years of age.
‡ Including children over fifteen years of age.
‖ Between five and seventeen years of age.
§ Including children over seventeen years of age.

XVI. HISTORICAL LIST OF COUNTY SUPERINTENDENTS.

From 1855 to 1876, inclusive.

NOTE.—From 1852 to 1854, the County Clerks were *ex-officio* County Superintendents. Those marked * are known to have been practical teachers.

ALAMEDA.

Rev. A. H. Myers....... '55, '56
Rev. W. W. Brier....... '57, '58
Dr. Henry Gibbons...... '59, '60
Rev. J. D. Strong....... '61, '62
Rev. B. N. Seymour.. '63, '64, '65
Rev. Chas E. Rich .. '66, '66, '68
* A. L. Fuller........... '69, '70
Rev. W. F. B. Lynch.... '70, '78

ALPINE.

L. S. Greenlow......... '64, '68
S. W. Griffith........... '68, '69
Joseph Uncapher........ '70, '71
* John Bagnall.......... '72, '73
R. W. Foster.............. '74
* Mrs. C. M. Pitcher .... '76, '78

AMADOR.

E. B. McIntire.......... '56, '57
Rev. H. H. Rhees....... '58, '59
J. H. Bradley .... '60
Samuel Page........... '61, '63
* D. Townsend.......... '64, '65
Rev. S. G. Briggs .... '66, '74
W. H. Stowes........... '74, '78

BUTTE.

J. J. Cline.................. '56
Rev. B. N. Seymour......... '57
H. A. Gaston............ '58, '59
Rev. J. B. Thomas...... '60, '61
S. B. Osbourn.......... '62, '63
* Isaac Upham.......... '64, '65
* C. G. Warren.......... '66, '70
* Lewis Burnham....... '70, '71
* H. T. Batchelder ...... '72, '74
* S. T. Blake........... '74, '76
* Arthur McDermott..... '76, '78

CALAVERAS.

Robert Thompson....... '57, '63
Rev. W. C. Mosher...... '64, '65
* F. O. Barstow......... '66, '67
* C. V. Currier .... '68, '69
* J. H. Wells........... '70, '72
E. T. Walker .... '72, '76
* Chas R. Beale......... '76, '78

COLUSA.

B. M. Hand .... '57, '60
Frank Spaulding............ '61
Charles Street.............. '62
John C. Addington...... '63, '67
* S. W. Britton.......... '68, '69
* G. W. Howard .... '70, '71
E. J. Edwards.......... '72, '73
* J. E. Putnam..... .... '74, '75
Sam. Houchins.......... '76, '78

CONTRA COSTA.

Thomas Ewing .... '56
E. H. Cox.............. '57, '58
A. F. Dyer .... '59, '60
D. S. Woodruff......... '61, '63
Rev. H. R. Avery .... '64, '68
*Alfred Thurber. '68, '72, '76, '78
*H. S. Raven........... '72, '74

DEL NORTE.

H. W. McMillen............ '58
R. S. McLellan. '59, '61, '64, '65, '68, '70
Charles Hinckley .... '62, '63
John Mavity............ '66, '67
John R. Nickel .... '70, '74
*Max Lipowitz.......... '74, '78

EL DORADO.

H. S. Herrick ...'55, '56, '59, '60
J. G. Eustis ....'57
H. L. Pease ....'58
*M. A. Lynde ....'60, '64
*S. A. Penwell..........'64, '65
*C. C. Conklin..........'66, '67
*W. H. Hill............'68, '74
*John P. Munson.......'74, '78

FRESNO.

E. S. Kincaid...............'61
H. M. Quigley..........'62, '63
S. H. Hill ....'64, '68
Dr. S. O. Ellis, Sr.......'68, '76
R. H. Bramlet..........'76, '78

HUMBOLDT.

A. J. Heustis ....'55, '56
E. H. Howard ....'57, '58
H. H. Seaverns ....'59, '60
Rev. W. L. Jones ....'61, '68
*J. B. Brown ....'68, '74
E. C. Cummings ....'74, '78

INYO.

C. M. Joslin ....'68, '69
J. W. Symmes..........'70, '78

KLAMATH.

R. P. Hirst ....'60, '61, '63
J. H. Twombly ....'62
E. Lee ....'64, '65
James Gould ....'68, '69
H. P. Scott ....'71, '72

KERN.

E. W. Doss.............'68, '69
J. H. Cornwall..........'70, '74
*L. A. Bearsdsley ......'74, '78

LAKE.

W. R. Mathews ....'61, '66
*A. P. McCarty.........'66, '67
*Mack Mathews ....68, '74
Rev. Louis Wallace .....'74, '78

LASSEN.

William Young ....'64, '65
A. A. Smith ....'66, '70
L. M. Crill ....'70, '71
L. N. Spaulding ....'72, '76
S. A. Doyle ....'76, '78

LOS ANGELES.

Charles Johnson ....'57, '58
J. W. Shore............'59, '63
L. J. Rose..............'64, '65
Rev. E. Birdsall ....'66, '67
H. D. Barrows...........'68, '69
*W. M. McFadden......'70, '74
*Geo. H. Peck..........'74, '75
*Thos. A. Saxen ....'76, '78

MARIN.

John Simms............'57, '58
John Shore.............'59, '60
James Miller............'61, '63
J. W. Zuver ....'64, '65
A. Barney..............'66, '70
* Samuel Saunders......'70, '78

MARIPOSA.

A. Reynolds............'57, '60
J. R. McCready.........'60, '65
D. W. Washburn ....'66, '67
W. C. Hill ....'68, '69
J. W. Simmons.........'70, '71
David Egenhoff.........'72, '76
Richard Kane...........'76, '78

MENDOCINO.

A. L. Brayton...........'59, '61
C. R. Budd.............'62, '63
J. L. Broaddus..........'64, '65
*C. C. Cummings.......'66, '70
T. B. Bond.............'70, '71
*J. W. Covington.......'72, '73
*J. H. Seawell..........'74, '75
*J. C. Ruddock.........'76, '77

MERCED.

J. W. Robertson............'56
B. F. Howell ....'57, '58
F. J. Woodward........'58, '61
R. B. Huey.............'61, '65
T. O. Ellis.............'66, '67
M. C. Munroe..........'68, '72
J. K. Law ....'72, '73
B. F. Fowler ....'74, '78

MONO.

M. S. Clark ....'70
A. W. Crocker..........'71, '72
J. S. Kirkendale ....'73, '74
E. R. Miner ....'75, '76
* Miss Alice Walker.....'76, '78

MODOC.

W. F. Estes............'74, '78

MONTEREY.

J. H. Gleason...........'57, '58
T. S. Roberts...........'59, '60
G. W. Bird..............'61, '64
W. M. R. Parker.........'64, '65
Thomas Bralee..........'66, '67
* T. W. Clay............'69, '70
E. M. Alderman........'70, '71
* S. M. Shearer.........'72, '73
R. C. McCroskey.......'74, '78

NAPA.

J. E. Herron...............'57
Jas. Corwin................'58
J. M. Hamilton.........'59, '60
Rev. A. Higbie.........'62, '70
Rev. G. W. Ford........'70, '76
L. Fellows............'76, '78

NEVADA.

W. B. Ewer............'56, '57
C. T. Overton..........'58, '60
J. A. Chittenden........'60, '63
M. S. Deal..............'64, '68
* E. M. Preston. '68, '69; '76, '78
* Augustus Morse.......'70, '71
* B. J. Watson..........'72, '73
* Frank Powers.........'74, '75

PLACER.

T. B. Hotchkiss............'56
P. C. Millette..........'57, '58
S. S. Greenwood.........'59, '60
* A. H. Goodrich........'60, '66
S. R. Case..............'66, '70
J. T. Kinkade..........'70, '76
Eugene Calvin..........'76, '78

PLUMAS.

M. D. Sawyer...............'59
J. C. Church...........'58, '59
H. S. Titus..............'60 '66
G. W. Meybert..........'66 '70
*S. S. Boynton..........'70 '72
J. A. Edmon............'72, '73
*W. S. Church..........'74 '78

SACRAMENTO.

Dr. F. W. Hatch, '55, '56; '59-63; '66, '67.
Nelson Slater...........'57, '58
*Sparrow Smith.........'64, '65
Dr. A. Trafton..........'68 '72
*S. H. Jackman.........'73, '74
Dr. G. R. Kelley........'75, '76
*F. L. Landis...........'76 '78

SAN BENITO.

*H. L. Morris...........'76 '78

SAN BERNARDINO.

H. A. Skinner...........'55 '57
R. R. Pearce................'58
Ellis Robbins...........'59, '60
A. F. McKinney.........'60 '64
W. S. Clark.....'64, '65; '68, '69
W. L. Ragsdale.........'66, '67
H. C. Brooks...........'70, '71
John Brown, Jr..........'72, '73
*Henry Goodcel, Jr......'74, '75
C. R. Payne............'76 '78

SAN DIEGO.

Frank Ames............'56, '57
J. M. Estudillo..'58-'62; '64, '65
Geo. Pendleton.........'62, '63
Marcus Schiller..........'68, '69
H. H. Dougherty........'70, '72
B. S. McLafferty........'73, '74
J. H. S. Jamison........'75, '76
*F. N. Pauly............'76, '78

SAN FRANCISCO.

*John C. Pelton, Co. Sup't...'54
City and Co. Sup't....'55

CITY AND COUNTY SUPERINTENDENTS.

E. A. Theller...............'56
Henry B. Janes..........'57, '58
*James Denman, '59, '60; '68, '69, '70; '74, '75
*Geo. Tait......'61, '62, '63, '64
*John C. Pelton........'66, '67
J. H. Widber.......'71, '72, '73
*H. N. Bolander.........'76, '78

SAN JOAQUIN.

*L. C. Van Allen....'58, '59, '60
*Cyrus Collins..........'60, '64
*Melville Cottle..........'64, '70
*W. R. Leadbetter.......'70, '74
*T. O. Crawford.........'74, '75
*S. G. S. Dunbar........'76, '78

SAN LUIS OBISPO.

P. A. Forrester..'58–'60; '66–'68; '70, '74
Alex. Murray............'60, '68
J. H. Gooch.............'68, '69
J. M. Felts..............'74, '78

SAN MATEO.

*W. C. Crook...........'62, '66
Robt. Greer.............'66, '67
*H. N. Nutting..........'68, '72
Rev. H. E. Jewet........'73, '74
*C. G. Warren..........'75, '76
G. P. Hartley...........'76, '78

SANTA BARBARA.

A. B. Thompson.........'64 '70
Rev. J. C. Hamer........'70 '76
G. E. Thurmond.........'70 '78

SANTA CLARA.

*Freeman Gates.........'55, '56
Mathew Mitchell........'56, '60
S. S. Niles..............'60, '64
Wesley Tonner..........'64, '67
*J. R. Brierly..............'68
*J. H. Braly............'68, '69
*N. Furlong.............'70, 71
*Geo. F. Baker..........'72, '73
*J. G. Kennedy.........'74, '75
*E. Rousseau...........'76, '78

SANTA CRUZ.

D. J. Haslam...........'59, '63
Rev. P. Y. Cool........'64, '65
*H. P. Stone...........'66, '67
*H. E. Makinney........'68, '74
*W. H. Hobbs..........'74, '78

SHASTA.

*Y. N. Chappelle.............'55
H. A. Curtin..................'56
*Grove K. Godfrey......'57, '64
John Conmy............'64, '65
W. L. Carter..........'66, '74
*G. W. Welch..........'75, '76
*Mrs. D. M. Coleman....'76, '78

SIERRA.

Rev. W. C. Pond........'61, '66
J. M. Haven............'67, '68
*J. H. Thorpe..........'68, '72
A. M. Phalin............'72, '78

SISKIYOU.

G. F. Price............'57, '58
R. S. McEwan..........'59, '60
*Thos. N. Stone.........'62, '68
*Grove K. Godfrey......'68, '74
*Wm. Duenkel..........'74, '78

SOLANO.

Rev. S. Woodbridge....'58, '61
Rev. J. W. Hines........'61, '64
*Geo. W. Simonton......'64, '68
*Milton Wasson.............'69
*W. H. Fry............'70, '74
*C. W. Childs..........'74, '78

SONOMA.

*Charles G. Ames......'61, '70
*G. W. Jones..........'70, '74
*A. C. McMeans........'74, '78

STANISLAUS.

A. B. Anderson........'61, '64
G. W. Schell..........'64, '65
T. T. Hamlin..........'68, '72
James Burney..........'73, '74
W. B. Howard..........'76, '78

SUTTER.

C. Wilcoxon........'56, '58, '61
A. S. Long.............'59, '60
J. E. Stevens..........'62, '63
*N. Furlong............'64, '65
*J. H. Clark............'70, '74
*M. C. Clark............'74, '78

TEHAMA.

W. L. Bradley..........'59, '60
W. H. Bahney..........'61, '66
*Geo. F. Morris........'67, '68
G. W. Jeffries..........'68, '72
F. A. Vestal............'73, '74
C. D. Woodman........'75, '76
E. S. Campbell........'76, '78

TRINITY.

M. Ruch....................'57, '60
Henry Martin....................'61
F. Walter....................'62, '63
David Gordon....................'64, '70
C. W. Smith....................'70, '71
Wm. Lovett....................'72, '73
H. H. Bragdon....................'75, '76
* Mary N. Wadleigh.....'76, '78

TUOLUMNE.

G. S. Evans....................'57, '58
B. A. Mardis....................'59, '60
R. E. Gardiner....................'61
Charles Pease....................'62, '63
* John Graham....................'64, '65
J. Spencer....................'66, '67
W. J. Clark....................'68, '69
* C. L. Metzger....................'70, '71
* John York, Jr....................'72, '73
John Murman....................'75, '76
* Rose R. Morgan......'76, '77

TULARE.

O. R. Smith....................'59, '60
T. O. Ellis....................'61, '64
M. S. Merrill....................'64, '68
J. W. Williams....................'68, '70
S. G. Creighton....................'70, '74
R. P. Merrill....................'74, '78

VENTURA.

T. S. S. Buckman....................'76, '78

YOLO.

Henry Gaddis....................'57, '65
* M. A. Woods....................'66, '68
R. R. Darby....................'68, '72
* G. N. Freeman....................'72, '76

YUBA.

Rev. E. B. Walsworth....'57, '61
W. C. Belcher....................'62, '66
* D. C. Stone....................'67, '68
* Isaac Upham....................'69, '70
Rev. A. A. McAllister....'71, '72
* Thos. H. Steel....................'72, '78

NOTES.—Among the County Superintendents distinguished for long terms of office, or for educational labors may be named:

Dr. F. W. Hatch, for ten years Superintendent of Sacramento County; a careful and popular officer, whose reports rank among the best.

Chas. G. Ames, for ten years Superintendent of Sonoma County; an accurate and capable school officer.

Rev. A. Higbie, of Napa County, seven years; and Rev. G. W. Ford, six years.

Grove K. Godfrey, six years in Shasta County and six years in Siskiyou.

Rev. W. C. Pond, Sierra County, five years.

George W. Simonton, Solano County, four years.

David Gordon, Trinity County, six years.

W. C. Belcher, Yuba County, four years; and Rev. E. B. Walsworth, same county, four years.

Rev. W. T. B. Lynch, Alameda County, six years.

PART III.

PRESENT CONDITION OF THE SCHOOL SYSTEM.

I. SCHOOL SUPERVISION.

I. State Superintendent of Public Instruction.
II. State Board of Education.
III. State Board of Examination.
IV. County Superintendents.
V. City Superintendents.
VI. City Boards of Education.
VII. Boards of District School Trustees.
VIII. County Boards of Examination.
IX. Board of Regents of the State University.
X. Board of Normal School Trustees.

I. STATE SUPERINTENDENT.—Elected every four years, at the Special Judicial Election, in the October following the General Election for Governor and other State officers in September. Salary, $3,000 a year; traveling expenses, $1,500 a year. Deputy Superintendent: salary, $1,800 a year. Clerk: salary, $1,500.

II. STATE BOARD OF EDUCATION.—It consists of the Governor, State Superintendent, Principal State Normal School, and the County Superintendents of San Francisco, Sacramento, Santa Clara, San Joaquin, Alameda, and Sonoma. *Powers.*—To issue life diplomas; to prescribe rules and regulations and a course of study for all schools, except those in incorporated cities; to adopt a State series of text-books.

[The power of adopting text-books repealed by the Legislature of 1876.]

Board required to meet at least four times a year. No salary, but traveling expenses allowed.

III. STATE BOARD OF EXAMINATION.—It consists of the State Superintendent, and four professional teachers appointed by him. Salary, $200 a year. *Powers.*—To prepare questions for the examination of teachers for county and city examinations; to issue State diplomas, valid for six years; first grade certificates, valid for four years; second and third grades, valid for two years—all on county and city examinations. Also to issue certificates on State Normal School diplomas of any State Normal School in the United States, and on *life diplomas* of other States.

IV. County Superintendents.—Elected every two years, at the general election.

Powers.—To apportion school moneys, draw warrants for the payments of teachers, conduct examinations of teachers, to visit schools, conduct County Institutes, and make a biennial report to the State Superintendent.

Salary.—From $200 to $1,800 a year; average, $830.

V. City Superintendents.—Elected, in general, by direct vote of the people, for two years. They have the usual powers of superintendents in other cities in the United States.

Salaries.—San Francisco, $4,000; Oakland, $2,400; San Jose, $1,200.

VI. City Boards of Education.—Elected by direct vote of the people, either at general or special elections, and consisting of from five to twelve members, elected for two years.

Powers.—To build schoolhouses, employ teachers, and manage school affairs generally.

No salary!

VII. Boards of District School Trustees.—Elected at special school elections, for a term of three years, one trustee being elected each year.

Powers.—To build schoolhouses, employ teachers, and manage local school affairs generally.

No salary.

VIII. County Boards of Examination.—Consist of County Superintendent, and of not less than three professional teachers, appointed by him.

Salary.—Three dollars a day, and traveling expenses.

Powers.—To hold quarterly examinations, using the questions prepared by the State Board of Examination, on the first Wednesday in the months of December, March, June, and September, and to issue 1st, 2d, and 3d grade county certificates.

IX. Regents of the State University.—Composed, partly, of *ex-officio* members, State officers; partly of members appointed by the Governor, for terms of sixteen years; and partly of members elective by the appointed members.

Powers.—To manage the affairs of the State University.

No salary.

X. Board of State Normal School Trustees.—Consists of the Governor and State Superintendent, and five members appointed by the Governor, for a term of sixteen years.

No salary.

ORGANIZATION OF DEPARTMENT OF PUBLIC INSTRUCTION, 1876.

I. OFFICE OF STATE SUPERINTENDENT.

Office located at the State Capital, Sacramento.

State Superintendent........................Ezra S. Carr.
Deputy .... Mrs. E. S. Carr.
Clerk...................................H. A. Moses.

II. STATE BOARD OF EDUCATION.

Office at Sacramento.

Gov. William Irwin..........................President.
Supt. E. S. Carr............................Secretary.
Chas H. Allen................Prin. State Normal School.

COUNTY SUPERINTENDENTS, EX-OFFICIO MEMBERS.

H. N. Bolander.........................San Francisco.
T. L. Landis.............................Sacramento.
W. F. B. Lynch..............................Alameda.
E. Rousseau..............................Santa Clara.
A. C. McMeans...............................Sonoma.
S. B. S. Dunbar..........................San Joaquin.

III. STATE BOARD OF EXAMINATION.

Place of Meeting, Sacramento.

Supt. E. S. Carr............................Chairman.
Chas H. Allen...............................San Jose.
John Swett.............................San Francisco.
Miss M. J. Watson ....Sacramento.
Mrs. Mary E. Michener...................Sacramento.

IV. COUNTY SUPERINTENDENTS.

Holding office from the first Monday in March, 1876, to March, 1878.

Counties.	Names.	Post-Office.
Alameda	Rev. W. F. B. Lynch	East Oakland.
Alpine	R. H. Ford	Silver Mountain.
Amador	W. H. Stowers	Plymouth.
Butte	Arthur McDermott	Oroville.
Calaveras	Charles R. Beal	San Andreas.
Colusa	Samuel Houchens	Princeton.
Contra Costa	A. Thurber	Pacheco.
Del Norte	Max Lipowitz	Crescent City.
El Dorado	John P. Munson	Placerville.
Fresno	R. H. Bramlet	Fresno.
Humboldt	E. C. Cummings	Rohnerville.
Inyo	John W. Symmes	Independence.
Kern	L. A. Beardsley	Bakersfield.
Lake	Louis Wallace	Lakeport.
Lassen	S. A. Doyle	Long Valley.
Los Angeles	Thomas A. Saxon	Los Angeles.
Marin	Samuel Saunders	San Rafael.
Mariposa	Richard Kane	Mariposa.
Mendocino	John C. Ruddock	Ukiah.
Merced	B. F. Fowler	Merced.
Modoc	W. T. Estes	Cedarville.
Mono	Miss Alice Walker	Bridgeport.
Monterey	R. C. McCroskey	Salinas City.
Napa	L. Fellers	Napa City.
Nevada	E. M. Preston	Nevada City.
Placer	Eugene Calvin	Auburn.
Plumas	W. S. Church	La Porte.
Sacramento	F. L. Landes	Sacramento.
San Benito	H. Z. Morris	Hollister.
San Bernardino	Charles R. Paine	San Bernardino.
San Diego	F. N. Pauley	San Diego.
San Francisco	H. N. Bolander	San Francisco.
San Joaquin	S. G. S. Dunbar	Stockton.
San Luis Obispo	J. M. Felts	Cambria.
San Mateo	G. P. Hartley	Spanishtown.
Santa Barbara	G. E. Thurmond	Carpenteria
Santa Clara	E. Rousseau	Santa Clara.
Santa Cruz	W. H. Hobbs	Soquel.
Shasta	Mrs. D. M. Coleman	Shasta.
Sierra	A. M. Phalin	Port Wine.
Siskiyou	William Duenkel	Yreka.
Solano	C. W. Childs	Suisun City.
Sonoma	A. C. McMeans	Santa Rosa.
Stanislaus	W. B. Howard	Modesto.
Sutter	M. C. Clark	Yuba City.
Tehama	E. S. Campbell	Red Bluff.
Trinity	Mary N. Wadleigh	Junction City.
Tulare	R. P. Merrill	Visalia.
Tuolumne	Rose E. Morgan	Columbia.
Ventura	F. S. S. Buckman	San Buenaventura.
Yolo	H. B. Pendergast	Woodland.
Yuba	Th. H. Steele	Marysville.

II. SCHOOL REVENUE.

The school revenue is derived from the following sources:

I. Interest on the State School Fund.
II. State School Tax.
III. County School Tax.
IV. City School Tax.
V. District Taxes voted at Special School Elections.

I. The State School Fund is derived from the proceeds of the sales of the 500,000 acres of land, granted by Congress to the State, for the purposes of internal improvement, and set apart by the State Constitution as an inviolable school fund, and from the sales of the 16th and 36th sections of township lands, consolidated into a general State fund.

It amounts to $1,737,500, invested in six per cent. and seven per cent. State bonds. The Endowment Fund of the State University consists of $1,500,000, yielding an annual revenue of about $128,000.

II. A direct State property tax is required to be levied annually, sufficient, with the interest on the State School Fund, to amount to $7 per census child, from 5 to 17 years of age. State apportionment, 1875, $1,210,808.

III. County School Tax. Rate determined by each County Board of Supervisors. Maximum rate, not to exceed 50 cents on each $100. Minimum rate, not less than $3 per each census child. Amount of County Taxes, 1875, $1,115,530.

IV. City School Tax. The rate is determined, in some cases, by the Board of Education, and in others, by the Common Councils, or Boards of Supervisors. In San Francisco, the amount required is $35 per child, on the average daily attendance for the preceding school year. Amount raised by City Tax, 1875, $391,364.

V. The District Taxes are voted at special school elections, generally for building purposes. Maximum rate, $1 on each $100. Amount raised in 1875, $315,000. Total School Revenue, 1875, $3,390,359. Total amount expended for Public Schools, from 1850 to 1876 inclusive, $25,000,000.

III. GENERAL PROVISIONS OF THE SCHOOL LAW.

ARTICLE X.

SCHOOLS.

SEC. 1662. Every school, unless otherwise provided by special statute, must be open for the admission of all white children between five and twenty-one years of age, residing in the district; and the Board of Trustees or Board of Education have power to admit adults, and children not residing in the district, whenever good reasons exist therefor.

SEC. 1663. All schools, unless otherwise provided by special statute, must be divided into first, second, and third grade. Each County Superintendent must, under instructions from the State Board of Education, determine the respective grade or class of schools in his county.

SEC. 1664. All schools must be taught in the English language.

SEC. 1665. Instruction must be given in the following branches—in the several grades in which each may be required—viz: reading, writing, orthography, arithmetic, geography, grammar, history of the United States, physiology, natural philosophy, natural history, elements of form, vocal music, and industrial drawing.

SEC. 1666. Other studies may be authorized by the State Board of Education, or Board of Education of any city, or city and county; but no such studies can be pursued to the neglect or exclusion of the studies in the preceding section specified.

SEC. 1667. Instruction must be given in all grades of schools, and in all classes, during the entire school course, in manners and morals.

SEC. 1668. Attention must be given to such physical exercises for the pupils, as may be conducive to health and vigor of body, as well as mind, and to the ventilation and temperature of school rooms.

SEC. 1669. The education of children of African descent, and of Indian children, must be provided for in separate schools; *provided*, that if the directors or trustees fail to provide such separate schools, then such children must be admitted into the schools for white children.

SEC. 1670. Upon the written application of the parents or guardians of such children, to any Board of Trustees or Board of Education, a separate school must be established for the education of such children.

SEC. 1671. The same laws, rules, and regulations, which apply to schools for white children, apply to schools for colored children.

SEC. 1672. No publication of a sectarian, partisan, or demoninational character, must be used or distributed in any school, or be made a part of any school library; nor must any sectarian or denominational doctrine be taught therein. Any school district, town, or city, the officers of which knowingly allow any schools to be taught in violation of these provisions, forfeits all right to any State or county apportionment of school moneys; and, upon satisfactory evidence of such violation, the Superintendent of Public Instruction and School Superintendent must withhold both State and county apportionments.

SEC. 1673. No school must be continued in session more than six hours a day; and no pupil under eight years of age must be kept in school more than four hours per day. Any violation of the provisions of this section must be treated in the same manner as a violation of the provisions of the preceding section.

ARTICLE XI.

PUPILS.

SECTION 1683. Pupils, how admitted.
1684. Must submit to regulations.
1685. Suspension and expulsion of.
1686. Defacing school property, liabilities for.
1687. Experienced teachers for beginners.

SEC. 1683. Pupils must be admitted into the schools in the order in which they apply to be registered.

SEC. 1684. All pupils must comply with the regulations, pursue the required course of study, and submit to the authority of the teachers of said schools.

SEC. 1685. Continued willful disobedience, or open defiance of the authority of the teacher, constitutes good cause for expulsion from school; and habitual profanity and vulgarity, good cause for suspension from school.

SEC. 1686. Any pupil who cuts, defaces, or otherwise injures any school house, fences, or outbuildings thereof, is liable to suspension or expulsion; and on the complaint of the teacher or trustees, the parents or guardians of such pupils shall be liable for all damages.

SEC. 1687. In cities having graded schools, beginners shall be taught, for the first two years, by teachers who have had at least four years experience; and such teachers shall rank, in point of salary, with those of first grade.

ARTICLE XII.

TEACHERS.

SECTION 1696. General duties of teachers.
1697. School month, in relation to salary of teachers, defined.
1698. Appeal allowed from order removing teacher for incompetency.
1699. Appeals in other cases.
1700. No warrant to be drawn in favor of a teacher unless he performs his duties.
1701. Nor unless he hold certificate, and was employed.
1702. Teacher's duty in regard to teaching morality, etc.

SEC. 1696. Every teacher in the public schools must:

First—Before assuming charge of a school, file his certificate with the County Superintendent;

Second—On taking charge of a school, or on closing a term of school, immediately notify the County Superintendent of such fact;

Third—Enforce the course of study, the use of text-books, and the rules and regulations prescribed for schools;

Fourth—Hold pupils to strict account for disorderly conduct on the way to and from school, on the play-ground, or during recess; suspend, for good cause, any pupil in the school, and report such suspension to the Board of Trustees or Education for review. If such action is not sustained by them, the teacher may appeal to the County Superintendent, whose decision shall be final;

Fifth—Keep a State school register;

Sixth—Make an annual report to the County Superintendent at the time, and in the manner, and on the blanks prescribed by the Superintendent of Public Instruction. Any school teacher who shall end any school term before the close of the school year, shall make a report to the County Superintendent, immediately after the close of such term; and any teacher who may be teaching any school at the end of the school year, shall, in his or her annual report, include all statistics for the entire school year, notwithstanding any previous report for a part of the year;

Seventh—Make such other reports as may be required by the Superintendent of Public Instruction, County Superintendent, or Board of Trustees or Education.

SEC. 1697. A school month is construed and taken to be twenty school days, or four weeks of five school days each.

SEC. 1698. In case of the dismissal of any teacher before the expiration of any written contract, entered into between such teacher and Board of Trustees, for alleged unfitness, or incompetence, or violation of rules, the teacher may appeal to the School Superintendent; and if the Superintendent decides that the removal was made without good cause, the teacher so removed must be reinstated.

SEC. 1699. Any teacher whose salary is withheld may appeal to the Superintendent of Public Instruction.

SEC. 1700. No warrant must be drawn in favor of any teacher, unless the officer whose duty it is to draw such warrant is satisfied that the teacher has faithfully performed all the duties prescribed in section sixteen hundred and ninety-six.

SEC. 1701. No warrant must be drawn in favor of any teacher, unless such teacher is the holder of a proper certificate, in force for the full time for which the warrant is drawn, nor unless he was employed by the Board of Trustees or Education; *provided*, that nothing in this section shall interfere with any special school laws now in existence for the counties of Trinity, Shasta, or Inyo.

SEC. 1702. It shall be the duty of all teachers to endeavor to impress on the minds of the pupils the principles of morality, truth, justice, and patriotism; to teach them to avoid idleness, profanity, and falsehood, and to instruct them in the principles of a free government, and to train them up to a true comprehension of the rights, duties, and dignity of American citizenship.

ARTICLE XIII.

DISTRICT LIBRARIES.

SEC. 1712. The Boards of Trustees and Education must expend the Library Fund, together with such moneys as may be added thereto by donation, in the purchase of school apparatus, and books for a school library.

SEC. 1713. Except in cities not divided into school districts, the Library Fund consists of ten per cent. of the State School Fund, annually apportioned to the district, unless ten per cent. exceed fifty dollars, in which event it consists of fifty dollars, annually taken from the fund so apportioned.

SEC. 1714. In cities not divided into school districts, the Library Fund consists of the sum of fifty dollars for every five hundred children between the ages of five and fifteen years, annually taken from the State School Fund apportioned to the city.

SEC. 1715. Libraries are under the control of the Board of Trustees or Education, and must be kept, when practicable, in the school houses.

SEC. 1716. The library is free to all pupils of a suitable age, belonging to the school; and any resident of the district may become entitled to its privileges by the payment of such a sum of money for life membership, or such annual or monthly fee as may be prescribed by the trustees.

SEC. 1717. The trustees shall be held accountable for the proper care and preservation of the library, and shall have power to assess and collect all fines, penalties, and fees of membership, and to make all needful rules and regulations, not provided for by the State Board of Education, and not inconsistent therewith; and they shall report annually to the County Superintendent, all library statistics which may be required by the blanks furnished for the purpose by the Superintendent of Public Instruction.

IV. CLASSIFICATION OF SCHOOLS.

I. State University.
II. State Normal School.
III. High Schools.
IV. Summary.

I. THE UNIVERSITY OF CALIFORNIA.—Location, Berkeley, five miles from Oakland. Value of buildings, grounds, etc., $500,-000. The University embraces seven courses of study, commonly called "Colleges," namely: *In Science*—Agriculture, Mechanics, Engineering, Chemistry, Mining, and Medicine. *In Letters*—Classical and Literary.

It is a free institution, open to young men and young women. The number of students in attendance from the beginning is as follows:

YEARS.	Science.	Letters.	Special and at large.	Total.	Ladies.
1869-70	14	21	5	40	..
1870-71	28	24	26	78	8
1871-72	75	28	50	153	27
1872-73	93	44	48	185	39
1873-74	100	44	47	191	22
1874-75	96	76	65	237	40
1875-76	162	139	65	366	..

II. STATE NORMAL SCHOOL.—Value of buildings, grounds, etc., $350,000. Free to both men and women. Number of students, 1876, 325. Annual appropriation for support, $23,000.

III. HIGH SCHOOLS.—The principal High Schools in the State are as follows:

		Pupils.	Teachers.
1.	San Francisco, Girls' High	650	21
2.	San Francisco, Boys' High	250	8
3.	Oakland, Boys' and Girls' High	135	4
4.	Sacramento, Boys' and Girls' High	101	4
5.	Stockton, " " "	65	2
6.	Los Angeles, " " "	57	2
7.	Marysville, " " "	21	1
8.	Santa Clara, " " "	19	1
9.	Vallejo, " " "	77	2
10.	San Jose, " " "	25	1
11.	Petaluma, " " "	52	2
12.	Grass Valley, " " "	20	1
13.	Nevada, " " "	20	1
14.	Santa Cruz, " " "	25	1
15.	Alameda, " " "	15	1
	Total	1532	52

In addition to the pupils in the schools specially classed as "High Schools," there are about 1,800 pupils in "First Grade Schools," pursuing an advanced, or partial, high school course.

SUMMARY OF CLASSIFICATION, 1875.

Number enrolled in State University	366
Number enrolled in State Normal School	350
Number enrolled in the High Schools, or the Advanced Grade	3,243
Number enrolled in Grammar, or First Grade Schools	16,177
Number enrolled in Intermediate, or Second Grade Schools	30,820
Number enrolled in Primary, or Third Grade Schools	79,532
Total	130,488

GIRLS' HIGH AND NORMAL SCHOOL.
Built, 1870. Cost, $35,000. Wood. Capacity, 500 pupils.

V. SUMMARY OF SCHOOL STATISTICS, 1875.

Population of California (estimated) 800,000.

Number of children between 5 and 17	171,563
Number that attended school	116,896
Average daily attendance in public schools	78,027
Attendance at private schools	15,000

CLASSIFICATION.

1. Attending State University	366
2. Attending State Normal School	350
3. Attending high schools, or in "advanced grades"	3,243
4. Attending grammar schools	16,177
5. Attending intermediate on second grade school	30,820
6. Attending primary or third grade schools	79,532

SCHOOLS AND TEACHERS.

Number of school districts	1,579
Number of schools	2,190
Number of male teachers	1,033
Number of female teachers	1,660
Average length of school in months	7.47
Number of teachers, graduates of some normal school	275

TEACHERS HOLDING STATE CERTIFICATES.

1. Holding life diplomas	292
2. Holding educational diplomas	421
3. Holding first grade certificates	615
4. Holding second grade certificates	210
Total	1,538
5. Number of graduates of the California State Normal School now teaching	240

SALARIES.

Average monthly salary paid men	$84 93
Average monthly salary paid women	68 00
Average annual salary paid men	672 00
Average annual salary paid women	543 00
Annual cost per scholar in average daily attendance	28 67
Annual cost of tuition per scholar in average daily attendance	21 59

15

FINANCIAL.

RECEIPTS.

Balance on hand at the beginning of the school year	$387,761 11
Received from State apportionments	1,210,808 49
Received from county apportionments	1,115,530 06
Received from city and district taxes	315,682 66
Received from miscellaneous sources (sale of bonds, rents, etc.)	360,576 98
Total receipts from all sources	$3,390,359 30

EXPENDITURES FOR SCHOOL PURPOSES.

Amount paid for teachers' salaries	1,810,479 62
Amount paid for rent, repairs, fuel, and contingent expenses	381,806 62
Amount paid for school libraries	33,962 72
Amount paid for school apparatus	10,713 02
Total current expenses	$2,236,961 98
Amount paid for sites, buildings, and school furniture	421,279 36
Total expenditures of all kinds	$2,658,241 34

VALUATION OF SCHOOL PROPERTY.

Valuation of sites, school houses, and furniture	$4,879,328 39
Valuation of school libraries	138,564 64
Valuation of school apparatus	50,785 27
Total valuation of school property	$5,068,678 30
Total expenditures for school purposes up to date	$24,542,775 00

VI. SCHOOL STATISTICS BY COUNTIES, 1875.

COUNTIES.	Census of Children 5 to 17 years old.	Average daily attendance.	Whole Number Enrolled.	No. of Teachers.
Alameda	9,330	4,458	6,261	121
Alpine	85	42	69	4
Amador	2,381	1,382	2,069	39
Butte	3,484	1,537	2,642	62
Calaveras	2,216	1,054	1,702	38
Colusa	2,346	963	1,787	43
Contra Costa	3,047	1,357	2,439	69
Del Norte	448	232	387	10
El Dorado	2,335	1,248	1,995	44
Fresno	1,398	457	939	30
Humboldt	2,863	1,248	2,320	50
Inyo	397	159	283	9
Kern	997	328	543	14
Lake	1,369	637	1,210	27
Lassen	667	390	544	14
Los Angeles	7,787	2,049	4,237	72
Marin	1,647	642	1,073	28
Mariposa	930	360	707	16
Mendocino	2,808	1,243	2,399	52
Merced	1,171	527	1,119	26
Modoc	846	441	604	24
Mono	112	57	102	5
Monterey	3,286	1,356	2,415	44
Napa	2,822	1,251	2,111	78
Nevada	4,705	2,356	3,774	63
Placer	2,519	1,338	2,262	52
Plumas	834	431	738	23
Sacramento	6,482	2,695	4,785	106
San Benito	1,456	592	1,037	22
San Bernardino	1,971	675	1,375	22
San Diego	1,834	440	818	25
San Francisco	41,021	20,830	32,075	507
San Joaquin	5,212	2,897	5,620	93
San Luis Obispo	2,012	679	1,134	26
San Mateo	2,340	815	1,439	37
Santa Barbara	2,282	608	1,229	22
Santa Clara	8,410	3,480	5,786	105
Santa Cruz	3,212	1,367	2,426	47
Shasta	1,517	694	1,205	33
Sierra	1,115	649	969	25
Siskiyou	1,705	906	1,387	39
Solano	4,630	2,229	3,594	78
Sonoma	7,003	3,437	5,900	132
Stanislaus	1,909	1,016	1,813	46
Sutter	1,549	710	1,423	38
Tehama	1,425	603	1,107	29
Trinity	642	316	443	17
Tulare	2,837	956	1,992	42
Tuolumne	1,872	1,058	1,577	28
Ventura	1,122	388	842	16
Yolo	2,566	1,273	2,156	53
Yuba	2,609	1,171	2,067	48
Totals	171,563	78,027	130,930	2,693

VII. RESUME OF THE CONDITION OF THE SCHOOLS.

1. BUILDINGS.—In general, the school houses are comfortable, are furnished with modern styles of desks, and fairly supplied with maps, charts, and simple school apparatus.

2. LENGTH OF SCHOOL.—The average length of school is 7½ months in the year, an average exceeded by only two or three States in the Union. There were only 34 schools in which the length of term was less than 6 months. In nearly 800 districts the length of term exceeded 8 months. The provision in making the county apportionment by which the minimum amount for each school, however small, is $500, has extended the means of education to the most remote settlements.

3. TEACHERS.—Of the 2800 teachers, 240, or nearly one tenth, are graduates of the California State Normal School. There are 292 holders of life diplomas; that is, about one tenth, who may be ranked as "professionals." There are about 400 holders of educational diplomas who have had at least 5 years' experience. In all, about one third of the teachers may be considered skilled in their profession, the remaining two thirds being mainly made up of "raw recruits."

4. INSTRUCTION.—There is a good course of study laid out by the State Board of Education; but, of course, this is carried out in the country districts to a very limited extent only. In a majority of the schools, the teaching consists of text-book recitations, with little or no instruction by the teacher.

5. LIBRARIES.—Each school is supplied with a small library, purchased by an annual appropriation of 10 per cent. of the State appropriation, not to exceed $50 yearly. The amount expended last year was about $50,000.

The libraries constitute one of the best features of the system.

6. SECULAR INSTRUCTION.—With a few unimportant exceptions, the schools are purely secular. The provisions of the State law are generally interpreted to exclude the reading of the Bible and prayer. In the State University, in the schools of

San Francisco, Oakland, and most other cities, and in most of the country districts, there are no religious exercises whatever.

The State Normal School is the only notable exception; there, the school is opened with prayer and the reading of the Bible.

7. DEFECTS.—There are two weak points in the system. 1. The short terms of school officers. 2. The frequent change of teachers.

Everywhere, except in San Francisco, the New England system of electing teachers annually is in full force and effect. Hence, a majority of the teachers are "circuit teachers."

The frequent change of school officers renders uniform and steady progress out of the question.

The most notable defect in the instruction given in the schools is the lack of thorough mental training, the work of the pupils consisting largely in memorizing text-book recitations.

The reforms of the next century will consist in the employment of skilled teachers, in common sense methods of teaching, and in the adaptation of courses of study to industrial pursuits.

8. EXPENSES.—The total amount expended for school purposes, during a quarter of a century, is, in round numbers, twenty-five millions of dollars. This is the best investment the State has ever made. Had fifty millions been expended, the State to-day would be the richer for it. Men, not money, make the true wealth of a nation.

9. WHAT WE NEED.—The following extract from an address by Hon. Ezra S. Carr, before the State Agricultural Society, September, 1875, outlines a want to be supplied during the next century:

CHILD CULTURE.

Our progress during the last six years is due to our increased facilities of travel and transportation. So many are now busy with plans for increasing immigration, that it may be useful to have one voice directing the public mind to the solution of a more important question, viz.: how to grow a crop of sound-bodied, right-minded, clean-hearted children, who will "take to work" as naturally and kindly as a duck takes to water. I hold that the end of the crop is the eater; the end of labor the betterment of the laborer; and that human improvement is as legitimate a subject for discussion in agricultural societies as that of colts or chickens. We have hitherto left this subject pretty much to the doctors—doctors of the body and of the soul—whose occupation will be gone when man truly reflects the Divine image. And although we need the help of these doctors still in the work of human improvement, and although we are immensely indebted to them for what has already been accomplished, I think it is better to pay them for the ounce of prevention than for the pound of cure. Nature herself protests when a lean, dwarfed apology for a man calls himself master of the noble brute creatures, which have become more than half human in their intelligence and beauty, through careful selections, breeding, and nurture. An organization like this, having for its object the improvement of the farmer, as well as the farm, will not love a horse less because it loves a child more. The interests of agriculture are bound up with those of education, especially in that modern form of it which is denominated "technical." The farmer's children are "the best working stock on the farm;" and the value of skill, intelligence, and good character applied there is more and more highly appreciated. This is the lowest, most material view of the subject, but it is one that the political economist will not overlook. Do our schools, do any of them, meet the great demands of agricultural and mechanical industry? Hundreds of the best and most progressive teachers say they do not; thousands and tens of thousands of anxious parents say they do not.

In a recent meeting of a State agricultural society in the East, it was said: "What we want is not mere culture, but culture applied, culture realized, culture put at work, and demonstrating, day by day, its uses." The masses of our people have little time to pursue branches of study which have not some direct bearing upon their callings or avocations. Aside from the elements, which all should receive, the importance of special knowledge, bearing upon special work, is paramount. Our system should be changed, so that from the highest classes in the country schools to the University, by unbroken gradations of the most liberal training in the acquisition of knowledge and skill, men and women should be fitted worthily to perform their appointed service in the industrial state.

It is fifteen years since the Massachusetts State Board of Agriculture asked the legislature for the passage of an act authorizing, as the first step in furnishing an agricultural education to the people—

First—"The engrafting upon her common school education the study of elementary geology, animal and vegetable physiology, and botany; to be taught in the usual form, by manuals, with suitable illustrations, simple and inexpensive; so prepared that it will not altogether depend upon the knowledge of the instructor to make them of use to the learner. With a slight change in their studies, our children would learn something which would every day become more deeply implanted in their minds by what they see going on around them." "These studies," they said, "cannot be commenced too early, for they are the germs of all future development, the vitality of which is never lost; they must be planted early if it is hoped to reach a full harvest."

Second—They asked for an agricultural school with a farm attached to it, where the practice of agriculture in its several departments, and the best methods of farm management could be practically learned. The committee, among whom I find the names of Marshal P. Wilder and George B. Loring, said: "If a person, who had the ability to perform whatever he undertook, should offer to the people of this commonwealth a secret, by which in twenty years the productive value of the lands throughout the whole State would be doubled, what would that secret be worth? The diffusion of general agricultural education would accomplish that object; nay, go far beyond it, in less time than has been named, and at an expense that would be trifling in proportion to the benefits that would flow from it."

Other States have taken similar action. The farmers of the West have recommended a revision of the school course, with this object in view.

In Illinois, an able defender of industrial education said: "We take the child out of God's natural industrial university and send him to school, where, at best, only a fraction of his entire manhood can be properly developed; and, after all, we do not fit pupils for actual life, even in those elemental studies after forty weeks' school per annum, as well as they were fitted in ten weeks, half a century ago. One prime cause of this is, that the bookmakers and publishers have assumed about as absolute control of our public schools as the politicians have of our post-offices. Rich publishing houses have offered as high as $70,000 for the introduction of a single text-book into a State. And yet not one of those books teaches us the things which it is our chief interest to know, and our protracted school drill leaves little time for anything else."

"I wish," says Professor Turner, "to make room for some of the subjects which underlie the industrial arts, botany, entomology, and zoology, for instance. The State of Illinois spends, say $12,000,000 a year on her public schools, and loses from $10,000,000 to $20,000,000 from obnoxious insects. Now, I would have every one of these insects, about a hundred in all, with pins in their backs, put up in a show-case in every public school in the State; and I would have every child know them as well as he knows his father's cows and horses; instead of having one or two lone men looking after them, I would turn millions of intelligent young eyes upon them, and thus prepare for their extermination. I would have this, whether the child knew there was such a word as 'en-tom-ol-o-gy' or not!

"The hard-working American people want to know something about our continent—our life-work, our bodies, and bones, and souls, our duties and destinies in the great republic in which we live.

"I look upon the agricultural classes to lift us out of this monkeydom of precedent, into the true freedom of American citizenship. All that is needed is that every man should quietly set about improving his own school, in his own district, as fast and as fully as he can."

I shall make no apology for quoting these educational authorities. I warn all those classes who do not believe in industrial education, that Broderick's words are fast coming to be true, that—

"WORKING-MEN WILL RULE THIS NATION."

The State Superintendent of Public Instruction in Connecticut, Mr. Northrop (and he has been saying these things from that office a good many years), says: "Every child's education is deficient who has not learned to work at some useful form of industry. Labor aids in disciplining the intellect, and energizing the character. Especially does farm work task and test the mind, leading a boy to plan and contrive to adapt means to ends. With all our improved gymnastics, none is better than manual labor, cheerfully and intelligently performed, especially farm work. The ambition for easier lives, and more genteel employments, and the silly but common notion that labor is menial, that the tools of the trades and the farms are badges of servility, have greatly lessened apprenticeships, and ought to be refuted in our common schools.

"Our youth should there be taught the dignity and necessity of labor, and its vital relations to all human excellence and progress, the evils of indolence, the absurdity of the present fashion for city life, and the wide-spread aversion to manual labor. A practical knowledge of some industrial pursuit is an important element in intellectual culture."

I fully indorse these sentiments. "Whatever you would have appear in a nation's life must be put into its schools," is a Prussian motto, and we put the same idea into section 1702 of our code, which makes it "the duty of teachers to instruct pupils to avoid idleness, and to train them to a comprehension of the rights, duties, and dignity of American citizenship." But Prussia *enforces* her principles in the most universal system of "real," or technical schools, which turn out able young farmers, carpenters, blacksmiths, and housekeepers, and nurses, while with us it all ends in an admonition to "avoid idleness."

The State must go further than this; it must fit its children for their places in the industrial ranks. The nation has two technical schools—one for training of navy, the other of army, officers. Each State has one for the training of teachers, and a few have real training schools or colleges of agriculture and the mechanic arts. If these are what they should be, they will do for those pursuits what West Point and Annapolis do for the army and navy, viz.: make men who are *proud* of their business. I wish some of the kid glove gentry who think the base-ball club and the boating club furnishes a more dignified employment for the muscles of our young men than manual labor, could have been with me at the annual examination of one of the nation's training schools, where high born and low born, without distinction of nationality or religion, learn—what? To scrub a deck, to furl a sail, to use every tool in the carpenter's shop, in the blacksmith's shop, to make and to mend everything that belongs to a ship, to be considerate, gentlemanly, orderly, to command themselves and others, to obey, to love their country's flag, and to die for it without a murmur, to go down with the ship if need be—all this while they learn everything that is required in literature and science for an education of the first class.

And must one be a soldier, or a sailor, to be thus furnished for his country's service, for his own service in the industrial state? Shall a man be trained in all manliness to walk the quarter deck, worthy of all obedience because he understands what he requires, and has himself performed, not once, but a thousand times, all that he exacts from subordinates; and may he not have an equal training for the post of foreman in a mechanic's shop, for the management of his own broad acres, and the laborers he requires to cultivate them? Do you suppose they would put a man in charge of the Naval Academy, or tolerate a single professor in West Point, who thought practical education in war and navigation would prove "a failure"—was, at best, a doubtful experiment? No; that isn't the way they manage. Those old admirals and army officers are seamen and soldiers through and through, from boots to buttons; they believe in their business. The men who lead in industrial education must believe in it also.

The kind of education wanted to-day is not that which has passed current, and which has proved a dead failure in making a generation of nobler youth, stronger in body, clearer in mind, and firmer in conscience, than the half-schooled frontier gave us a hundred years ago. Don't take this on my authority, but look through the Governors' messages and State Superintendents' reports. Why, only last year the Education Committee of the Massachusetts Legislature said: "The public school system of Massachusetts fails to meet the demands of modern civilization." Why and how? Civilization now demands skilled, intelligent labor; and, as Scott Russell says, "Occupations which require no skill, but only brute force, will necessarily be vacated by human hands." The substitution of steam culture for hand labor has thrown thousands of English workmen out of employment.

"Society, in the march of improvement, is as certain to do without the unskilled, the unintelligent, and uneducated, as it is to do without wild plants and animals. Nor will the laws be unjust which forbid those who cannot create their food to subsist on the labor of others."

Governor Hartranft, of Pennsylvania, calls attention to the scarcity of skilled labor in that State, and says, that although $10,000,000 are annually expended for education, none of the children who complete their terms in the public schools have any special fitness for trade, and few become artisans. He recommends schools where boys can be instructed in trades, and urges compulsory education. I might amplify this testimony almost indefinitely, but I turn to other aspects of the question.

I am not one of those who think a thing must be good because it is baldheaded with antiquity. Education is essentially conservative. You cannot make a move in the way of improvement without disturbing somebody, and we shall have to disturb a good many people sitting in comfortable chairs before we get our educational stream to turning mills and grinding corn.

While I do not think that bodily labor is specially desirable for its own sake, I think any scheme which leaves physical education out of the account is radically defective. If you can have this with training in useful arts, so much the better, but have it we must.

There was a training in those primitive New England times when a fellow had to lie down to his Lindley Murray before a fire of pine knots, after milking the cows, cutting the wood, and doing the "chores;" when the girl added the daily skein to the festoons of yarn for the family clothing, which is hard to get in these days. As soon as a child was old enough to pick up a basket of chips, it became an element in the productive wealth of the home. Surely it was none the worse for it to be taught by the statutes of law and filial duty that service was due for the care and support of its helpless years. These views may seem sordid, but the looseness with which children grow up to think their parents and the rest of the world owe them a living is filling our streets with hoodlums and with animated fashion plates, ready to be blown away by the first ill wind of temptation. What is a hoodlum? A boy gone to waste, rotten before he is ripe, because society does not know enough to preserve and economize him.

The education required by a people is not a fixed quantity, either in kind or degree, and the condition and circumstances of laboring men of every class have greatly changed since the idea of public education first dawned. Why, do you know that the experiment is historically so recent that a good many countries have not had time to make it?

The history of education fully explains why it is not more practical. Colleges and seminaries grew up out of the monasteries, which, for a long time, treasured all the learning there was in the world. Learning was a monopoly; first of the priest, then of priests and the nobles, then of these and the judges, and finally, and not without hard squeezing, the leech or doctor got into this good company, and then came the printed Bible to carry the art of reading wherever religious zeal could take it. There was nothing but literature for education to use; it covered the whole field, except mathematics. Columbus invented geography, and Galileo and Copernicus astronomy, long after the great European universities were founded. In England, where our college system came from, the aristocratic classes only were benefited by it, and it suited them very well. And when the common school got started, it simply took a few of the first leaves out of the college book. It is not so very long since men learned to read and spell in the Universities of Oxford and Cambridge. It took several centuries of human progress to bring rulers to consent that common folks should learn the alphabet; and, again, to get permission for women to tamper with the dangerous thing. It took a good while to get a spinning-jenny, and a power wheel, and a steam plow; and the education of the Oxford time don't suit the spinning-jenny age, as England has learned to her cost.

Until about the time of the gold discovery in California, England was domineering over the rest of Europe, through her commercial supremacy, and her command of the supplies of raw materials, which enabled her to take the lead in manufactures. These advantages she was likely to retain. But France and Germany, by the most magnificent provisions for technical schools, set themselves to compete with her on her own ground of manufactures, and not only distanced her completely, but almost drove her from the field. The Exposition of '67 proved that Germany could make better steel, and France better locomotives; "that England was beaten, not only on some points, but, by some nation, on nearly all the points on which she had prided herself." The English government then sent eighty skilled workmen over to the Continent, to find out the causes of defeat. The unanimous reply was: "Their industrial education has caused it."

Lord Stanley addressed the most careful inquiries to all the foreign Consuls in France, Prussia, Saxony, Switzerland, Belgium, and got the same answer, "industrial education." And lately there comes a plan from England for a national system of industrial instruction for the whole people, beginning in primary schools, and ending in a great "central technical university" for training professors and teachers of institutions of lower rank, devoted to raising the standard of industrial well-being. Instead of believing that money is the root of evil, the Englishman believes it to be the root of industry, and so of all good, and this change in the direction of popular education is due to the lesson the English nation received at Paris and Vienna.

The great natural advantages which we possess will not give us industrial supremacy, unless we follow these examples. The "*International Magazine*" emphasizes our duty and our opportunity in strong language: "With an agricultural wealth to which no limit can be assigned, with mineral riches everywhere bursting through the surface, with water power which no mills can exhaust; not to advance, not to rival the skilled industry of Europe, is not a loss merely, it is a crime." The California wheat-grower and wool-grower must compete in the Liverpool market with the wheat and wool of the world. Competition, in every branch of industry, has become world-wide, and unless the American farmer and manufacturer does his best, he is sure to take the lower place in the world's market.

With gold and silver mines that supply all nations, with forests shading our hillsides, with flocks, and vineyards, and great valleys teeming with their abundant harvests, we cannot be rich or great, unless we can compete in the enlightened employment of these natural means and forces. The experience of all Europe teaches, "Industrial supremacy is the prize of industrial education."

Let us lay the foundation of this supremacy in

OUR PRIMARY SCHOOLS.

Carry it forward by a well-devised system of secondary technical schools, and complete it in a University where prominence is given to different branches of learning, according to the directness and value of these as applied to the occupations and pursuits of our people.

Perhaps there was never a time when the relations of the Government to education need to be discussed so thoroughly, and yet so temperately. That universal intelligence is the only guarantee of universal liberty, is one of the fundamental ideas of the American's political faith; but the right and duty of the State to educate has been better stated in monarchical Germany than in republican

America. The great Fichte said: "The end of the State is not only to live, but to live nobly." And the clearest of writers upon the philosophy of education, Karl Rosencranz, said: "The idea that the Government has the right to oversee the school, lies in the very idea of the State, which is authorized and under obligations to secure the education of citizens, and cannot leave their fashioning to chance. The separation of the school from the State would be the destruction of the school."

With us it would be the destruction of the State; for here the diversity of the materials which form the State, requires the unifying influence of a broad and comprehensive system of public education.

The work of the State in education may be divided into three sections. The first is elementary and general (and should be universal and free), making every child familiar with reading, writing, drawing or picture writing, with elementary arithmetic and natural history, and with the geography and history of his own State and country. In the second stage, separation and specialization should begin, which will necessarily grow and perfect itself with the growth of culture, and the more perfect organization of the forces of civilization. We now specialize only in regard to classes of unfortunates, the deaf, dumb, blind, etc.; by and by we can specialize as to uses, and make our country schools more preparatory to agriculture, horticulture, and the like; while our city schools, by vacation classes, half-time schools, and other agencies, at first, and afterwards by special schools, render the same service to the mechanic and manufacturing arts. The certainties of science are swiftly taking the place of the hap-hazard pursuit of those arts, and a great part of secondary instruction should be in the simpler applications of scientific principles.

In the third, or University stage of education, the one-sidedness of a particular or strictly technological training is rounded off by a survey of the relations and value of each specialty to others, without losing sight of a specific individual purpose. The University is as necessary a part of public instruction as the elementary or technical school, and should be the crown and complement of these. Below this point the States say every child *shall* be furnished with the means for the rational development of his physical, moral, and intellectual powers; to this, instruction should be added which will enable the child to apply those powers in obtaining a livelihood; while at the gates of the University the State confers a privilege, and says to the youth: You *may* go up higher, and contend for the prizes of thought and activity. The University says: Here you shall find the natural sciences carried up into the science of nature; that the phenomena of society, of industry, of trade, of finance, of politics, are subject to fixed laws. The University is an organic encyclopedic representation of all the sciences, with their connections and relations. And this is equally true of the arts, architecture, music, painting, the drama—are like the sciences, bound together in a *Universitas Arcium.*

While this is the true conception of a University, and should not be lost sight of in laying the foundations of an institution for all time, it is not immediately practical or adapted to the wants of young and growing States. The reason of this is, that the lower stages of public education are yet imperfect and unorganized. To expect to have a great University without a good proportion of high schools, and before we have a single technical school, seems to me preposterous. We may have students crowding into our University to get what other colleges give—liberal literary or scientific education—without getting a step nearer the ideal University, while numbers of the students of older colleges are found among us seeking for second-rate clerkships, in threadbare clothes; but when we get the feeders to our University in running order, we shall find its utmost usefulness realized in the production of educated power instead of

EDUCATED HELPLESSNESS.

"We thank you," said the Iroquois Chief (in the year 1774) to the Government of Virginia, which had offered to educate some of their young men; "we have already had experience of your education, and some whom you have educated in all your sciences come back to us bad runners, ignorant of woodcraft, unable to trap a deer, snare a fish, to build a wigwam; we cannot accept your offer, though we appreciate your good will, but we will take a few of your sons and make men of them."

Something like this the people have been saying to the Universities founded upon the munificence of the State and nation, not because they do not appreciate education, but *because they do.* They know that it costs more to hang a man, to board and lodge a man at San Quentin, than it would to teach him the duties and responsibilities of American citizenship, and how to get an honest living; that it costs far more to maintain a system of demagogy than of pedagogy! They know that where five agricultural scientists could obtain employment, five thousand skillful, intelligent farmers are needed to-day in our own State. The friends of the so-called higher education should be willing to see the University filling the present need of technical training in agriculture and the arts, making practical workers, as well as thinkers, of its students, thus supplying the means of its ideal perfection.

The technical school in which we are most directly interested, is that which gives us teachers. Without the right kind of teachers, no reform is possible. The one business which it should be the special concern of the State to maintain in honor, which should be kept free from political or sectarian influences, which should be entered into with zeal and consecrated ability, and never as a makeshift—is education. The educator, whether of the school or the press, stands at the point of power, and holds the highest office in the social economy.

The work of organizing the national education is now claiming the attention of scholars and patriots. Such an organization, in its higher and lower stages, will be impartial in its bearings upon intellect and industry, impartial as to sex, making a boy's training preparatory to a man's work, and girl's to a woman's, wife's, mother's work, and in both will recognize the intrinsic dignity of self-support.

The graduate of the National School of Pedagogy, or Normal

School, will have the same relation to the Government that the graduate of West Point or of the Naval Academy has, and thus step by step the hitherto unrewarded and despised profession of teaching shall be exalted and ennobled. Do I believe in this good time coming? Most assuredly I do. The time has already come when war is no longer a necessity, and that nation is the most civilized which can most easily dispense with it. The reign of words, too, is almost over; dogmas, religious or political, no longer fetter the nations; thought is free as air. Literature must take the back seat; while the arts, leading science, make the circuit of the world. Between the standing armies of soldiers, which tell how imperfect still is human government, and the sitting armies of sophists, whose mission it is to perpetuate existing evils, another great army is being drilled—the army of labor—in which we shall find the most practical philosophy, the broadest intelligence, and the most Christian patriotism.

Little more than two hundred years ago, Sir William Berkeley, Governor of Virginia, said: "Thank God, there are no free schools nor printing presses here, and I hope there will be none for an hundred years, for learning has brought heresy and sects into the world, and printing has divulged these and other libels." The ghost of Sir William flits in a few remote corners of our land, but the spirit of modern inquiry forbids that it shall be materialized. With conscious pride, the farmers and laboring men of America are building a commonwealth whose spirit shall be peace on earth and good will to man; whose weapon, suffrage; whose conservatism, education; whose objects are freedom, order, and economy within our own boundaries, and an eternal brotherhood with those who are our wider neighbors.

ERRATA.

Page 20, Sec. 8, read "approved May 3, 1852," instead of "approved May 3, 1862."

Page 24, See. 15, read "1855," instead of "1856."

Page 25, Sec. 17, read "seventh," instead of "seventeenth."

OMISSION.

In the section of legislation, 1874, on page 65, no mention is made of the Compulsory Education Bill passed during that year; but as the law has proved a dead letter, the omission is of little consequence.

www.ingramcontent.com/pod-product-compliance
Lightning Source LLC
LaVergne TN
LVHW010245110826
845151LV00004B/1393

* 9 7 8 1 4 2 5 5 2 3 6 6 4 *